D0045529

TEETH

The Story of Beauty, Inequality, and
the Struggle for Oral Health in America

Mary Otto

THE NEW PRESS

25 YEARS

NEW YORK
LONDON

Requests for permission to reproduce selections from this book should be mailed to: Permissions Department, The New Press, 120 Wall Street, 31st floor, New York, NY 10005.

Published in the United States by The New Press, New York, 2016
Distributed by Perseus Distribution

LIBRARY OF CONGRESS CATALOGING-IN-PUBLICATION DATA

Names: Otto, Mary, author.
Title: Teeth : the untold story of beauty, inequality, and the struggle for
   oral health in America / Mary Otto.
Description: New York : New Press, 2016. | Beauty—Suffering—Emergencies
   —The world beneath our noses—The birth of American dentistry—
   Separate lives—Adventurers and auxiliaries—The system—Color lines
   Deamonte's world—Riding into the epidemic—Sons and daughters of
   Chapin Harris. | Includes bibliographical references and index.
Identifiers: LCCN 2016041484 (print) | LCCN 2016043002 (ebook) | ISBN
   9781620971444 (hc : alk. paper) | ISBN 9781620972816 (e-book)
Subjects: | MESH: Dental Care—economics | Healthcare Disparities | Tooth
   Diseases—complications | Dental Care—history | Poverty | Health Policy |
   United States
Classification: LCC RK58.5 (print) | LCC RK58.5 (ebook) | NLM WU 29 | DDC
   617.600973—dc23
LC record available at https://lccn.loc.gov/2016041484

The New Press publishes books that promote and enrich public discussion and understanding of the issues vital to our democracy and to a more equitable world. These books are made possible by the enthusiasm of our readers; the support of a committed group of donors, large and small; the collaboration of our many partners in the independent media and the not-for-profit sector; booksellers, who often hand-sell New Press books; librarians; and above all by our authors.

www.thenewpress.com

Book design and composition by Bookbright Media
This book was set in Bembo and Oswold

Printed in the United States of America

10 9 8 7 6 5 4 3 2 1

Contents

Preface

AIDA BASNIGHT STOOD ON A WINTRY STREET CORNER IN DOWN-town Washington, D.C. She was dressed in a bright, hand-knit hat and scarf and a heavy coat. She was working to sell a newspaper produced by the city's homeless. There was solemn beauty in her dark eyes, in her high cheekbones, in her smooth skin, but she was careful to smile with her mouth closed.

Her missing teeth bore testimony to her life's hardships.

Her molars had been the first to go. She lost them to infection in her thirties when she was working as a secretary in Chicago. She woke up in terrible pain with a swollen face, and the molars were extracted. Amid other difficulties, other teeth went bad.

When she was in her mid-fifties she lost a steady job working with computers. Then she fell behind on her rent and lost her home. She slept in a park for a while. "It's really scary being out there in the street and being homeless," she said.

She eventually found help through a women's supportive hous-ing program. But Basnight, who always prided herself on her work ethic and skills, had been unable to find a lasting job, in spite of dozens of applications. "Nobody's gonna hire you with that bunch of gaps in your teeth," her elderly mother warned her. Basnight feared her mother was right. "I always feel self-conscious about them in the interviews. I can't smile because I've got no teeth."

She said she kept hoping for something better. But in the meantime she stood in the cold with her newspapers, facing the well-dressed commuters. They hurried past her, toward the rush-hour trains.

Shame is common among the millions of Americans who lack dental care. More than one out of three low-income adults avoids smiling, according to a Harris poll conducted on behalf of the American Dental Association in 2015.[1]

America's social welfare programs continually emphasize the importance of self-advancement, but, lacking dental care, the poor and working poor find it especially difficult to improve their lives. In the competition for service jobs, working at restaurants or retail counters or reception desks, they are often passed over. "Unless they look good, you don't want to hire them," observed dentist Judith Allen, who spends her days working with poor and uninsured patients in a city health department clinic in Cincinnati, Ohio.

When patients get to Allen they are often in pain. Their lips and even eyes may be swollen by oral infections. Their teeth are diseased and ruined. Many have gone for so long without dental care, extraction is the only option. "We remove what we can't save. And then we go in and we restore what we have left." Without her help their teeth will continue to mark them as broken people. And across the country, millions go without help. There is a shortage of places like the Cincinnati clinic where Allen works.

Stigma is an ancient word: a brand or mark of subjection or disgrace. In the way that they disfigure the face, bad teeth depersonalize the sufferer. They confer the stigma of economic and even moral failure. People are held personally accountable for the state of their teeth in ways that they are not held accountable for many other health conditions.

There has been a scarcity of sociological research on this subject, but a team of British researchers looked at the phenomenon. "Although tooth decay and gum disease involve diseased tissue, those experiencing these physical states are not generally regarded as being ill," observed the author of their study. "In part, this may be because oral health problems are seen as a failure of individual responsibility rather than misfortune."

In the study, participants, who lost their teeth through disease and trauma, discussed their feelings. "It's almost as if I feel as if I've failed because I've got dentures," said one woman. "I don't think people feel the same way about knee replacements, do they?" responded the researcher. "No, that's right," the woman said.[2]

For reasons including poverty, isolation, and the lack of private insurance and providers available to treat the poor, roughly one-third of the people living in America face significant barriers to obtaining dental care. Medicaid, the federal-state health program that now covers more than 72 million poor Americans, treats adult dental benefits as optional. It is up to states to decide whether to offer them. In hard times, coverage of even the most basic dental procedures often ends up on state chopping blocks.

The young and the old also suffer. More than 35 million poor children are entitled by federal law to dental benefits under Medicaid, but more than half go without care. Fewer than half the nation's roughly one hundred fifty thousand working dentists participate in the program. Only a tiny fraction work in federally funded safety net clinics. Approximately 49 million Americans live in communities that are federally designated as dental professional shortage areas. Medicare, the federal health care program that currently provides benefits to more than 55 million aged and disabled people, has never included coverage for routine dental care.

In the seventeenth century, French philosopher René Descartes introduced a theory that changed the world. He uncoupled the indivisible spiritual human mind from the divisible working machinery of the human anatomy, thus liberating scientific inquiry from religious dogma. He also, it could be said, removed the head from the body.

In the wake of Descartes, increasingly specialized healers began laying claim to parts of the body for study and treatment. For centuries, along with shaving and tonsuring, leeching and cupping, barber surgeons had counted tooth extractions among the deeply personal services they performed. But the teeth were worthy of science too, Pierre Fauchard, the eminent eighteenth-century surgeon–dentist, insisted. He advanced the idea that dentistry was a unique and important branch of surgery.

Cartesian dualism served its purpose, opening new possibilities for physiological exploration. Yet at the same time, medical research became more reductive and mechanistic, less personal and less holistic. Some have suggested that the formative influence of Descartes stubbornly persists in the ways the modern health care system fails to integrate care.[3] Perhaps, too, it lingers in the gulf between the head and the body, the understanding of oral health and overall health. It has been said that this gulf must be bridged to bring a more complete kind of health to America. "Just as we now understand that nature and nurture are inextricably linked, and mind and body are both expressions of our human biology, so, too, we must recognize that oral health and general health are inseparable," declared the then U.S. surgeon general David Satcher in his landmark report, *Oral Health in America*, published in 2000.[4] In the ways they connect us to the world, in the ways they allow us to survive and to express ourselves, the teeth and other tissues of the mouth and face "represent the very essence of our humanity," noted Satcher.

Systemic health and disease are mirrored in the components of our saliva. Our first permanent molars bear the time stamp of our births. Pain, loss of function, serious illness, and even death result from untreated oral conditions and offer harrowing reminders that the mouth is part of the body and that oral health is essential to overall health. Yet the separate, carefully guarded, largely private system that provides dental care in America can be enormously difficult to reach for those without mobility or money or adequate dental benefits.

In his report, Satcher warned of a "silent epidemic" of oral disease.

This book began in 2007, at the heart of that epidemic, at the bedside of a Maryland schoolboy who was dying of complications from an untreated dental infection. The story of the death of twelve-year-old Deamonte Driver, which appeared in the *Washington Post*, helped inspire reforms in Maryland and in Medicaid dental systems nationwide.

But America's silent epidemic of oral disease persists.

This book provides a look into the insular world of dental care in America. It examines the enduring tension between the need of all Americans for dental services and the lack of services available to millions of us under the current system.

Beginning with the world's first dental college that opened in Baltimore in 1840, not far from where Deamonte died, this book explores dentistry's evolution in isolation from the rest of the nation's health care system. Its narrative seeks to explain why obtaining dental services may require a journey that some patients never manage to make.

My reporting took me from Florida to Alaska, and in my travels, patients, providers, policy makers, researchers, and public health leaders spoke of their own experiences, their own journeys. Their stories were by turns agonizing, challenging, confounding, and hopeful. They described the raw physical suffering of disease and exquisite moments of understanding. They explained the intricacies of enormous government programs, the hidden worlds of microbiology, the vagaries of diagnostic coding. Some proudly defended the current system of providing dental care in America. Some described a vision for a transformed oral health care system— one that incentivizes disease prevention over drilling, that uses new kinds of teams to reach the millions currently not receiving oral health care, a system where dentists spend less time extracting and more time healing and where patients break the cycle of disease and pain and loss.

Some spoke of bridging the gap between oral health and overall health. Some spoke of ending the silent epidemic.

Part I

BAD TEETH

1

Beauty

The mouth is a portal, an interface, an erogenous zone.

It is our first connection with the world and our last.

It is the domain of the breath, the self-expressing lips. The grotto of the tongue.

The realm of the teeth.

The teeth that are part animal, part mineral.

The teeth, inlaid with jade by the ancient Mayans, still fetishized today.

The teeth, rotting and aching at the dawn of agriculture, still tormenting today.

The teeth that are whitened and straightened.

The teeth that are amputated and thrown away.

The teeth that endure longer than the bones, that withstand fires, floods, time.

The teeth that identify us, scattered in deserts, buried in caves.

The teeth keep a record of our lives, locked in their enamel. They identify us even beyond the grave . . .

"Your hair is like a flock of goats moving down the slopes of Gilead," sang Solomon. "Your teeth are like a flock of ewes that have come up from the washing; All of them bear twins. And not one of them is bereaved. . . . Your cheeks are like the halves of a pomegranate behind your veil."[1]

On a cold evening, in the ballroom of a suburban hotel, seventy-nine young women shimmied in stilettos. Across their short black cocktail dresses, each wore a sash bearing the name of a place in Maryland; Annapolis, Towson, College Park, Baltimore. They were bouncing in unison to the blare of an Iggy Azalea tune.

Many of the beauties moved with certainty born of long experience on pageant runways, but this was the first pageant for a dark, slender contestant from Silver Spring, twenty-three-year-old Mamé Adjei. She was trying not to show her shyness. She had no fairy godmother. Her parents were far away.

The evening gown she brought for the final round had been sewn by a friend.

She prepared for this pageant as she prepared for assignments back in college, doing her research, seeking out advice. She read and she trained in the ways of pageant walking and talking. She practiced the all-important pageant smile. The pageant smile, she knew, must shine, must radiate. It must never flag or falter, grow stiff or weary. In spite of intense anxiety, hunger, or boredom, the pageant smile must project brightness, allure, inexhaustible pleasure. So she trained the muscles in her small exotic face. Her lips lifted into an enchanting bow. She trained holding the smile for one minute; five minutes; ten minutes; twenty, forty, sixty minutes. She was working in downtown Washington and she challenged herself to smile for the entire train ride home, out to the end of the line, where she lived with family guardians in a small apartment decorated with enigmatic African dolls.

Her fellow passengers smiled back.

She grew up in Ghana and Switzerland and Maryland, the daughter of African diplomats. She had to repeat a grade in elementary school because of all the moving around. In her adolescence, her parents decided to leave her in Silver Spring, Maryland, with relatives. From then on, years elapsed between their visits. The way she explained it, she was raised by telephone. On some level, she felt abandoned. She worked hard to excel. In high school she was on the track team and a cheerleader but she always felt alone. On this runway, in the sparkling lights, as the crowd of families and friends cheered for other contestants, she missed her mother and father badly.

After graduating from college, she got an internship at a think tank on K Street in Washington, working for human rights. She thought sometimes about studying law.

But she had done a little modeling, starting when she was six, posing for a church brochure. She always felt there was something exciting about facing the camera, about being photographed.

She decided to enter the Miss Maryland USA pageant. She figured that if she lost, she would apply to law school.

The pageant started on a Friday and went on for two more days. On Saturday, the prospect of law school loomed large. Her smile nearly let her down. At a crucial moment, her facial muscles rebelled. Her mouth began to quiver. Her upper lip stuck to her fine white incisors. She had forgotten a most basic pageant rule. She had forgotten to put Vaseline on her front teeth. On this Sunday night, the final night, she remembered the Vaseline. And again she took a breath. And again she glided forward, into the lights.

And once again, she smiled.

Some contestants were eliminated. Some kept bravely smiling, even as they left the stage. Others went with heads bent, like spent flowers. Adjei remained, among sixteen finalists, strutting in high heels, her dark skin glowing against a white swimsuit, her white teeth glowing against her red lipstick. She smiled as she walked forward and, as she turned away, she cast another lingering smile. Nine more women were eliminated in the bathing suit round. There were only five now. One was Adjei.

Dressed in her modest golden gown, she drew a question out of a fishbowl.

What advice would she offer a young woman just arriving in America from a foreign country?

"Culture is a beautiful thing," she said. "You should hang on to it."

Suddenly, she was being crowned Miss Maryland USA. The pageant host asked her if she had words for what she was feeling. "I am so happy and extremely blessed," she said, weeping.

Adjei walked the runway once again, wearing her new rhinestone tiara, clutching a huge bouquet of dark red roses against her golden breast. She won cash and a year's worth of eyelash extensions, new jewelry and a new gown. She won fitness and coaching sessions. And she won $10,000 worth of "smile enhancement" services from the pageant's official "smile sponsors." The prizes would help her prepare for a higher level of competition, the Miss USA pageant.

"There is this pressure to be perfect in every regard," explained Ryann Richardson, a tall, willowy former Miss Philadelphia who lost to Adjei.

"Perfect hair. Perfect skin. Perfect body. Of course the perfect smile, which comes down to perfect teeth."

A few evenings later, Mamé Adjei emerged from the cold darkness of downtown Washington into the warmth of a K Street coffee shop. She was muffled in a paisley scarf, a short jacket, slacks, and long boots, like a thousand other young working women, heading home at rush hour. She was quiet, thoughtful, tired, still trying to reconcile her full-time internship at the think tank with her new responsibilities as Miss Maryland USA. There were official appearances and meetings with the pageant sponsors who were outfitting her and training her to compete for Miss USA—including the "smile sponsors."

She said she could not remember the last time she had visited a dentist, but it had been years. And she said she saw the chance to get her teeth improved as an opportunity that came with success.

A certain kind of smile is expected of people who are rising. "It's a right of way. A rite of passage," she explained. "As soon as you get money that's your way of saying 'I'm here. I've come up. I've got my smile.'"

Still, she lingered on the meaning of the opportunity. She said she admired the music of an upstart rapper named J. Cole, a military brat turned college graduate known for his blend of skillful rhymes and social messages. One of his songs was called "Crooked Smile."

In the song, he talks about his teeth, and his decision not to get them straightened since he hit it big. Cole says he kept his "twisted grill" as a way of staying "real."

The song questions the whole social script about the "perfect smile," she mused.

"He says, 'I went through life and I got here with my crooked smile so it must be okay,'" Adjei explained. "What he is saying in his rap, it's so true. Why do we always feel like we have to change ourselves?" she wondered. "Maybe that's us needing to change our perception of what a perfect smile is."

Still, she had made her first appointment with the cosmetic dentists. On their website, Drs. Linda and Chip Steel alluded to the rewards their patients might enjoy.

> *A beautiful smile could be a gateway to the best things in*
> *life . . .*
> *Finding your perfect job,*
> *meeting the perfect mate*
> *or just feeling good when you look in the mirror*
> *Sometimes, it all starts with a great smile!*

It was easy to pass right by their office, located in a plain, neat brick house on a busy road in Sandy Spring, Maryland, a quaint enclave an hour's drive from Washington, D.C. "Parking in the rear," the sign said. The office was there in the back, in the ground-level basement of the house. There was a holiday wreath on the door and, inside, burgundy wall-to-wall carpeting and a coffee table with an arrangement of artificial pomegranates. Behind the glass of the reception desk, arrayed upon the wall, there were framed glossy photos of many of the past Miss Maryland USAs and Miss Maryland Teen USAs who had their smiles perfected in the office.

"Oooh!" whispered Adjei, when she spotted their crowned images. The receptionist asked her for her form and asked how to pronounce her name. "Mah-May," she said. She was ushered in for her appointment.

In the waiting room, among the reading materials, was a book entitled *Billion Dollar Smile*. The author, smiling broadly on the cover, was Beverly Hills cosmetic dentist Bill Dorfman, a pageant judge and celebrity dentist, famous for repositioning gums and applying veneers on *Extreme Makeover*, one of the popular television shows celebrating the nation's cosmetic surgery juggernaut.

"Before you read another word, walk over to the mirror. Now say 'cheese.' What do you see? Is your smile dingy and dark—or healthy and bright?" asked Dorfman from the pages of his book. "Like they say with the lottery, you gotta be in it to win it. You have to play the game. Life is hard enough and a bright, beautiful smile can help open doors and hearts."[2] He acknowledged "critics out there who dismiss cosmetic surgery as superficial." But for them, he had a ready response: "So what! It is superficial. But so are many of the things in our lives; clothing, haircuts, cars and houses. If you want to do something about your appearance and you can, then go for it!"

An hour later, when her appointment was over, Adjei saw her teeth more critically.

Back in the car, she pulled down the sun visor and pondered them in the mirror.

They had been examined and cleaned. They had been judged to be sound and healthy. Yet she learned she had an overbite. And there were tiny spaces, uneven spaces between some of them. She thought of the upcoming pageant, the national stage. "I've definitely got to get them all aligned and straight so they look the part," she said. "Whitening," she said. "And aligning them."

Adjei and the dentists settled on a treatment plan that included Invisalign braces. There would be a new set of clear plastic appliances every two weeks, which would press her teeth into an improved configuration. There would be a bleaching solution to place in the trays that would whiten them at the same time. There was also the possibility she would get her gums contoured, to make her teeth look longer.

"We talked about the gum that goes over your enamel. How it recedes over time anyway. They could go ahead and shave it off me now," she explained. "I'll have the appearance of having my longer teeth. It looks like I'm short-teethed but it's really just gums covering my enamel."

After the braces were done, she would need to wear a retainer for two years.

She herself had watched the smile makeovers on television shows. She had thought about the powerful, even magical way a smile can play with the imagination,

"Getting dental work can make a world of difference in someone's life," she said.

"It's a first impression thing. People show you respect. People give you more love when your teeth are just straight and fixed. And more presentable. People are more approachable. Because if there are black and missing teeth all over, it's sad to say, but you look poor. You know what I mean?"

Some of her friends were still in college. Some, drawn to political activism, were joining a nationwide protest over aggressive police tactics. In early December, she read about the campus demonstrations, students marching and blocking roads near her old school, plans for a poetry slam. Sometimes she missed those college days when she was majoring in political science and African American studies. At the same time, she was trying to stay focused on her internship and her work as Miss Maryland USA. She learned to change clothes and make herself up in the car in order to keep up with her public appearances.

Near Christmas she had another dental appointment. As she waited in the office she read the history of Sandy Spring, the little community where the dental office was located—the pastures and rolling lawns, she learned, had once been plantations.

She read about a slave who bought his own freedom and then bought the freedom of his wife and children. When she was called in for her appointment, this time, she had to bite into a tray of plastery paste to make impressions of her teeth. Photos were taken of her face, from every angle.

"They want to see where everything is placed, how it looks," explained Adjei. "Smiling, profile, mouth open, mouth closed. To keep a log of the progression."

The braces would be delivered after the holidays. "I have to make sure I wear them twenty-two hours out of the day if I really want to see the best and quickest results. So it's really my commitment and my time."

On the way home the road was dark and there was a historical marker saying this was an Underground Railroad route. Slaves fled to freedom through these woods. Some people don't understand why history is important, she said. When she switched on the radio there was a new J. Cole song playing. He wrote it in honor of Michael Brown, a young black man, left dead after a confrontation with police in Ferguson, Missouri.

The new song "Be Free" echoed on the dark road.

The trade show at the annual session of the American Dental Association (ADA) was a vast and stunning display, befitting an industry valued at more than $110 billion a year. The exhibits went on for blocks—office furnishings and x-ray machines, disposable bibs and tissue lasers, lab coats and business management software, extractor forceps and teaching puppets, disembodied dentures and pearly laminate veneers, adult braces and medical credit card services, portable wooden chairs to take missionary care to jungle villages and bleaching solutions to make teeth four shades whiter in five minutes.

"Twenty-five years ago, A1 was a white tooth. Now it's a brown tooth," noted David Hornbrook, an athletic-looking California dentist well known for his cosmetic work. He was preparing to do a live veneer demonstration before an audience of colleagues attending the ADA meeting. The large room where Hornbrook was working was set up like a darkened theater in the round. At the center of the room, inside a lighted pavilion, a neatly coiffed dental assistant sat beside a dental chair where a young woman wearing jeans was reclining. She was waiting for her final veneer treatment.

She was introduced as Cherish. Her four front teeth had been prepared at an earlier appointment—depth cuts made, biting edges shortened and reshaped, some enamel removed to accommodate the new porcelain surfaces. She was administered a local anesthetic, and while it took effect Hornbrook talked about his dental practice in San Diego, about his system of predictably and efficiently delivering "smile designs."

"We have the opportunity to change somebody's life with a beautiful smile," Hornbrook told the crowd.

Then at the chair, three big screens showed Hornbrook chipping away the provisional veneers that the patient had been wearing over her cut-down teeth.

The finished porcelain veneers needed to be etched and bonded. But first Cherish had a chance to try them on. They were symmetrical and straight and very white. They fit over her old teeth a little like sparkling glass slippers. "Smile real big," the dentist told Cherish, and she did.

The dental meeting spanned several days and the thick program included listings for scores of continuing education courses, among them twenty-two listings for cosmetic dentistry.

It is difficult to find definitive statistics on how many of America's dentists perform cosmetic procedures these days. The services range from simple bleaching treatments to complex full-mouth restorations. Neither the American Dental Association nor other groups such as the Dental Trade Alliance or the American Academy of Cosmetic Dentistry say they can offer figures on the national trend. But as they did in the 1980s, when the modern cosmetic dental boom really took off, some industry analysts have continued to estimate that more than 80 percent of dental practices offer at least some cosmetic procedures.[3]

At "Veneers for Noncosmetic Dentists," practitioners lined up along workbenches to listen to a lecture on "off-the-shelf smiles" and "template-driven smile rehabs."

"Paint-by-number dentistry is in essence template-driven," explained dentist and instructor Martin Goldstein, showing a slide of a sad clown painting. For dentists, the templates can take the guesswork out of designing new smiles for their patients.

There are also services to help dentists sell their patients on the designs. Smile-Vision, an imaging company based in Newton, Massachusetts, transforms "before" photos of patients into customized "after" photos that simulate how they will look with their new teeth. There are medical credit card companies that offer smiles on installment plans.

"In my area of practice, in central Connecticut, the economy is depressed and people try to finance things," said Goldstein. "We need financing available and CareCredit has been very good about that."

Veneers alone regularly cost one thousand dollars per tooth, and extensive smile makeovers involving procedures such as bleaching, orthodontics, crowns, implants, or gum contouring can cost many thousands. But demand is strong.

"Weddings are a terrific way to incentivize people to get their smiles done because they want to look good in the albums," noted Goldstein. "Keep that in the back of your mind." He advised the roomful of dentists to be sure to schedule enough time to allow for the task of placing six, eight, and even ten veneers. "It's a very profitable morning," he said with a smile.

The dentists were given sets of stone teeth for the practice session, as well as other supplies. "This is a reduction guide," said Goldstein. "You can place it over your prepared teeth at the time you are doing your cases to make sure that you reduced enough of the dentition to allow for the porcelain. That's very important."

Then diamond burs were distributed. The dentists fitted the burs into their handpieces and, with a rising hum, they bent to the work of cutting and shaping the model teeth to accommodate the veneers.

The cosmetic dental boom that began in earnest in America back in the 1980s keeps on booming. These days, Americans spend more than one billion dollars a year on teeth-whitening products alone, industry studies have shown.[4] And the shining white American smile is now a commodity marketed around the globe.

Europeans still tend to prefer a subtler look, teeth that appear more natural. Some have joked about the perfection and "lavatorial" whiteness of American smiles.

But like Americans, consumers in emerging economies claiming billions of teeth—China, India, and Brazil—want movie star smiles. They are eagerly seeking that flashing set of white front teeth known as the "social six." A veneer job has become a globally recognized badge of success.

"You know I call a smile the ultimate jewelry," Ohio dentist Dan Ward told his class on Smile Design. "Every year in Columbus we have quite a large jewelry show," he said. "I see all these people spending all this money on jewelry and some of the smiles I see I want to say, 'You know what? If you would take the $50,000 you are spending on that diamond and get your teeth done you might look better than that piece of jewelry you are buying.'"

Dentists, once exclusively focused upon fillings and extractions, are nowadays considered providers of beauty, Ward said. Instead of dreading their dental appointments, patients are careful to keep them and even look forward to them. The trend has made life pleasanter for dentists, Ward noted.

But the stakes are high.

"Just think about it," Ward said. "People are coming to you for esthetic procedures expecting for you to change their lives. That's pretty heavy. That's a big deal.

"How many of you have had 'If you will fix my smile I am going to get married'? I've had it. . . . And it worked. Now obviously what I did was important. But more important, I made her feel good about herself. You see we forget sometimes. We are psychologists."

Success can be sweet. But failure can mean a lawsuit, Ward warned.

Cosmetic dentists endow the six top front teeth with particular esthetic significance that goes beyond their biological importance. The paired central incisors, flanked by the lateral incisors and the curving canines or cuspids, are given specific roles in the configuration of the smile.

"The central incisor is your age tooth," Ward explained to his class. "The lateral incisor: now we are talking about the sex tooth—the tooth that tends to be different in the different sexes. The feminine tooth tends to be more rounded, the masculine tooth tends to be more flat. Finally we have the personality. And of course that is shown in the cuspid." Dentists like Ward aim to achieve a harmonious balance in the relative sizes and shapes of the teeth, but they don't all agree about the ideal proportion to employ when reconfiguring them. Many have relied upon the Golden Proportion—found in nature and revered since ancient times as a kind of mystical formula for beauty—as their guide.

"It is shown in nautilus shells. It is used in designing cars. Credit cards are pretty close to the Golden Proportion," Ward told his class. In a smile conforming with this enigmatically pleasing scale, the widths of adjacent teeth are proportioned in accord with the ratio represented by the Greek letter *phi*.

Others have developed their own formulas they believe deliver better-looking smiles. Ward has called his the Recurring Esthetic Dental proportion. His research has convinced him that the use of this formula results in a smile that features the dominant front teeth, which cosmetic patients and dentists prefer.

This smile "does not come out of nature," he explained. On that point, he made no apologies. "Somebody is coming in to pay us. Do they want to get what they saw in nature? Or would they rather have what people think looks better?"

What has come to be known as the Hollywood smile—the American smile—known for its bold, ultra-white, star-quality teeth may not be naturally occurring. But over the course of much of the last century, and particularly over the past three decades, the bleaching, bonding, and laminating materials that help achieve it have evolved in response to demand. That demand has been driven by a confluence of powerful forces: fashion, mass media, easy credit, marketing, and the popularity of elective surgical procedures of all kinds.

"So how do we diagnose a smile?" Ward asked the dentists. New digital cameras were distributed and participants were asked to pair up and take photographs of one another. "Now that we have taken that picture we are going to talk about evaluating a smile using a photograph," he explained. A photograph bares flaws that might be fleeting in real time. It reveals gaps, asymmetries, stains, and misalignments ripe for cosmetic correction. The pictures serve as a guide for the dental laboratories in fabricating the finished veneers and crowns. And, Ward noted, they can protect the dentist if things don't go as planned.

"Heaven forbid if you get sued," he told his fellow dentists.

"The judge says, 'This lady says you messed up her teeth. Let me see a picture of the way she looked before we started.'" Without a photograph "you are dead," Ward added. "You lost the case."

"In my opinion, you cannot do predictable esthetic or cosmetic dentistry without a camera. Bottom line."

An increasing number of dentists do not limit their cosmetic work to the teeth, participants in a "Botox for Every Dental Practice" workshop learned. The teeth can be perfect, but the dentist who ignores the rest of the face is not really completing the job, according to the teacher of the class, Ohio dentist Louis Malcmacher.

"This has got nothing to do with a wrinkle dentist trying to grab money from patients," Malcmacher explained as class participants took a break before opening the vials of botulinum toxin that they had purchased for their practice session.

"This is real treatment, real evaluation, real examination," he said.

"Botox is only a tool to get the best esthetic and therapeutic outcome. That is what all this is really about and that is the way every dentist should approach it, just like any other part of their practice."

Each $575 vial contained a tear-sized drop of the elixir. The dentists learned to dilute the botox with saline solution, and to use alcohol to wipe down the faces of their volunteers: mostly their dental assistants and other staffers, husbands and wives. They marked the injection sites with pens. Then, with rows of loaded needles, they attacked crow's feet, wrinkles, and frown lines.

A photograph is more than a mirror. In the face of mortality, it offers hope for a permanent self. Wedding albums, family portraits, the images of stars and models on screens and in glossy magazines dwell in an idealized place, separate from time and space. Photography offers a parallel universe, graven by light, a chance for perfection. Photography and professional dentistry were born at precisely the same moment in history. The disciplines have enjoyed a complex and synergistic relationship ever since. Both, in their own ways, have built empires upon the smile.

It was in 1840 that the world's first dental college opened in Baltimore, Maryland. One of the school's co-founders, Chapin Harris, was deeply concerned with the clinical aspects of dentistry. But he was also a devout admirer of teeth.

"In every age and country, even among the rudest and most barbarous nations, these useful and beautiful organs have attracted attention, and been regarded as being of great importance for the purpose of giving beauty and symmetry to the face," Harris wrote in what would become the world's first dental college textbook: *The Dental Art: A Practical Treatise on Dental Surgery.*[5]

It was also in 1840 that the first U.S. patent was awarded for a camera.

The device was a wooden box fitted with a concave reflector and a plate for "taking likenesses."

The patent was granted to Alexander S. Wolcott, a dentist.[6]

It was that same year that William Henry Fox Talbot invented the photographic negative. He called his images calotypes, taken from the Greek word *kalos* for beautiful.

The photograph offered a new way of seeing.

"We learn to see ourselves photographically; to regard oneself as attractive is, precisely, to judge that one would look good in a photograph," wrote essayist Susan Sontag in *On Photography*.[7]

The negative process made the images reproducible. Soon photography was a widely consumed commodity. The mass-produced photographs held up a new kind of mirror. They standardized beauty.

Faster films—and, by the end of the nineteenth century, moving pictures—offered increasingly candid images. Then, in the early twentieth century, the first sound films arrived in America's theaters. Eager audiences gazed into the flickering silver light, into the great, luminous faces on the screen. The stars opened their mouths and spoke.

Some of the actors had been poor, or lived hard and fast. It showed in their teeth.

There were shantytowns around the studio gates, where aspiring performers camped and hoped for big breaks. The director King Vidor found many of the stars for one of his films adrift on the streets of Los Angeles.

The Great Depression of the 1930s could have spelled disaster for Hollywood. Instead the motion picture industry found a powerful role in the crisis, capturing the nation's fears and fantasies, offering distraction and dramatic catharsis. Even in the depths of the depression, 60 million to 80 million Americans went to the movies each week.

Audiences thrilled to dramas like *Our Daily Bread* and laughed aloud to garish and spectacular comedies like *Gold Diggers of 1933*.

A young dentist named Charles Pincus went to the movies too. When the stock market crashed, he had just opened an office on the corner of Hollywood and Vine. Watching the actors up on the screen, he realized there was a place for a dentist in the dream factory. "The camera is cruel in its relentless exposure of the smallest flaw in the mouth," he wrote. "A tooth turned even slightly out of line casts a shadow before it."[8] Pincus invented a mixture of powdered plastic and porcelain that he shaped into snap-on caps to cover the flawed teeth of the actors. The appliances were known as Hollywood veneers.

There were plenty of stars who needed the dentist's help. Montgomery Clift, Fanny Brice, Mae West, Joan Crawford, and Bob Hope were among his patients. So was James Dean, who died in an accident at twenty-four. "He was a farm boy. But he was missing all of his back teeth. He wore partials," remembered Los Angeles dentist Timothy Gogan, a longtime student and protégé of Pincus. "Judy Garland had a bunch of spaces in her front teeth. So he would make these little slip-ons. In the '50s when she was running out of money she didn't have the veneers and there are some pictures of her without them," Gogan recalled. There was also Shirley Temple: "You never saw Shirley Temple without hers."

The child star was under contract to Fox by the time she was six. Her breakout role came that same year. It was in 1934 in the film *Stand Up and Cheer*. In a climactic scene, the little girl helps to lead an "Out of the Red" parade where legions of joyful workers fill the streets, celebrating the country's return to financial health. The child danced and beamed through nearly two dozen feature films by the time she was twelve. Yet America never saw her lose her baby teeth. "In Europe they thought she was a midget because a midget would have all the teeth," said Gogan.

Those dainty teeth, like a matched set of pearls, were among Pincus's proudest achievements.

"Shirley Temple was quite a problem as a moppet star," explained

Pincus, in a talk to fellow dentists—illustrated with before and after photos of the girl. "Losing her deciduous teeth during the production entailed many different types of restorations which had to be constantly changed," Pincus noted. "All this had to be planned so as not to hold up the shooting schedule, as one day's loss meant approximately 15 to 20 thousand dollars cost to the studio."[9]

The millions of fans who adored Temple included President Franklin Delano Roosevelt. He recognized the tiny actress as a powerful antidote to hard times.

"It is a splendid thing that for just 15 cents an American can go to a movie and look at the smiling face of a baby and forget his troubles," Roosevelt said.[10]

In 1938 Roosevelt invited Shirley Temple to the White House. The president got a rare and unexpected glimpse of the child's natural teeth.

Years later in her memoir, the actress would remember her visit with Roosevelt.

"Why aren't you smiling?" he suddenly inquired. "I thought you were famous for your smile."

"'Smile for him,' Mother urged, who up to then had said nothing.

"'The reason is I lost a tooth. See?' I pulled back the upper lip and went on to describe how the tooth had fallen out during a bite of sandwich. He threw his big head back and broke into loud laughter."

The little girl was not laughing, though. She was worried about the tooth, which had disappeared from the hotel dresser where she was keeping it until she could place it beneath her pillow for a tooth fairy reward. "It seems as if I have been losing teeth all my life," she remembered telling Roosevelt wistfully. "'That's the way with all of us,' the President said, looking slightly uncomfortable."[11]

At the time of their conversation, Temple and Roosevelt had two of the most photographed smiles in the world. Their exchange served as an acknowledgment of the growing currency of the smile in public life.

The powerful blend of personality and optimism the two of

them managed to project with their open smiles left a permanent imprint on America's national character, historian John F. Kasson has argued.

"The forces set in motion by their smiling faces have shaped American life ever since," wrote Kasson.[12]

And dentists would learn from Hollywood, Pincus predicted.

They would shape the American smile.

"A captivating smile showing an even row of natural appearing gleaming teeth is a major factor in achieving that elusive dominant characteristic known as personality," he counseled his fellow dentists.

"One must always keep in mind that one is dealing with organs which can change an individual's entire visual personality. Few things will cause a patient to enthuse as much as the results which may be obtained by a little simple rounding of very long sharp cusps. . . . Long narrow teeth may be made into well proportioned centrals and laterals through shortening and recontouring."[13]

The end of World War II brought dramatic change to America. Prosperity and science offered new potential in peacetime. Women, who had entered the workplace in vast numbers during the war, were now vying with returning men for jobs. They were discovering new roles and new identities. Popular women's magazines redefined beauty in the nuclear age. "Farewell to Ugliness" declared the headline for one series of articles.

"To the homely girl, life may seem an endless succession of Embarrassments, Frustrations and anguish until she decides, one day, to . . . have a plastic surgery operation. Then a remodeled nose, a rounded chin, may alter her personality—and her whole life."[14]

Cosmetic dentistry was part of that same wave.

The February 1956 issue of *Cosmopolitan* magazine featured a movie star on its mauve cover sporting sparkling diamond earrings and a dazzling smile.

But the real star of the issue was a working woman, a twenty-seven-year-old secretary identified only as Jane, whose

dental "miracle" was described in a story headlined: "DENTAL
COSMETICS Now *your teeth* can be made beautiful."

"Jane had been having trouble with her teeth all her life. Nothing seemed to stop the formation of new cavities. She had them
taken care of promptly, but countless fillings of all colors, sizes
and shapes made her mouth an unsightly hodgepodge. As a result,
Jane seldom smiled, didn't 'meet' people easily, had never been able
to get the good job her ability merited. Now her friend Sally was
going to get married; in three weeks she would be quitting just the
kind of job Jane had always wanted. This was Jane's big chance, and
she decided to do something about her teeth—but fast!'"

Jane had heard of a newly popular treatment, "porcelain jacket
crowns," which, the article explained, were "delicate individual
thimbles of gold and porcelain or acrylic . . . once considered the-
atrical luxuries" that "now enable the dentist to save mere stumps"
and "restore a healthy bite along with a healthy ego."

She opted to have a full-mouth treatment.

Placed under a sedative that kept her "relaxed and dreamy for
several hours," the dentist "drilled and shaped for a jacket every
tooth in her lower jaw." She was fitted with temporary crowns and,
a few days later, the entire process was repeated on her upper teeth.
"Fitting her permanent jackets required three brief additional
appointments. Within three weeks from start to finish, every
tooth in her mouth was crowned with beauty and armored against
future decay," the story reported. The cost per crown ranged from
between $60 to $150.

"Expensive? Jane doesn't think so, even though she borrowed to
meet her bill. Her payments are just about covered by the big raise
in earnings on the new job."

The four-page article included, in a small box near the end, a
few cautionary words on cosmetic dentistry, offered by Charles
A. Wilkie, secretary of the Dental Society of the State of New
York. "Except in isolated cases, dentistry frowns on the sacrifice of
healthy tooth tissue for purely cosmetic effect," Wilkie noted. He
observed that crowns were a preferable alternative to the extraction

of sound teeth, but his three-paragraph statement ended with this: "Today, dentists treat the patient as a total personality. The psychology of the individual is important, and a mouth that is merely healthy without being attractive may be unsuited to the patient's urgent psychological demands."

Those urgent psychological demands did not go away. Cosmetic dentistry became part of the same quest for physical self-improvement that brought the nation tummy tucks and liposuction. Creating the perfect smile might have gotten its start in the dream factory that was Depression-era Hollywood. But the multibillion-dollar cosmetic dental industry that makes Americans' teeth look bigger, straighter, shinier, and whiter really took off in the 1980s. By that decade it began to seem that dentists would need to find something to do besides drilling and filling cavities.

"End of Most Tooth Decay Predicted for the Near Future" read the headline in a 1983 issue of the *New York Times*. Community water fluoridation programs, which got under way after World War II, had brought the decay-fighting properties of fluoride to the municipal water supplies of 125 million Americans—over half the nation's population. The growing use of professionally applied topical fluorides, protective dental sealants, and other innovations were also credited with reducing decay. "For the first time in the history of man, we are seeing a decrease in tooth decay," a federal health official told the newspaper.[15]

In the wake of such news, dentists embraced cosmetic procedures in earnest.

By 1987, the *New York Times* weighed in on that trend as well. "Going into the 1980s, the dental industry appeared headed for some trouble—brought on ironically by its own impressive achievement by reducing decay in this country by 50 percent in two decades," reporter Warren Berger wrote. "But just as the need for traditional dental work declined, cosmetic dental surgery began to flourish.

"Today more than 80 percent of the nation's 130,000 dentists do cosmetic work and many report it is the fastest growing part of their practice," wrote Berger.

"Studies show nearly half the country's dentists are installing porcelain laminates."[16]

Product innovations meant dentists had better materials at their disposal, as Berger noted. But other factors have helped drive the trend as well.

The smiles of Shirley Temple and Franklin Delano Roosevelt may have stood as emblems of American solidarity during the hard times of the Great Depression and World War II. But it was the Hollywood smile of President Ronald Reagan that gleamed over the glamour, conspicuous consumption, and individualism that marked the 1980s. The decade also brought a dramatic shift in the business climate for health care services, including dental care. Following a 1982 decision by the U.S. Supreme Court, longtime restrictions on medical advertising were lifted. The decision served as a milestone in a larger federal challenge to organized medicine's control over the market for medical procedures.

The ruling not only opened the way to more competition in the marketplace; it created a way for providers to sell procedures to the public. And the marketing of procedures, particularly cosmetic procedures, began to recast the doctor-patient relationship. "Advertising changed the way we think of plastic surgery from a medical relationship between a surgeon and a patient to a commercial relationship between a consumer and a service provider," noted Laurie Essig in *American Plastic: Boob Jobs, Credit Cards and Our Quest for Perfection.*[17]

In their advertisements, providers offer the hope of cosmetic transformation. Before and after photographs invite the consumer to imagine a sagging jaw made sleek, a wrinkled brow made smooth, a crooked smile made straight.

Perfection comes at a price. But the banking deregulation of the 1980s and 1990s gave rise to another catalyst that continues to drive elective procedures, including cosmetic dentistry: the medical credit card. The cards, which typically offer long-term, deferred-interest financing, are marketed as a way of helping consumers to get the treatments they desire, at the time they want them. By 2013, 79 percent of the members of the American Academy of Cosmetic Dentistry responding to a survey reported that they offered their cosmetic dentistry patients third-party external financing services. The same 79 percent said that the offer of that financing option boosted "case acceptance" and "helped patients get to a 'yes' decision."

"With CareCredit I'm able to get the care I need instead of waiting. That means I'll have a beautiful smile for my wedding next year!" declared a woman named Pamela Z. on the website of one of the leading medical credit card companies.

But the cards can be risky and consumers do not always understand the terms. In 2013, CareCredit was ordered to refund cardholders up to $34.1 million by the federal Consumer Financial Protection Bureau (CFPB) after the consumer watchdog agency determined that the company, and the service providers, had enrolled customers without adequately explaining the terms. "At doctors' and dentists' offices around the country, consumers were signed up for CareCredit credit cards they thought were interest free, but were actually accruing interest that kicked in if the full balance was not paid at the end of a promotional period," the agency found.

CFPB determined more than one million consumers were potential victims of misleading practices and that many "incurred substantial debt." The agency could not provide specific data on the number of consumers who went into debt paying for new smiles.

Beyond the cost of the care, a few dentists have raised warnings about the emotional forces that underlie the demand for cosmetic dental treatments, and the biological consequences of some of the procedures. In some cases, the mental health of the patient in search of a Hollywood smile can cause concerns, according to Chris Herren, a Kentucky dentist and former professor at the University of Kentucky College of Dentistry.

"You think certain procedures are going to be cut and dried but you may be dealing with things that are emotional and psychological with a patient that go beyond just a veneer or a bleaching," said Herren. "They bring in all their experiences."

An encounter with a patient early in his career taught him this. He went on to publish a much-cited paper about the case.

"A twenty-seven-year old woman goes to her general dentist's office for bleaching. She is extremely preoccupied with the shade of her teeth," the paper began. "She was using tooth whitening products both over the counter and prescribed by a dentist to maintain her goal of achieving 'a movie star smile.'" The patient turned out to be suffering from a condition called body dysmorphic disorder, or BDD, which manifests itself as a fear of ugliness, an obsession with perceived physical flaws. Researchers have estimated that up to 15 percent of patients seeking cosmetic surgeries suffer from BDD. Even after a number of bleaching procedures, the patient continued to insist her teeth were too dark. Finally, she told the dentist that tooth whitening had become an all-consuming obsession.

"The floodgates opened," recalled Herren. "I wasn't prepared for the emotional response." The patient was referred to her primary care physician, who diagnosed her with BDD and placed her on a regimen of cognitive therapy and medication. Herren's paper, which appeared in a peer-reviewed journal, cautioned other dentists to be aware of the problem.

"With the number of elective cosmetic dentistry procedures being performed on the rise, dentists may be the first health care provider to notice BDD and intervene," the paper warned.[18]

Though techniques and technologies have advanced since the early days, many cosmetic procedures permanently alter the teeth. Treatments such as veneers typically require lifetime maintenance. Sometimes they fail. These are factors that patients and dentists need to candidly discuss. "It is well known that patients elect to have radical esthetic surgery on various parts of their bodies knowing that the procedures are elective," warned prominent Utah dentist and lecturer Gordon Christensen in an online editorial. "But oral overtreatment in the name of esthetic dentistry without total informed consent of patients, primarily for dentist financial gain is nothing less than overt dishonesty in its worst form," he wrote. "You cannot put tooth structure back after it has been removed."[19]

By early in the new year, Mamé Adjei had left her internship at the human rights think tank. She said she didn't feel it was fair to the organization, taking off time for her pageant work. She found a part-time job at a friend's beauty business, where the hours were more flexible, allowing her to make her Miss Maryland USA appearances and get ready for the national stage.

By February she was tired and feeling stressed. She needed to choose her gown for the Miss USA pageant and have it fitted but she seemed to be losing weight. Her dental work was lagging, too, and she was blaming herself. She was supposed to switch to a new set of Invisalign braces every two weeks. "I made the mistake of keeping my second set almost three weeks and you cannot deviate from the plan or else it sets you back." To make matters worse she left them out in the evening sometimes, she admitted. "But I can't afford to because the competition is very close," she said. If the dentists could not close the tiny gaps with the braces in time for the pageant, Adjei said, Linda Steel told her they could use other methods.

"She told me they can make my teeth look as perfect as they can with bonding. For the spaces." She said the regime using the Invisalign braces had been harder than she expected. She had headaches from the pressure on her teeth and the whitening solution had been somewhat painful too. "I didn't realize those little clear plastic trays would do that," she said stoically. "With the sensitivity and the shifting and the headaches all at once. I can't stand my own teeth right now. But I'm gonna whiten a little bit more before the official photo shoot for the headshots."

She was going to take the bus into New York City to have her photographs made for the official pageant program, but first she needed the dentist to temporarily remove the tiny hooks for her braces, so they did not show in the photographs.

Around the parking lot outside the dental office, the trees were filled with birds. A woodpecker drummed on a tree trunk.

Adjei emerged from the dental office, wrapped in her coat and scarf. She walked across the icy parking lot. She was carrying something that the dentist gave her.

It fit into her graceful palm. It was a plaster cast of her teeth. The teeth curved along the dental arches, uppers and lowers, each one shaped, specific to its task, an orderly, businesslike set—incisors, canines, premolars, and molars. She gently opened them and traced their delicate cusps.

"So funny. . . . Little baby teeth."

She joined the upper and lower parts together and studied them. They regarded her back, cryptically. "It's a model of my teeth, at the first days, without seeing a dentist," she explained. Linda Steel had made it. "She went in there and sculpted and shaved off the stuff, so I could see how I have an overbite and the spaces I have in between my teeth. . . . That will all be fixed by the time of the pageant."

She appreciated the careful smoothness of the model. She said she planned to keep it on her dresser. She hoped the dentist would give her another one, when the work was done. "If that's not standard procedure I'll ask her if I can have one for a keepsake. My year as Miss Maryland USA." Now that the hooks were off, she said she was ready for her official portrait for the Miss USA pageant book. "Yeah, it's the beginning," she said quietly and seriously.

She went to New York. Then, in the winter another opportunity arose that she needed to keep secret for a while. She was chosen to go to Los Angeles to compete in the television series *America's Next Top Model*. By late spring, when she got back to Maryland, she had reached tray number ten of her Invisaligns. Her sojourn in Los Angeles left her sleek and buoyant.

By early June there was a final push to get ready for the Miss USA pageant.

After a morning appearance in Baltimore, she was an hour late for her dental appointment. Dressed casually in dark green slacks and jacket, her hair a soft mahogany-colored mane, her eyes laughing, her teeth sparkling, she looked like some glamorous wood nymph.

But her teeth were not done yet.

She had missed a two-week cycle of Invisaligns in Los Angeles. She did not tell the dentist. Each new set hurt, she said. "These new ones . . . they don't fit properly. But my teeth will wriggle and move into the trays and sit in them perfectly in a couple of days." She moved her long brown fingers and curled them, like teeth.

"It's never gonna start fitting perfectly at the very first. It moves in slowly. That's when it hurts. You get headaches."

There was more whitening scheduled before the pageant. And laser gum contouring.

"So my next appointment will be next week on Tuesday where he will shave my gums a little bit. Contouring. So they can reveal more enamel so I can have a bigger smile, like more teeth showing because I have what they call Chicklets. Like very baby teeth. They want to elongate my teeth and my smile. I don't know. I don't want to have horse-looking teeth, though. I don't want to look like a horse. But . . . just shaving a little bit of the gum. They are talking like millimeters. Barely noticeable . . . but that's it. I am going to continue bleaching until I go to Miss USA."

The following week she was back at the dentists' office. When she emerged from her appointment, high spirits were not in evidence. "They shaved and cut my gums, see?" she said, lifting her lips to reveal the places, faintly dark.

She studied herself in the car's sunshade mirror. In the rearview mirror too.

She reapplied her lipgloss and lip liner but continued to examine herself.

"He just took just like two millimeters off my teeth so that they look longer," she said.

"I really didn't even need it because I don't smile that huge," she said.

"When I smile it's like . . ." She turned on that expression, that beam, which arranged all her features, eyes, cheeks, mouth, into the configuration of beauty and serenity. But the radiance was clouded by worry and confusion.

She was tired. She remembered the burning smell of the procedure. She was given vitamin E to rub on her gums to help them heal. She said she needed to find her friends who were waiting to meet her.

"Oh Jesus. And I have so much to do today. I have to go to my dress sponsor to figure dresses out. I didn't realize my mouth would be like this.

"God, I hope my lip is not messed up from this," she said gravely.

"I'm just creeped out. My gum is shaved off. I'm like an art project. I hope it heals over. They are just revealing more enamel. I don't think I needed it. My teeth were just really short. I don't mind my little special things about me. Now my teeth look like everyone else's."

2

Suffering

THE LIGHT OF A FRIDAY MORNING IN AUTUMN GENTLY TOUCHED THE little town: the Farmers and Miners Bank, the grocery store with the hand-lettered signboard advertising sugar on sale, the squat yellow brick courthouse. It was Jonesville, the county seat of Lee County, by many measures the poorest county in Virginia, and the farthest flung, here, in Appalachia. On this day, all attention was focused upon the outskirts, where at the small airport, preparations were under way for a free health clinic, to be held over the weekend.

In a few hours, the first of the patients would start arriving. They would come from the roads and the highways, the nearby towns and the more distant hollows, from southwestern Virginia and Kentucky and farther away. Some barely had the gas money to get to Jonesville. One woman was driving from Tennessee holding her broken glasses to her eyes. The truck with the chest x-ray machine was already parked at one end of the runway. And when the sky cleared a little more, an old airplane would be flying over the mountains, bringing in folding dental chairs and medical equipment and crates of surgical gauze and gloves from Knoxville.

The free clinic was organized by the Remote Area Medical Volunteer Corps (RAM), a nonprofit that, since its beginnings in 1985, had headed hundreds of missions and brought medical relief to some of the poorest places on the planet. This would be RAM's first visit to Jonesville. But the health problems in this pocket of Appalachia—the cancers, the diabetes, the ruined joints—were nothing new. The rotten teeth were nothing new. The toothaches were nothing new. In Lee County—remote, isolated, poor—the shortages of all kinds of health care had been a chronic problem. There were not enough primary and mental health care workers. And the shortage of dental providers was most acute.[1]

By federal estimates, roughly 49 million Americans live in communities that have been designated dental professional shortage areas—Lee County is one of them.[2]

And if dentists are in short supply in places such as Lee County, so is the money to pay them. "These are not forgotten people," explained RAM dental director John Osborn, a Knoxville dentist. "The system has passed them up."

Hundreds, sometimes thousands of aching teeth are extracted at these free weekend clinics.

The loss of a tooth to disease may prefigure other losses in life quality. In terms of oral health, complete tooth loss, or edentulism, has been called the "final marker of disease burden."[3] An extraction is emblematic of defeat. The extracted tooth will not grow back. But when routine care is long deferred, when more complex procedures are out of reach or not an option, the extractions serve the urgent need of relieving infection and relieving pain.

The news of the plans for the RAM clinic in Lee County claimed top headlines in the local paper. People talked about it for days in church and at the gas station and in the coffee shop out on the U.S. 58 bypass. On this Friday, at the airport, there was excitement in the air as volunteers worked to set up a sort of field hospital with tents and folding tables. Volunteer doctors and nurses, dentists and hygienists were coming from "out of town." A man with a "Friends of Coal" bumper sticker on his truck arrived with pizzas. Members of the high school football team, the Lee County Generals, who were waiting in their red numbered jerseys to help unload the plane, ate the pizza quietly and hungrily, out by the runway. Then a great deep-throated roar could be heard and everyone looked up to the pale clearing sky.

"Here's the plane!" someone shouted.

The World War II–vintage C-47 cargo plane landed smoothly, then stood there shimmering on the narrow landing strip at the foot of the mountains. RAM's founder, Stan Brock, a lean, charismatic British-born adventurer, greeted the small crowd in his calm, serious way. He was, as always, tan and, as always, dressed in a khaki shirt and pants.

Brock became famous in the 1960s as the anaconda-wrestling co-star of the television program *Mutual of Omaha's Wild Kingdom*. When he started RAM, his original goal was to get health care to the people living in the far-flung, third world places he had visited in his travels. But when he discovered that there were people in desperate need right in the United States, he began organizing clinics much closer to home.

Brock told the football players the plane they were seeing was used for the invasion on D-day, that young men about their own age had parachuted out of this very plane on June 6, 1944. "A lot of those young guys didn't make it back," he explained, as the football players listened with a kind of shy attention. Then it was time to get to work. There was a military precision to these operations that Brock had honed over the years that helped convey their urgency. At Brock's direction, the football players began hauling carefully organized crates of supplies out of the plane.

Slowly, methodically, the weekend hospital took shape. Areas were set up for medical tests and exams. Eyeglasses would be provided free of charge. The airport waiting room was transformed into a six-chair dental clinic. By the time the chill of evening fell upon the mountains, a line of cars and pickup trucks had formed on the road coming up to the airport. In the predawn darkness of Saturday, about four hundred people were waiting. Worn-out miners, old farmers, tired homemakers, unemployed workers took their numbers at the gate, wrapped in coats and blankets. Charlton Strader, a retired construction superintendent with tremors and chronic obstructive pulmonary disease, said he used to have dental benefits but that he lost them. He said his teeth had started "snapping off and breaking." "I've got one that bothers me all the time," he said.

Randy Peters, a former miner and mattress factory worker with multiple sclerosis, was also troubled by his teeth. "I've got a couple broken ones and a couple of bad cavities," he said. "It's getting so I can't eat."

Ernest Holdway, a disabled miner, said he came to get a tooth extracted. "It ain't hurting but it will," he predicted. His dental insurance ended when he had to leave the coal mine. Now his teeth were starting to fail him. "I always had good teeth until I started the arthritis medicine," he explained. "Nobody wants to lose their teeth. I've heard it takes years off your life." He said he just finished paying off the $1,500 he'd owed for the extraction of three bad molars, which he was told to get removed before a knee surgery. He was still fighting to save his leg. He showed it. It was fearfully swollen.

"I'm a good person, but I sure have been tested," he said.

By the time the sun was fully up, Jonesville's small downtown was empty. "Everybody is down at RAM getting their teeth pulled," said the waitress at the coffee shop.

Throughout the day, patients emerged from the dental clinic with gauze clenched between their remaining teeth. They took seats in folding chairs underneath a tent to recover, or waited for friends and relatives still receiving services. "I had two pulled," said Emma Marsee, an unemployed nurse. "One had an infection underneath the filling." Marsee's daughter, a waitress, was also in the tent waiting for care. She depended on her smile for her economic security, Marsee said. "It's all about appearance anymore," said Marsee, a striking woman, strawberry blonde with golden eyes. Who wanted a waitress with bad teeth? "If you are not a healthy-looking individual, you don't want that person taking care of you."

Everyone in that big tent was struggling.

"It's tough in this area because there are no jobs," said Marsee.

Even as people sat in their folding chairs, the behavior of some suggested fatalism, weary self-destruction: the girl with the deeply decaying teeth taking another drink of Coke. A baby with a sippy cup of sweet juice in the arms of a gaunt mother waiting to see a dentist. The woman with the rasping cough, taking a drag from a cigarette.

"Nerves" are a common complaint in this region, research by the Southwest Virginia Graduate Medical Education Consortium found.

"A frequently reported cause of nerves was having too many problems and too few solutions," the authors of a study on the problem found. The consortium concluded that residents of the area were 70 percent more likely to commit suicide than people living elsewhere in the state.[4]

Marsee, too, was familiar with the dark side. "Drug abuse in this area is horrible," she said. It showed in some of the hopeless, drug-blackened teeth.

The area has been poor for a long time, yet people hate to move on. "All your roots are here," said Marsee. "It's hard to leave it." There was the old beauty of the mist-shrouded mountains, the green woods. The love of family, the kindness of neighbors, of strangers.

The teeth flame out when they die. That is a very old kind of pain.

The human fossil record bears mute testimony: the ancient Egyptian mummy unearthed with packing in the jaw. The Alaskan incisor, bored with a simple tool sometime between 1300 and 1700 A.D., apparently to relieve an abscess. The tooth of a medieval Dane, with a rosary bead tucked into a cavity.[5]

Decay is a progressive disease and, unchecked, it results in excruciating pain and tooth loss. Many factors contribute; diet plays a major role. In the very old days, when refined foods were rarer, the toothache was a curse of privilege. When sugar became cheaper, tooth decay, the main cause of toothaches, became more widespread. The habit of sipping sweet sodas has been widely implicated. The steady bath of sugar never allows the teeth to repair and remineralize themselves.

These days, too, hundreds of common over-the-counter and prescription medications taken by millions of Americans make teeth more susceptible to disease.

One of their side effects is dry mouth, a condition that reduces the natural flow of saliva that cleanses and buffers the teeth, helping to protect them from decay. Without fluoride to strengthen the teeth, without enough routine home care, without timely professional care, the disease process progresses.

The excruciating pain of toothache is not rare. Millions of Americans experience toothaches.

Financial factors are the main reason Americans delay getting needed professional dental care, a study by the American Dental Association found.[6]

Private and even public dental benefits can help defray the cost of services.

But more than 114 million Americans lack them entirely. While the national health care reform program signed into law in 2010 took significant steps to broaden access to dental services for children, it did less to address the broken system for adults. Even many working adults with private health insurance lack adequate coverage for dental care. While routine preventive visits may be covered, beneficiaries are typically required to pay a percentage of the cost of procedures such as fillings, crowns, root canals, and implants, which can run to hundreds and thousands of dollars. Among U.S adults who struggled with unpaid medical bills, 12 percent reported dental bills made up the largest share of the bills they had problems paying, a 2015 survey found. "Insurance is not a panacea against these problems," the researchers concluded.[7]

And most people who have dental benefits lose them when they retire. Medicare, the nation's health care program covering roughly 55 million elderly and disabled Americans, does not cover routine dental services.

The dental suffering among many of the more than one million residents of American nursing homes is particularly acute. Since 1987, when federal law set new standards for institutions receiving Medicare and Medicaid funding, nursing homes have been required to provide oral health services. Yet amid the daily cycle of washing, turning, and changing bedridden and disabled patients, simple tooth brushing and denture care have often been overlooked. "Most clinical studies of nursing home residents report widespread inadequate oral hygiene and associated dental, gingival and periodontal conditions," noted the authors of one survey. "Medical and nursing services were almost uniformly provided while dental and mental health services were provided much more infrequently."[8]

Visits by dental professionals are also rare in many institutions. Many of the patients Louisiana dentist Gregory Folse said he has visited on his rounds of nursing homes have not had care in years. When he looks into a new patient's mouth, he is not surprised to find decay, rampant infection, the broken stumps of teeth, and even oral cancers. He is paid a stipend to serve as the dental director for the homes. Most of the patients are covered by Medicaid, but adult dental benefits in the state are extremely scant. Folse estimated he has donated more services than he has billed to Medicaid. He said he travels forty to fifty thousand miles a year through the backwoods and bayous, driving a pickup truck, carrying portable tools and instruments, setting up in nursing home community rooms and beauty parlors, repairing dentures, pulling teeth. "Nine hundred patients with severe gum disease or abscess. Half of my patients. I take everybody that has swelling. Everybody in pain. Everybody that's got loose teeth. And I help them as best I can. With funding, without funding. The family pays some, the nursing homes. Sometimes no one pays. I do it."

Some of the patients suffer from dementia and getting them to open their mouths is a challenge. The work is rewarding, just the same, he said. "I had a patient in a wheelchair. She had a stroke. She was so happy to get her dentures. She reached down and grabbed her purse. She reached inside. She found a piece of bread. 'Here doc. Take it.' I didn't want to take her last piece of bread," said Folse, with a laugh. "No telling how long it had been at the bottom of her purse. We have to give out of being wealthy. She gave to me out of her poverty."[9]

The rate of dental suffering is a grim kind of economic indicator.

The poor are more likely to suffer from toothaches. Their oral health is worse and it can be hard to find a dentist who will treat them. The lack of money to pay for care is a major barrier: roughly one in five Americans is covered by Medicaid, the enormous federal-state health care program for the poor. But coverage is no guarantee of access to treatment, as only a minority of dentists see Medicaid patients.

Children are entitled to dental care under Medicaid but often face difficulties obtaining services. Fewer than half of dentists saw any Medicaid patients in the majority of states included in a 2010 study by the U.S. Government Accountability Office.[10]

A 2016 study by the American Dental Association found that 42 percent of the nation's dentists had registered as Medicaid providers on the program's Insure Kids Now database. But the percentage did not necessarily reflect the percentage of dentists actually participating in the program. "It does not mean you are seeing Medicaid kids. It does not mean you have open appointments," said economist Marko Vujicic, who helped lead the study. "Take it for what it is. It is the best data we have."[11]

The situation is harder for Medicaid's adult beneficiaries. Dental benefits for adults are an optional part of state Medicaid programs. They are among the first line items to end up on budget chopping blocks in times of fiscal austerity.

Toothaches are destroyers of sleep. They make eating painful, working and parenting overwhelming. It is the poor who are most likely to pray to heaven for relief. They turn to drugs, both legal and illegal, and folk remedies. In desperation, some even pull out their own teeth.

Out at the free clinic in Lee County, among the solid, stoic mountain people, Tabitha Hay, with her fragile face and darkly mascaraed eyes, looked like a lost tropical bird, blown off course by a storm. She and her mother-in-law and husband arrived at the clinic after a thirteen-hour drive from Belleview, Florida. They were self-employed. They cleaned houses and took care of pets for well-off retirees. They left after work on Friday evening and drove all night to get to Jonesville. All three of them needed care, but Tabitha, twenty-six, needed it most. She was tormented by a molar, decayed beneath a filling.

"I feel like my jaw is being crushed," she said. "Sometimes the pressure is like it is going to explode. I'm hungry but I can't eat. To sleep I have to put a heating pad on it and nothing takes the pain away." After missing a week of work she tried to get back to the job on the day before the trip.

"I tried to work. I couldn't do anything. I sat in the back seat and cried."

She said a Florida dentist told her the extraction would cost $500. It was money she did not have. She arrived too late to get care at the free clinic on Saturday. She was told she would need to wait until Sunday. As night fell upon the mountains, she bedded down in the red Kia with her husband and mother-in-law to face another night of pain.

Researchers have found choice words for the pain of toothaches —sharp, throbbing, lancinating. Heat and pressure on the affected tooth can result in paroxysms. Capillary dilation that comes with the approach of sleep seems to worsen the anguish.

Writers have reflected upon the way the toothache works upon the mind in the darkness. "I once read the sentence 'I lay awake with a toothache, thinking about the toothache and about lying awake,'" C.S. Lewis wrote in *A Grief Observed*.[12]

"Part of misery is, so to speak, the misery's shadow or reflection:

the fact that you don't merely suffer but have to keep on thinking about the fact that you suffer."

Fear makes the pain worse. And fear is the reason that millions of American adults—one out of ten—do not visit the dentist for their oral health problems, according to federal statistics.[13]

"The issues of pain, anxiety and fear have always been a major part of dentistry," wrote researcher Robert Pawlicki.[14] Yet a better understanding of these factors is needed. Dental fear is a ripe area for study, particularly as the definition of pain itself has continued to evolve.

"Pain is no longer viewed as a sensation," Pawlicki noted. "It is understood as a perception."

Some dental patients experience panic, lying prone in the chair, the dentist standing above, in a position of power. For others, it is opening up the intimate territory of the mouth, submitting it for inspection, for judgment, that inspires dread. The one-way conversations, the sharp instruments, the sounds and smells of dental offices cause fear in others. Some patients gag. Some squirm. Some delay care until their problems are very far advanced. Then the ordeal of treatment creates further fear and avoidance.[15] Pawlicki found that people who feared the dentist were more than three times as likely to miss appointments as the nonfearful.

Dentists lose money when patients miss their appointments. They tend to blame the patients. Missed appointments are one of the main reasons dentists give for not participating in Medicaid.

Some say dental schools do not do enough to train dentists to address patients' fears. In private practice, many rely upon anesthesia to treat the deeply fearful. But anesthesia comes with its own expenses and risks.

Experts on dental fear suggest dentists try building confidence over time, meeting with frightened patients in a setting other than a dental chair to talk with them about the care they need. But that takes a long-term relationship, afforded by what health care policy experts call a "dental home." In the free clinics, there are only well-intentioned strangers and the urgent crush of the pain.

Dawn on Sunday found Tabitha Hay's small face very pale. Her makeup was gone. She was dressed in rumpled clothes and wrapped in a fleece pirate blanket printed with skulls and crossbones. She wore black rubber flip-flop sandals on her feet.

As she got her x-ray and approached the head of the line for dental care she got paler still.

She stood at the threshold of the airport waiting room with the six portable dental chairs and the dentists working. She paused at the row of plastic seats against the wall where the patients at the head of the line were to sit and wait to be called.

There was that strong insistent dental office odor, the high, clinging note of clove oil, with the mineral undertones of tooth dust.

"That smell," she murmured.

Then there was the sound of the drilling and the sight of the shining instruments laid out on trays. "I don't like needles," she said. "I'm freaking out."

When it was Hay's turn to go, she climbed into the folding dental chair. Then she gripped it, sobbing. "You're gonna be okay," volunteer Dana Williams, a nursing student at Mountain Empire College, told her softly. "If you get really emotional they won't be able to work on you." That would mean the thirteen-hour trip from Florida would have been a wasted effort. That would mean driving home in pain.

"Just calm down. Take a deep breath," the volunteer dentist, Michael Pignato, told her. Williams took Hay's hand and held it, murmuring soothing words. Pignato gave her a shot of anesthetic and then another. Hay writhed on the chair. She said she could still feel pain, as anxious people often do. Moaning, she finally gathered herself enough to allow the dentist to begin his work with his instruments, his elevator and his forceps. Her toes curled up. Her rubber sandals fell to the floor.

It took a struggle to extract the tooth but it finally emerged.

Pignato set it on the tray and it lay there, with its long red roots gleaming. Then Hay was calmer.

Pignato had flown down from Rochester, New York, to help out at the clinic.

It was still early but he, too, looked pale and tired. He reminded Hay that another one of her teeth needed attention and suggested that they might as well press forward.

"I'm gonna tell you," he told her. "You are taking a couple of years off my life."

They went ahead with the work.

Speaking later, Pignato said he found satisfaction in volunteering his skills, in helping people who needed care. "I'm sort of blue collar," he said. "I'm soft. If somebody needs something done I do it for them." A dentist for more than thirty years, he said he still had some of his first patients in his practice in upstate New York. "They still have their teeth," he said.

He won their trust by providing for their needs. "I can do dentistry," he said. "But I don't sell dentistry. I just do what people need to have done." The profession's increasing emphasis upon cosmetic procedures can make it harder to find dentists interested in providing basic care, he said. "Nobody wants to do the low-end stuff."

It was easier to find dental care in these Appalachian communities before the mining industry dwindled, others have observed. "You had U.S. Steel and there were better benefits," said dentist Chris Herren. He was not at the free clinic but spoke in a telephone interview from his office, located over the mountains, ninety miles away from Jonesville in the town of London, Kentucky.

"The town I am in had well-paying jobs. While we didn't have mines in the town I'm in, the supporting businesses were here. As the mines went down, the supporting businesses went down. There has been a big shift." Nothing has come to replace the mines, or the paychecks or the benefits. It is harder now to keep dentists in places like these. People enter the profession these days with heightened expectations, he said. "It's not glamorous anymore just to do certain procedures, do fillings, do basic things," said Herren. "A lot of young dentists are leaving. We have dentists in my society who want to sell their practices."

Then, too, new dentists may begin their professional lives in heavy debt. The average educational debt per graduating dental school senior was estimated to be $247,227 in 2014, according to the American Dental Education Association.

If they want to go into private practice as most do, they need to buy equipment and hire staff. "Dentistry is a business too," said Herren.

Medicaid does not pay dentists as well as private insurance does, or as well as patients who pay for elective procedures out of their own pockets. Rates vary from state to state. But on average, Medicaid pays about half of what private dental plans pay for children's dental care, according to the American Dental Association.[16]

At the free clinic, dental coordinator John Osborn said the business of dentistry works against caring for the poor. "I have a son who is at Meharry [School of Dentistry]. That is where I graduated from. They talk us into helping people. He'll have between $300,000 and $400,000 in student debt. Can he take TennCare Medicaid patients or go out and help people?" If he does, said Osborn, he will still need to figure out how to pay his bills. "He's gotta do something else to make up the money."

The incentives drive a lot of dentists to set up practices in affluent places and cater to the wealthy. The community of Falls Church, Virginia, a suburb of Washington, D.C., and one of the richest places in the United States, had plenty of dentists—one dentist for every 350 residents in 2015. Meanwhile, Dickenson County, Virginia, next door to Lee County, had one dentist for 15,486 residents.[17] There are vast swaths of Alaska and a number of counties in Kansas with no dentist at all. There are shortages in struggling urban and rural places across the country.

So poor places have their own kind of dental archaeology, as distinct as the lonely mountains enfolding Jonesville, as distinct as the crumbling schools and roll-down steel gates in some of the crime-ridden communities outside Washington, D.C.

By the time they reach adulthood, many poor Americans think of toothaches as a fact of life. Research has shown that millions of American children suffer from them. The pain takes a toll on every aspect of their lives. Nearly 11 percent of U.S. children—and 14 percent of six- to twelve-year-olds—experienced a toothache during a six-month period, for a total of about 7.5 million children overall, concluded one study, based upon extensive federal data gathered in 2007 and 2008. The report found that poor and low-income minority children and those with special needs were significantly more likely to have had a toothache than better-off children.[18] "Until the early twentieth century, toothache was so common that few escaped the experience during a lifetime," wrote the authors. "As fluoride became more widely available and dental care has advanced, toothache is fortunately no longer universal. Even so, results from this study indicate that toothache is far from eradicated. The difference now is that toothache disproportionately affects vulnerable groups—poor minority and special needs children—and further compounds the other challenges they face."

Children with poor oral health were nearly three times more likely than their peers to miss school as a result of dental pain, another study found.[19]

In a mobile dental clinic, making the rounds of poor schools in suburban Maryland, dentist Hazel Harper put new blue barrier tape on the handles of the chairside light and prepared for the next child. Harper, a former dental school professor and a longtime professional leader, corralled dental students and colleagues to organize the mobile clinic program after an area schoolchild died of complications from untreated tooth decay in 2007.

The van began its journey, getting dental services to children who might otherwise go without. Sometimes they were in pain. Sometimes they were already afraid of dental care. Sometimes they were both.

"What are you gonna do?" asked little Olivia Davis when she climbed into the dental chair. She was wearing sneakers that looked like they had been sprinkled in rainbow-colored glitter.

"See how your shoes are all sparkly? We're gonna make your teeth all sparkly too," Harper told her. "We're gonna count your teeth."

But the worry on Olivia's face just deepened.

"Don't be scared," said Harper. "We're not going to do anything to hurt you."

Big silent tears began rolling down the girl's brown cheeks.

"Why are you crying?" asked Harper kindly, peering into the child's mouth.

The dentist read the story within Olivia's dental arches. About five years old. No adult molars yet, but her teeth were already carrying a record of disease. A deciduous or baby molar and a canine missing, extracted. The other three deciduous molars decayed.

"Are any of your teeth hurting?" Harper asked Olivia. The child just sobbed.

Harper gave her the purple plush lion to hug. The puppet, who wore a big toothy grin, was used to teach children good brushing habits. "Hold Mr. Courage," said Harper as she forged ahead. As the child clutched the toy, Harper took out her motorized dental handpiece and showed Olivia the colorful disposable animal-shaped brushes she used for cleaning.

"Which one do you want? The penguin or the zebra?"

As the dentist worked, she made note of the decay she found. She wrote on the chart that the little girl would need to be seen in a dentist's office soon. She would need treatment or her cavities would only get worse.

In Maryland, in the years before the 2007 death of twelve-year-old Deamonte Driver, researchers at the state dental school had sounded warnings about dental pain and its impact upon the lives of the poor in that state, among the nation's richest. They decried the lack of attention to the problem. "Nearly 12 percent of school children in Maryland have had at least one episode of dental pain as reported by a parent or guardian. Furthermore, almost a third of the children who have had a history of dental caries also have had dental pain," noted public health dentist and researcher Clemencia Vargas and her team from the University of Maryland School of Dentistry in their 2005 paper. "Any other preventable pain that affects almost a third of any social group would be subject to multiple studies. Unfortunately dental pain is considered by many a common occurrence and for this reason is less likely to be studied than other less prevalent health conditions." Many of the victims were so resigned to their suffering they did not even complain, the researchers suggested.

"It is probable that many children learn to live with pain, taking pain as part of their normal lives, similar to the perception of dental pain in the earlier centuries," they wrote.[20]

For poor adults in Maryland, dental suffering has also been common.

Waiting in a predawn line to have eleven teeth extracted at a free clinic in Laurel, Maryland, Mandy LeQuay described the pain as a mind-numbing, incapacitating fact of life. "It affects my ability to be a good parent," she said. She explained she had been temporarily hospitalized for the infection in her mouth, but was then sent home. She sometimes resorted to cutting the infected lesions in her gums in an attempt to relieve the excruciating pressure.

A team of University of Maryland dental school researchers examined the role of toothache pain in the lives of poor Maryland adults, and the strategies they used to cope with it. Almost half of the respondents reported having suffered more than five toothaches over the past five years. "The intensity of pain associated with the most recent toothache was pronounced. Almost half (45.1 percent) reported the highest pain possible," the researchers wrote. More respondents sought out nonprescription medicines and home remedies than professional help. A vast majority turned to a higher power for relief. "The use of prayer in our study was used by a large majority (75.4 percent) with respondents who were Black reporting the highest use (85.4 percent)."[21]

They have been praying in other states too.

"I pray constantly," said Gregory Fulton, whose teeth were a set of mismatched, ravaged stumps. Sometimes the pain they caused was beyond description, he said.

"I pray in my mind. I pray all the time." He sat heavily upon a low wall in Tampa, Florida, cane in hand. He wore a John Deere cap and an uneven beard.

He was well known in the line for the good free lunch at the Trinity Café.

"You have a ticket, Poppa?" asked a volunteer who wore a large medal, shaped like a cross, around his neck. Fulton nodded in assent. He counted out 30 cents in change and handed it to another man. "Buy a cigarette and we can smoke it together."

In his circle, Fulton was called "the walking Bible." He said he had read the book forty times from cover to cover. He was fifty-five but seemed ancient. He had lived a hard life that included a period of crack addiction, a stint in prison he compared to Jonah's time in the belly of the whale, and a born-again experience. He had type 2 diabetes.

He said he was hoping for dentures but first needed to get his teeth extracted. He said he was seeking help from the county in getting the procedure done.

The infection in his teeth caused his mouth to flare up intermittently and his face to swell. Antibiotics helped temporarily. Then the swelling returned.

The teeth are made from stern stuff. They can withstand floods, fires, even centuries in the grave. But the teeth are no match for the slow-motion catastrophe that is a life of poverty: its burdens, distractions, diseases, privations, low expectations, transience, the addictive antidotes that offer temporary relief at usurious rates.

Others waiting for lunch at the Trinity Café also spoke with deep familiarity about the pain. With his curly hair and blond eyelashes, David Hill looked something like a troubled Charles Lindbergh. He had a wild light in his blue eyes, and he cried easily.

His teeth were dark at the roots. He pointed to a lower incisor that was gray. It had broken open.

At some moments, he said the pain was so deep it became like a partner. "Really the pain almost feels good after a while. The medula takes over and you waltz through it." At other times, he said he was its slave. "I'm in a lot of pain but I can't do anything about it," he said. "I don't beg, borrow, or steal. Shoot me in the head, please. It would be a lot easier if you put me out of my misery."

Donald Solomon, who used a stout bamboo stick as a cane, was missing one of his front teeth. "I ain't gonna lie. I drank a few beers and I pulled it myself," he related. "I ain't hurting no more." That was more than a decade ago, after he fell off his bicycle. On another occasion, he found the money to have a wisdom tooth professionally extracted. "It had a big hole down in it," he said, and it was infected. He knew it needed to go. He heard about a young man in Tampa, just seventeen, who died of a similar infection some years ago.

"It gets in the bloodstream and it kills you," he said quietly. "That is why I got it pulled. That is why Mr. Donald is still here. That is my story and I'm sticking to it."

Stephanie Oliva pushed her sleeping infant son in a carriage as she waited for lunch.

"The back of my teeth hurt," she said. "I probably have a cavity," she added with a shrug.

When it was time to go in for lunch, Fulton allowed others in the line to go ahead of him. "The first shall be last and the last shall be first," he said gently, lingering in the sunshine. He finally made his way with much difficulty to the cheerful dining room, which was decorated with a holiday tree and enlivened by two volunteers playing mariachi music. Pork cutlets were served, and macaroni, green beans, and salads. Fulton began having chest pains. An ambulance was called and he was loaded on a gurney and disappeared in a flurry of lights and sirens.

Across the long blue causeway in St. Petersburg, a nonprofit clinic, one of the oldest free clinics in the nation, has been attempting to provide dental care to working poor patients, who labor in the city's sparkling restaurants and hotels, who build and clean homes and care for the sick and the elderly.

"It's just astounding to me how many grown adults, even older adults come in and say this is their first dental appointment," said Susan Easter, health center director at the St. Petersburg Free Clinic. "We had a couple here this morning. They were shaking because this was their first time for dental care." After the 2010 passage of the nation's health care reform law, some of the longtime clients were able to get private health insurance. They no longer needed the medical services of the free clinic, Easter said. But the need for dental care only seemed to grow.

The free clinic had no dental chairs of its own, so the dental services were provided after hours, in borrowed space at a nearby county health clinic. In most cases, the patients had deferred needed care for a very long time.

"Most of them, believe it or not, have not been to the dentist for ten years, or they have never been to the dentist," said the clinic's dental project supervisor, Claudia Rosas. She said she had worked as a dentist in her native Colombia but would have needed to go to dental school all over again to practice in the United States, so after she emigrated she trained as a dental hygienist. At the free clinic, her staff consisted of one dental assistant. A major part of Rosas's job involved cajoling local dentists into volunteering to see patients a few at a time. Some of the patients were attempting to rebuild their lives after periods of addiction.

"Their teeth are melted," said Rosas.

After the teeth were extracted, Rosas tried to find the patients dentures so they could return to work. Rosas hoped to break the cycle of disease and pain, but she knew the messages about oral health often came too late. Parents need to teach their children: "Your teeth are pearls. You should keep them," she said.

—◦◦◦—

In one coup, Rosas and her colleagues managed to land a $5,000 grant to hold a daylong dental clinic. The money came from a charity dedicated to the memory of the Rev. Dr. Martin Luther King Jr. On one day in 2015, more than fifty patients were scheduled for care and three volunteer dentists were on hand to see them.

Among the patients was Lakecia Gathers, a tall, slender woman who managed vacation rentals. She had been working for months with a swollen mouth and an infection throbbing in her gums. She had one bad tooth extracted the month before.

At the MLK Day clinic, volunteer dentist and clinic board member Silas Daniel studied Gathers's x-ray for the remaining problem. The image showed what looked like two thorns embedded in her jaw, surrounded by a gray shadow. They were the two roots of a broken molar enclosed by an infection, a cyst inside her gum.

"Pain in dentistry is pressure," explained Daniel. "Your tooth is like a Coke bottle that has been shaken up. The pressure builds." Gathers kept her hands folded on her lap as the dentist went to work on the procedure. The roots were hard to extract. When she saw blood on her bib she expressed worry. "I'm gonna pass out," she warned. She would feel much better when the rotten roots were gone, Daniel assured her. "That infection grew and grew," the dentist said. "That messes with your blood pressure and your white blood cells and your blood sugar."

Her body was being relieved of a burden. "You'll be a new person," he told her.

There was also Donna Johnson Agate, an unemployed certified nursing assistant whose terror of the dentist was adding to her pain. She was too frightened and nauseous to even sleep the night before the clinic, she said. She lay in her bed obsessing.

"I had a real bad experience as a kid with a dentist."

When her name was called, she tried to settle into the dental chair but kept jumping up. Finally two student dental assistants from Pinellas Technical College joined forces to calm her. The tall, slender young assistant, Emrah Kuc, reminded her to breathe. The grandmotherly one, Connie Leonard, took her hand. They helped

her get through it. "Just knowing they were there made a difference," said Agate gratefully as she left.

The last patient of the day was Sean Cuffie, who has been in pain
for months.

The anguish reached the point where a couple of times he went
to the emergency room of nearby St. Anthony's Hospital. But the
medications he was offered only brought temporary relief. He
was a tall, handsome man with long dreadlocks and delicate long-
fingered hands. After some drifting in his early adulthood, Cuffie
said he was back in school, working on a business degree. His volunteer dentist, John Thee, studied his x-ray and shook his head. In
addition to serious decay, Cuffie had advanced gum disease that
could eventually cost him all his teeth, Thee warned.

Cuffie murmured that he was prepared for bad news.

The dentist gave him injections of local anesthetic and went to
work. He extracted the two teeth that seemed to be the source of
most of Cuffie's pain. The first one took a long time to come out.
There was a large cavity in the side of the second one. The ruined
teeth lay there on the chairside tray, the blood drying on their roots
and cusps.

Cuffie thanked the dentist and his assistants and disappeared out
into the Florida afternoon. His teeth waited behind, to be tossed
into the bin for medical waste.

3

Emergencies

THE AMERICAN HEALTH CARE SYSTEM IS SET UP AS IF THE MOUTH was separate from the body. That is the way it has worked for more than a century, and yet nearly every emergency room visit for a toothache challenges this arrangement. Hundreds of thousands of times each year, people with toothaches show up in emergency rooms. These visits cost hundreds of millions of dollars annually. Still, the patients' needs are seldom met.

Late on the warm, clear Tuesday morning of August 23, 2011, Kyle Willis went to the emergency room of Mercy Hospital, a community hospital located in Batavia, Ohio. The hospital was a few miles north of the tiny town of Amelia, where Willis was living. He was twenty-four, renting a trailer home on the four-lane Ohio Pike, not far from where he grew up. He worked at a fast food restaurant, ten miles away, past laundromats and check-cashing shops and hardware stores, closer to the city of Cincinnati. He was raising his six-year-old daughter, Kylie.

He had no insurance and little money. He had an aching wisdom tooth. At the emergency room, according to hospital records, he was diagnosed with an unspecified dental disorder. He was given prescriptions for a painkiller and an antibiotic and sent on his way, recounted his aunt, Patti Willis Collins.

"The pain one was like four bucks. And the other prescription was twenty-six dollars," said Collins. "So he had the four dollars. And he said 'Well I'm in pain.' So he went and filled the scrip for pain." He did not, however, fill the prescription for the more expensive medicine, the antibiotic.

The wisdom tooth was abscessed and the infection got worse.

At the time, Collins said she was not aware that her nephew, whom she had known and loved since birth, was suffering. She only pieced together the details of what happened later on. She was returning from a trip to Los Angeles when she first learned about her nephew's problem, she said. When she was in the airport, she received a call from her mother, his grandmother.

"My mom said, 'Kyle has really got a bad toothache, Patti.' And I said, 'When I get home I will call my dentist and call Kyle and see if maybe he wants to go to my dentist,'" Patti Collins recalled.

But she did not have the chance to arrange the appointment for her nephew.

In the predawn hours of the next day, Tuesday, August 30, Kyle Willis was back at Mercy Hospital. This time he was taken there in an ambulance, said Collins.

His face was swollen. The hospital records showed that this time his admitting diagnosis was a possible allergic reaction. But the swelling turned out to be orbital cellulitis, a condition signaling that the infection from his wisdom tooth had spread through his facial tissues. Then Willis suffered a subarachnoid hemorrhage, doctors determined, bleeding in the lining of the brain. The toothache had escalated into a systemic crisis.

"He was in convulsions at that point," said Collins. "He was out of his mind." Later that morning, another ambulance rushed Willis the twenty miles from the quiet suburban hospital in Batavia to the neurosurgery department at the towering University Hospital in downtown Cincinnati. "So he was in the ambulance going to University," said Collins. "That's when he went into a coma."

"Pt pronounced brain dead at 1442," noted the careful printing on the University Hospital record. "Family informed. . . . Pt placed back on ventilator."

"My daughter called me: 'Mom. You gotta come. We gotta go right now.'" Collins did not believe what she was hearing, she said. No one in the family could grasp the news. "There were two doctors, saying that 'we had him on life support and you need to make a decision because he is not going to make it.'"

They all prayed. "God, give us back our Kyle. What is this? Why?" But it was over. "We went in and looked at him. I wanted to make sure. You know. And they said the way you tell is his eyes. There was nothing there. His pupils. Nothing. . . . I went up and looked at him. I was just, 'Kyle? Can you see me?' Nothing."

Patti Collins's brother, Kyle Willis's father, told the doctors to discontinue the life support. "And they pulled it. About twenty minutes later everything went flat," she said. "That was it." The cause of death, the record read, was cerebral edema due to dental abscess.

Kyle Willis was remembered at a funeral at the simple white cinder block Church of God in New Richmond, the little Ohio River town where he grew up. He was buried in an old cemetery on a steep wooded hillside just outside of town. His daughter, Kylie, has missed talking with her dad, Collins said. The child was being raised by her grandfather.

It was a bitter-cold day in February when Patti Collins recounted the story. She was dressed in deep brown. She wore a hat that framed her elegant face in soft brown and white feathers. She is a former Cincinnati Bengals cheerleader, married to the famous and flamboyant funk bassist Bootsy Collins, who played with James Brown and Parliament. She met her husband when she was teaching aerobics. After they were married, she went on to manage his musical and philanthropic work, both highly regarded in the city of Cincinnati.

After their nephew died the couple began speaking publicly about the importance of dental care. The two of them appeared at a city council meeting that focused upon the death of Kyle Willis and the wider unmet dental needs in Cincinnati and the surrounding communities. City officials discussed ways to avert more such tragedies. The hours at a city clinic in downtown Cincinnati were expanded in an effort to help more needy people get timely care. In the narrow hallway leading to the dental chairs, a plaque memorialized Kyle Willis.

On a visit to the clinic Collins studied the image of her nephew, with that lively grin. "Look at that smile. Look at those teeth," she said. "He had one bad tooth."

In 2011, the year Kyle Willis died, more than 84,000 Ohioans who had public insurance or who were uninsured went to hospital emergency rooms for dental problems, according to the grassroots group Dental Access Now. "One of the reasons Ohioans may be using the emergency room is because they cannot find affordable dental care in their community. The state of Ohio has eighty-four federally designated dental health professional shortage areas," noted the group in a 2014 report.[1]

Semirural Clermont County, where Willis was living, was one of them.

In times of pain the doors of the emergency department slide open, quietly, automatically. The patient does not need to have a dollar in his pocket, or an appointment, or even an identification card to enter, to present himself at the desk and ask for help. Any hospital that accepts Medicaid and Medicare is required to screen and stabilize anyone who shows up, without regard for legal status, citizenship, or the ability to pay. The red lettered sign gives hope of at least some form of temporary relief.

These emergency room visits are enormously expensive to the health care system as a whole. And they seldom address the patient's needs, because without dental care, the problems only get worse. In rare cases, they end in death, like in the old days before antibiotics even existed. Dental emergencies seldom work out well for anyone: the hurting patients, the overwhelmed emergency departments, or the taxpayers.

Dental visits to emergency departments nearly doubled in the decade between 2000 and 2010. Tooth decay, oral lesions, abscesses, gum infections, and related complaints were the reason for more than four million emergency room visits during the three-year period spanning the recession years of 2008 and 2010. The visits cost a total of $2.7 billion, according to one major 2014 study. The patients seldom received actual dental care on the visits, only prescription medications, the researchers concluded. During that decade, a total of 101 of the patients died in the emergency rooms.[2]

On the whole, with routine professional and home care, most of those millions of problems could be resolved in less costly and more effective ways, or prevented altogether, noted the researchers, who gleaned their findings from data drawn from a nationwide set of hospital emergency department databases. But the lack of insurance or the means to pay for care, the lack of regular preventive services, geographical isolation, poor diet, and poor oral hygiene all go on to contribute to the oral conditions that land people in emergency rooms, noted the authors of the paper. Overuse of emergency departments for all kinds of aches and pains, fevers, and injuries is a national concern. But the number of patients making visits for dental problems has been growing faster than the numbers making visits for other needs, research has shown. More than 2 percent of all emergency department visits are now related to nontraumatic dental conditions, a 2015 study showed.[3]

In medical terms, more than half of the myriad health problems that drive people to emergency departments would not require hospital care if there were some other readily available source of attention, experts have found. People often turn to emergency rooms for these kinds of problems when their doctor's office is closed, noted *New York Times* health writer Jane Brody in a column on the crisis. "The medical profession has thus far failed to adequately fill the gap left by doctors who no longer make house calls or answer the phone 24/7," she wrote.[4]

Many of the people who go to emergency rooms for dental problems are not there because their dentist's office is closed. They go because they do not have a dentist. "Most of the visits to the ER occurred on weekdays when many dentist offices are open," wrote the authors of a study from the University of Minnesota. "Almost 75 percent of the visits were during the week and of those, about three-quarters were between 8 a.m. and 8 p.m. Thus, for a majority of these visits, the patients were not going to the hospital because dentists' offices were closed. . . . In other words, the use of the ER was often not related to the need for after-hour care." The more than ten thousand visits they studied were made to five major hospital systems in the Minneapolis–St. Paul area over the course of a year. The charges for the visits amounted to nearly $5 million. The majority of the patients lacked private insurance. They were covered by Medicaid and other publicly funded programs, so taxpayers footed the bills for the care that did not meet the patients' needs. Because they were covered by publicly funded programs they faced a shortage of dentists who would see them, a barrier to care that is common nationwide. "Fewer than half of all dentists participate in public dental insurance programs, and even those who do may restrict the number served," wrote the authors.[5]

Medicaid expansion under the 2010 Patient Protection and Affordable Care Act brought health coverage to millions of new beneficiaries. But dental services, long provided separately, remained scarce for many and hard to find. The newly covered adults in many states were still likely to lack dental care and would continue to turn to emergency rooms, a team of researchers concluded in a 2015 paper. "The large number of visits to emergency rooms for dental conditions that could be treated in outpatient settings is indicative of the fact that our health-care system treats dental care differently from other preventive care when, in fact, dental care should be considered part of a person's overall health and well-being," noted lead researcher Maria Raven, an associate professor of emergency room medicine at the University of California–San Francisco.[6] The study, which examined county-level rates of emergency room visits for nontraumatic dental problems in twenty-nine states, found that in urban areas, where the vast majority of dental emergency room visits occur, Medicaid dental coverage did not appear to reduce the number of emergency room visits. The lack of Medicaid dental providers continued to drive beneficiaries to seek care in emergency rooms, the researchers found.

Taking steps to help patients bridge the long-standing gulf between medical care and dental care could help solve the problem, according to the authors. They suggested setting up on-site dental clinics in emergency rooms and employing midlevel dental providers similar to the nurse practitioners who have been used for decades to expand medical care to underserved communities. They also recommended providing incentives to medical providers and health insurers to refer patients for preventive dental visits, similar to the way the physicians and insurers routinely refer patients for colon and cervical cancer screenings. Raven and her team were not the first to study dental emergencies, or to recognize them as a manifestation of the disconnect between the dental care system and the larger health care system. They were not the first to make such recommendations. Health care policy experts have been observing the gap and suggesting ways to bridge it for many years.

"Dental service in hospitals and dispensaries has been developing but as yet is generally deficient," wrote William J. Gies, in a major critique of the dental system, published in 1926. "The need for dental internes in hospitals is apparent."[7]

Very recently, in response to the crisis, some steps have been taken on state and community levels. Emergency room diversion programs, organized by dental and public health groups, have aimed to get patients out of ERs and into dental offices. Public and private nonprofit community health centers, which provided care to about 4.7 million dental patients in 2014, have obtained federal grants to create or expand oral health programs in the poor and rural communities they serve.[8] Midlevel dental providers, who are less expensive to train and employ than dentists but who have been fiercely opposed by organized dental groups, are being tried in a handful of states and tribal areas. But closing the divide between dental care and the larger health care system presents challenges. The two systems have been largely separate for so long.

Two centuries ago the boundaries were not so well defined. An hour's drive northeast of the trailer park where Kyle Willis lived lies the town of Bainbridge, Ohio. A small home, now kept as a museum, marks the place where back in the 1820s a local physician named John Harris offered classes designed to help aspiring physicians prepare to enter medical school. There were no formal dental schools back then. Dentistry was widely considered more of a trade than a healing art. But by some accounts, Harris also taught a little dentistry to those who were interested. "He used a rocking chair for patients and alcohol for anesthetic. Among his resources were an Indian skull and text books imported from England," the authors of a pictorial history of American dentistry reported.[9] John Harris's younger brother, Chapin, may have learned some dentistry from him. Chapin Harris then went out on his own. He practiced in Ohio for a while in those early years. He spent 1828 in Greenfield "extracting, cleaning teeth and inserting a few fillings," moving on to Bloomfield, Ohio, for two or three more years, practicing "dentistry, medicine and surgery," according to one early account of his life.[10]

By the time he settled in Baltimore, in the 1830s, Chapin Harris would have recognized an infection like the one that killed Kyle Willis. In his travels, he had been observing cases of his own and collecting accounts from other practitioners. Dental abscesses, the accompanying pain and resulting havoc, figured heavily among the case histories that he gathered. Sometimes the infections spread to the brain, other times they closed the throat. Either way they ended terribly. "My friend, Dr. L—, of Frederick was called to visit a young gentleman who labored under the violent pain of the face and inferior maxillary," Harris wrote. "His sufferings were traced to the roots of one of his molar teeth."

The infection advanced, Harris reported, "The inflammation, not withstanding the skilful exertions of the physician, rapidly increased; high and intractable fever supervened . . . and in a few days, he died."[11]

Deaths from dental abscesses are far rarer in America than they were in those days, researchers are quick to note. The infections are preventable and treatable. Yet patients continue to be hospitalized for them. And deaths continue to occur. "Nearly two hundred years ago, a dental abscess, a result of an infection in the root canal system, was considered a death sentence and often a leading cause of death," noted the authors of a large study published in the *Journal of Endodontics*.[12]

"Through advances in dental science, a periapical abscess has become a preventable and treatable condition, typically managed with a high success rate in the dental office setting," the researchers observed. "Left untreated, periapical abscesses can have serious consequences that can lead to hospitalization." Nationwide, a total of 61,439 hospitalizations were primarily attributed to periapical abscesses during the nine years between 2000 and 2009. The inflation-adjusted cost of the hospital stays came to $858.9 million. The average patient stayed nearly three days in the hospital, the study authors wrote. A total of sixty-six of the patients died. "Without dental insurance, access to dental care is difficult, and with the limited government-assisted coverage for dental treatment, fewer individuals are likely to seek preventative and routine care that can ultimately prevent hospitalization for periapical abscesses," the authors noted. Nearly 44 percent of the patients were publicly funded Medicare and Medicaid beneficiaries, so taxpayers shouldered their costs.

It was an infected wisdom tooth that killed Kyle Willis. Yet wisdom tooth removal is a rite of passage for many young adults, particularly those who have dental benefits and money to pay for care. Americans spend an estimated $3 billion a year removing wisdom teeth, according to an April 2014 study published in the *American Journal of Public Health*. The biggest predictor of having the surgery is "availability of insurance," the study concluded. Yet even a person with good coverage might have to pay 20 percent of the fee out-of-pocket, or up to $500 for the removal of four wisdom teeth, the *Los Angeles Times* reported in a 2015 story on wisdom tooth removal. As the article observed, some experts have challenged the need for the "prophylactic" extraction of wisdom teeth that show no potential for causing problems.[13]

Meanwhile poor, uninsured, and publicly insured adults often go without needed care, particularly in fiscally hard times.

State decisions to cut adult dental benefits under Medicaid, which occur frequently during economic downturns just when more people need them, lead to an increase in emergency department use for dental problems, research has shown. But the same financially stressed states and their taxpayers end up bearing the cost of deferred dental care in expensive emergency treatment for decay, abscesses, and other dental ailments anyway, according to a study released by the Pew Center on the States, a division of the Pew Charitable Trusts. The philanthropic organization concluded that in the recession year of 2009 alone, preventable dental conditions were the primary diagnosis in 830,590 visits to hospital emergency rooms—a 16 percent increase from the prerecession year of 2006. "States are saddled with some of these expenses through Medicaid and other public programs. Especially large bills result when severe decay-related problems require hospitals to use general anesthesia," noted the philanthropy in its report "A Costly Dental Destination: Hospital Care Means States Pay Dearly." Pew concluded that states could reduce hospital visits, strengthen oral health, and cut their costs by making investments to expand community water fluoridation programs to reach the 25 percent of Americans who currently lack access to fluoridated water. The philanthropy recommended getting the larger health care system involved in increasing access to preventive dental care in underserved places—spanning the gap between dental and medical care. "Medical professionals should play more of a role in prevention," the group wrote. Pediatricians, nurse practitioners, and other medical providers could perform oral exams and offer preventive fluoride varnishes to young patients. They could refer children to dentists for additional care. "Involving medical providers is important because young children see them earlier and more frequently than they see dentists," the study noted.[14]

University Hospital is a sprawling level-one trauma center in the heart of Newark, New Jersey. Amid a steady flood of horrific injuries, rampant infections, and major heart attacks, the hospital also deals with toothaches. The hospital was included in a 2014 study of emergency department visits for dental problems in poor regions of New Jersey. Young adults, particularly those lacking insurance or covered by Medicaid, were the biggest users, according to researchers from the Rutgers Center for Health Care Policy and the Rutgers School of Dental Medicine. "The reliance on emergency room dental treatment is symptomatic of a larger problem: a public that is alarmingly uneducated about the severe consequences of inadequate dental care and a system that refuses to acknowledge oral health as a crucial aspect of overall medical health," wrote Cecile A. Feldman, the dean of the Rutgers School of Dental Medicine, after the study was released. "There is still the misconception among many that dental care is a luxury, a mostly cosmetic process that helps ensure straight, white teeth," she noted, in a guest editorial that ran in the Newark *Star-Ledger*. Feldman also faulted the system for contributing to the rise in emergency room usage for dental problems. "For many," she added, "a visit to the dentist is unaffordable and inaccessible." The doors of private dental offices may remain closed to them. But the doors of the emergency room are always open.

On this day, with every bay in the emergency department at University Hospital filled with slumped, bleeding, and curled people, toothache patient Shatiyna Giles had already been moved to a special area where she was awaiting a nurse. Huddled on a hospital bed, dressed in her street clothes and covered with a sheet, the twenty-six-year-old community college student said she felt bad about neglecting her teeth, particularly the upper molar that was causing her the most pain.

"It tastes so nasty. It's decayed," she said. "I'm so ashamed I let it get like that." Her face looked swollen. "I've been up all night crying," she said. "My head feels like it's about to explode."

Her chances of getting care were better than those faced by Kyle Willis. A large teaching hospital like University has resources to deal with dental emergencies that many community hospitals lack. A person with a dangerous dental abscess could have it drained here, said the chief emergency department (ED) resident, Dave Woodkotch, a physician. University Hospital usually has a dental resident on rotation or on call for consultation. The hospital is located next door to Rutgers School of Dental Medicine, which operates several dental clinics, including one right off the main lobby of the hospital.

Patients who arrive at the emergency department with dental problems typically follow the route Giles was taking, explained the ED's chief of service, Gregory Sugalski, an energetic, youthful physician with a military bearing. "Most of them get funneled through our fast-track section, to get seen by the nurse practitioner," said Sugalski. "If they have facial cellulitis or an abscess, we may get a consult from dental to come and look at the patient." Usually, after being seen, the patient receives not only prescriptions for antibiotics and pain control but also a referral to the dental clinic. The health care workers who serve this poor urban neighborhood remain mindful of the cost of medications and the other barriers patients face in getting their health problems successfully resolved, said Sugalski.

"Whenever possible, when we know the patients don't have insurance or resources, we try to go to the Walmart list to make sure we give them one of those $5 prescriptions or something cheap.

So we are not giving them prescriptions that won't get filled." Even so, Sugalski said he was realistic about which medication a suffering patient would purchase if he or she could only afford to buy one. The patient would be likely to do what Kyle Willis did. "Given the choice, they will probably pick the pain medication over the antibiotic."

Following up with actual dental care is essential, said Sugalski. Yet the dental clinic located in the hospital fills up quickly each morning. Getting necessary treatment there may require a return visit. "In this community, the biggest angst I have is making sure my patient gets follow-up," Sugalski said.

He has heard the talk of better coordination between the worlds of dentistry and medicine. Still, Sugalski said he had trouble imagining a time when the emergency department would not play a role in addressing dental pain. "If I have a toothache at two in the morning and the only thing that is open is the ED, do all the coordinating you want to do. You are gonna go to the ED." And you will still most likely need to navigate from there into another system, the dental system, for care.

In that gulf that separates the teeth from America's modern $2.9 trillion health care system, there remains a kind of mystery, bordering on taboo. It can be difficult, even for battle-hardened emergency room physicians, to talk about. During his residency at University Hospital, Dave Woodkotch said he learned to cope with every kind of emergency imaginable. He even spent two weeks in the hospital's oral and maxillofacial surgery department, where he learned to perform extractions. "Our primary objective was to learn anesthesia. But there was an extraction clinic and everyone is there to get a tooth pulled, so when we rotated through we pulled teeth." He has seen all sorts of horrific trauma. But extractions still make him uneasy.

"For some reason I'm just not one for dentists," he explained. "I had my first cavity when I was twenty-two. . . . It was like the worst experience I've ever had in my life. I don't like someone drilling in my mouth. . . . I guess if you are not used to it . . . it's one of those things that make me really uncomfortable. I didn't like pulling teeth. Or really bad eye injuries."

Sugalski listened quietly, then said he understood. "I don't think Dave is unique for it. I think most of us are just not comfortable pulling teeth."

He could not explain the source of this feeling. Before Sugalski came to University to run the emergency room, he was an army doctor. He served in Iraq and Afghanistan, ministering to troops who had been shot and blasted by landmines. He has seen more trauma since. "We put tubes in chests. We crack people's chests wide open and all that kind of stuff, that doesn't faze me, but I don't know. Pulling a tooth is just somehow . . . maybe it's more personal. I don't know."

4

The World Beneath Our Noses

"SHOW ME YOUR TEETH," THE GREAT NATURALIST GEORGES CUVIER, is credited with saying, "and I will tell you who you are." That a tooth could tell a life story, he was certain. Working in late eighteenth- and early nineteenth-century France, Cuvier saw each animal as an exquisitely organized whole. He found a "constant harmony" between the incisor and the tarsal bone of the camel, the canine and the fibula of the small deer known as the chevrotain. The tooth of a carnivore corresponded with the eye, the leg, the intestine, the brain, and the instinct of a carnivore, Cuvier observed. From the tooth, he deduced the creature and its place in the world. Revolutions, upheavals, catastrophes might wipe out entire species. Of the truth of extinction, Cuvier was certain. He found the evidence in the teeth and bones of vanished animals. Yet in his view of the body as a closed system, Cuvier found no place for significant change and adaptation.[1]

The father of paleontology went to his grave in 1832 rejecting the possibility of evolution. His protégé, Louis Agassiz, was likewise unconvinced, even when the work of Charles Darwin rocked the world of science. Through it all, though, Agassiz remained a firm believer in collecting. Many of the treasures Agassiz acquired during his explorations ended up at Harvard, where he accepted a professorship in 1848.

With its cases of bones and crystals and relics, the brick Peabody Museum of Archaeology and Ethnology on Divinity Street in Cambridge, Massachusetts, retains the curious appeal of an enormous Victorian collector's cabinet. On this day, walking through the collections on her way to her office at Peabody, Harvard paleoanthropologist Tanya Smith paused at a showcase to admire an old artifact, a tribal war club. It was studded with long curving teeth, their white, striated enamel glowing richly behind the glass.

Smith, too, can take a tooth and tell you a life story. But far from seeing a tooth as evidence of a closed system, Smith finds in a tooth both the records of developmental milestones and environmental shifts. For Smith, a tooth is a time capsule. With help from technology, she is able to read the story lines that are invisible to the naked eye, the deep records of a life that are stored in the dental microanatomy.

"We have this faithful clock in our mouths," she explained. The development of our teeth begins long before birth, when we are an embryo, the size of a bean, just a few weeks old. The tooth bud ripens in the fold that becomes our jaws, and the prisms of the enamel are secreted in daily pulses. As we grow, the rhythms of time, the disruptions of traumas and transitions are documented in the striations of the enamel. The teeth contain a mineralized chronicle of daily growth. The record of the physiological changes that occur with birth are embedded as a "neonatal line" in the enamel of our baby teeth and our first permanent molars, the ones that emerge when we are about six years old, heading off to first grade.

People are often startled to learn that they carry a birth certificate in their teeth, said Smith. "Everybody knows about tree rings, but nobody knows about the time lines in teeth. Why is that?" she wondered. "They are so much more personal."

The teeth are deeply intimate in that way. Beyond individual history, the teeth are powerful tools for reconstructing evolutionary processes that help constitute our collective history as well. Looking across all primates, dental development correlates strongly with attributes such as brain size, reproduction, and weaning age, Smith said. For that reason, fossil teeth hold clues to the path of evolution. Their microanatomy offers a deeper look into the timing of developmental stages that may have opened the way to the crucial evolutionary transformations that made us human. A shift to a longer, slower childhood is believed to have provided our early ancestors with the additional time for brain growth and learning that were necessary to build more sophisticated survival skills and more complex, more recognizably human societies. But when, Smith and her colleagues wondered, did the shift from a live-fast die-young approach to a longer, slower childhood begin?

They turned to ancient teeth for answers.

When Smith started doing her research, reading the lines in the dental enamel required slicing into the fossils. Obtaining permission to section such treasures was extremely difficult. Then a "super microscope" at the European Synchrotron Radiation Facility in Grenoble, France, gave Smith and her team a noninvasive alternative. Using high-energy x-rays, the synchrotron can produce a series of images of the fossil that are transformed by software into cross-sectional views. The process enabled Smith and her team to study and compare the infinitesimal striations found in the dental enamel of a collection of some of the rarest juvenile fossils ever unearthed. The images revealed records of the daily rhythms of the growth of these ancient children. And in the dental remains of an eight-year-old Stone Age child found in a Moroccan cave, Smith and her colleagues traced the earliest recorded evidence of a modern childhood. They determined that the young hominid, who lived one hundred sixty thousand years ago, was developing at the same rate as an eight-year-old living today.[2]

Microanatomical examinations of ancient teeth have challenged previously held age assessments for famous juvenile fossils including the enigmatic Taung child, discovered in a South African mine in 1924. The skull of the little *Australopithecus*, discovered by anatomist Raymond Dart, had a full set of baby teeth, with first molars just beginning to emerge. Based on that developmental evidence, scientists long believed the hominid had died at the age of six. But a deeper look at the enamel rings revealed the Taung child was only about three and a half years old when it got its first molars. Childhood was much faster one to two million years ago, when the Taung child lived and died.

Such findings have added more complexity to what was already a complicated and emotionally charged effort to chronicle human ancestry. It would be easier if the narrative were simpler, Smith admitted. "People are looking for these *Just So Stories*," she said. But science doesn't work that way.

Locked inside fossil teeth, more clues remain. Smith said she is eager to go on.

"There is something really satisfying to me about studying biological rhythms," she said, "the intimacy of looking at the days of an individual's life."

Chemical traces contained in teeth for millennia have their own stories to tell.

The element barium, for instance, serves as a biomarker for breastfeeding in both ancient and modern primates, enabling Smith and colleagues to document nursing and weaning back to Paleolithic times. Studying the barium patterns and growth lines in prehistoric teeth, they concluded that a young Neanderthal, whose remains were found in a cave in Sclayn, Belgium, was breastfed until the age of seven months.[3]

Lately, Smith has been scanning the teeth of wild chimpanzees for evidence of stress, disease cycles, and rainfall patterns. The results at this point are inconclusive but she has pressed on with the labyrinthine study of life. "This is biology," she said with the trace of a sigh. "There is so much variation."

For millennia, healers understood the body in environmental terms. They explained the causes of aches and plagues using the humoral theory, a sweeping system that has been described as a kind of "human ecology."[4] Dental problems, like other physical ailments, were attributed to shifts in the qualities of the humors: hot and cold, dry and wet; imbalances among the elements: fire, water, earth, and air. "Cold is bad for the bones, teeth, nerves, brain, and the spinal cord; heat is good for these structures," notes one Hippocratic aphorism. The coming of spring presaged outbreaks of consumption, fevers, and oral afflictions. "Some people were very ill with swellings in the throat, inflammation of the tongue and abscesses in connection with the teeth," a case history reported in *Epidemics III*. Sometimes, a diseased tooth appeared to inflame the entire body. An ancient case of rheumatism was reputed to have been cured by an extraction, though Hippocrates was said to have been leery of pulling teeth.

The glimpses of tiny animalcules came much later. Dutch draper Anton van Leeuwenhoek was the first to marvel over the wild diversity of microbial life within the human mouth. Peering into his handmade microscope in the seventeenth century, he was awed by the creatures he found amid his own plaque and spittle. "I . . . saw, with great wonder . . . there were many very little living animalcules, very prettily a moving," he wrote in his beautiful curving script in September 1683. "The biggest sort . . . had a very strong and swift motion, and shot through the water (or spittle) like a pike does through the water." Others "spun round like a top." Still others "hovered so together, that you might imagine them to be a big swarm of gnats or flies, flying in and out of one another."[5] The mesmerizing worlds revealed by such lenses eventually transformed the understanding of health and disease. But it would take more than two centuries for researchers to begin to link microbes with oral diseases such as caries.

Tooth decay and toothaches would continue to be seen as inevitable parts of life, and the care of the teeth was widely considered a mechanical concern.

In the seventeenth century, a barber surgeon ministered to the dental needs of the Plymouth Colony. In the eighteenth century, goldsmith and ivory turner Paul Revere, a hero of the American Revolution, constructed false teeth in Boston.[6]

By the turn of the nineteenth century, science and specialization were transforming many aspects of Western medicine. A growing emphasis upon clinical observation and an increasing array of instruments—stethoscopes, bronchoscopes, laryngoscopes, endoscopes—brought a sharper and narrower focus to the study of disease. Physicians and surgeons, increasingly working together, developed new approaches to treating specific ailments of the heart, the lungs, the larynx, the stomach, the bowel.

They left the teeth to the tradesmen.

But Chapin Harris, who began his career as an itinerant dental practitioner, led the effort to elevate his trade to a profession. Within the span of a year, between 1839 and 1840, Harris worked with a small group of others, including Horace Hayden, a Baltimore colleague, to establish dentistry's first scientific journal, a national dental organization, and the world's first college of dentistry. After the Baltimore College of Dental Surgery opened in 1840, the first two graduates, given credit for previous education, were granted degrees in just five months. "This day, for the first time in the history of the world, the practice of dentistry is recognized as a profession, and you are the first who are permitted by public authority to be distinguished by the title of Doctor of Dental Surgery," they were told by Thomas Bond, a physician and the school's professor of dental anatomy and physiology. "Gentlemen, I bid you farewell!"[7]

The second dental college opened in Cincinnati in 1845.

By 1870, there were ten.

Dental students learned the mechanics of drilling and filling teeth and constructing dentures. They learned to perform extractions. Then they went out to practice in the villages, towns, and cities of a growing nation.

—⁂—

The ancient humoral theory of disease still held sway at the time the world's first dental college was founded. Chapin Harris's own studies suggested to him that the causes of toothache were as varied as the types of pain. There was "inflammation," caused by "the direct contact of acrid humors," as well as "irritating and exciting agents," such as hot and cold foods; "mechanical violence"; "tumefaction of the gums"; "mercurial medicines"; "improperly performed dental operations"; "colds, cachexy, blows and jarring of the teeth," to list some of them. In other cases, the origins seemed more occult. "We often meet with cases of tooth-ache that are the result of none of the causes that have been just enumerated," Harris advised. "These are induced by a morbid sympathy between the teeth and some other part of the body. Persons of a nervous temperament, and pregnant females, are particularly subject to this sort of tooth-ache; and sometimes it is a symptom of a disordered state of the stomach."[8]

With causes seemingly so elusive it was left to the dentist to treat the symptoms. In cases where the tooth remained relatively intact, two or three leeches applied to the gum or "soothing astringent preparations" sometimes worked to relieve inflammation and pain. Often the pain eclipsed such measures and extraction was seen as the only recourse.

It was only after Chapin Harris was gone that miasmas and acrid humors were laid aside in favor of the germ theory. The germ theory revolutionized clinical and public health medicine in the late nineteenth century. It engendered new approaches to everything from city sanitation to hospital design to tooth-brushing habits.

Countless lives would be saved by new understandings of contagion, treatment, and prevention. But for a while, new fears about germs wrapped dentistry in another kind of miasma.

It was in 1880 that an Ohio-born American dentist named Willoughby D. Miller traveled to Germany to work in the laboratory of physician and scientist Robert Koch. Germany was a great center of medical research, drawing many eager and curious American doctors. By the time Miller arrived, Koch had traced the cause of the disease of anthrax to a specific bacterium. In two more years, he would present his discovery of the microbe responsible for tuberculosis, a killer of millions. The lecture in which Koch explained his findings about tuberculosis, and displayed his microscope slides and tissue samples, is still remembered as one of the most important in medical history. Through his methods, Koch helped transform the study of disease. He invented techniques for culturing and staining bacteria. And he laid down a set of conditions, known as Koch's postulates, that needed to be met in order to establish a causal relationship between a specific bacterium and a specific disease. In 1905, he was awarded the Nobel Prize.

Meanwhile, Willoughby Miller studied oral bacteria. He catalogued the rosary-like strands and spirals of microscopic life he found within the teeth and gums of patients, dogs, even his errand boy, "who had a very carious right inferior molar, covered with tartar and deposits, the surrounding gum being slightly inflamed." In his writings, including a landmark book, he generated a late nineteenth-century field guide to the human mouth. He also laid out pathbreaking ideas about the causes of tooth decay. He classified the organisms he found in decayed teeth as parasites, at least some of which had destructive powers at their disposal. They thrived upon the carbohydrates contained in foods consumed by their human hosts. Miller observed bacteria fermenting sugars from foods and producing acids. These acids were capable of attacking and destroying the enamel of the teeth. "The destruction of the enamel as it occurs in decay must be regarded as essentially a parasitico-chemical process," Miller concluded. "The loosening of the enamel-prisms is caused by acids concerning whose origin there can be no doubt; they arise in the mouth by fermentation of carbohydrates," he wrote.

Sectioning samples of decayed lesions, he surveyed the ruined landscape beneath his microscope lens. "Successfully stained cuts of decayed dentine furnish preparations which to the eye of the bacteriologist and pathologist are not only of exceeding great beauty, but also demonstrate with such clearness the intense action of microorganisms upon dentine that no doubting Thomas can look at them and then have the hardihood to deny their significance," Miller wrote. "The dentine is completely riddled by masses of bacilli and threads." Once through the dentine layer, the infection reached the tooth's pulp and inflamed the vital nerve. With a condition Miller classified as gangrene of the pulp, the tooth's fate was sealed.

Here, on a microscopic level, Miller was witnessing the process of the disease that had plagued humanity for generations. And, as Miller preached, dental infections claimed many lives. If the infection spread to the throat or the brain, the consequences were often fatal in those days before the discovery of antibiotics.

Spurred by his beliefs about the infective powers of oral bacteria, Miller preached about the importance of hygienic practices. To patients, he recommended strong mouthwashes to battle the pathogens lurking in saliva. To his fellow dentists, he stressed the scrupulous washing of hands and sterilization of instruments.

But Miller took his case further. In fact, he began to see the mouth as the vector for all manner of human suffering. He warned his fellow dentists of the dangers in a landmark 1891 paper, "The Human Mouth as a Focus of Infection," published in the *Dental Cosmos*, a leading dental journal of the time. "During the last few years the conviction has grown continually stronger, among physicians as well as dentists, that the human mouth, as a gathering-place and incubator of diverse pathogenic germs, performs a significant role in the production of varied disorders of the body, and that if many diseases whose origin is enveloped in mystery could be traced to their source, they would be found to have originated in the oral cavity," Miller wrote.[9]

Bacteria invaded the bodies of people and animals by way of their mouths, causing deadly epidemics such as cholera and anthrax. But the mouth was not just a passive portal for illness. Miller saw it as an active reservoir for disease, a dark, wet incubator where virulent pathogens were able to multiply.

Miller died in 1907 after suffering complications from a ruptured appendix.[10] His fascination with the workings of oral bacteria was not universally embraced by his fellow dentists. Many of them remained focused upon the intense and physically demanding work of drilling, filling, and extracting teeth. The study of the causes of oral disease was not a major emphasis of American dental education. But amid growing speculations about the dangers of oral bacteria, the medical profession would begin to take an unusual and fierce interest in the mouth. A speech by British physician William Hunter delivered to the medical faculty at McGill University in Montreal in October 1910 and republished in the British medical journal *The Lancet* helped to start the furor. Hunter argued that the mouth was *the* preeminent focus for human disease. His speech galvanized the clinical and public imagination. The ideas he articulated would shape attitudes toward dentistry—and oral health and disease—for the next three decades.

Hunter opened with a brief paean to the sanctity of antiseptic surgery. Then he warmed to his main topics: oral sepsis and the "focal theory." Hunter painted in lurid terms the rampant state of oral disease. He described the "septic roots" of the neglected teeth of the poor "lying exposed in all their nakedness surrounded with tartar, overgrown it may be by foul, septic fumigating gums." But far worse, Hunter argued, was the rot to be found festering in the mouths of wealthier people.

It was the dentists who were to blame, Hunter contended.

"No one has probably had more reason than I have had to admire the sheer ingenuity and mechanical skill constantly displayed by the dental surgeon. And no one has had more reason to appreciate the ghastly tragedies of oral sepsis which his misplaced ingenuity so often carries in its train. Gold fillings, gold caps, gold bridges, gold crowns, fixed dentures, built in, on and around diseased teeth, form a veritable mausoleum of gold over a mass of sepsis to which there is no parallel in the whole realm of medicine or surgery," he asserted.[11] The sepsis infected the entire system, manifesting itself in a host of ailments including colitis, anemia, nephritis, ulcers, and scarlet fever, Hunter warned.

Since dentistry's professional beginnings seventy years before, dentists could point to contributions they had made to healing. Dentists Horace Wells and Edmund Kells had been hailed for their pioneering work in early anesthesia and x-ray technology. By the early twentieth century, increasingly sophisticated electrically powered drills and local anesthetics were making dentistry less painful. American restorative materials and techniques had won international repute. American dentists felt they had come a long way since the days of the itinerant tooth pullers. Hunter's indictment hit dentistry like a broadside.

Other medical leaders were quick to spread the alarm. In a succession of high-profile speeches and papers, leading American and British physicians concurred: the human mouth was a veritable cesspool. Aching teeth and inflamed tonsils were teeming with newly discovered germs. Dental restorations were dangerous. So were bites. The teeth were weapons. Saliva was septic.

British researcher F. St. John Steadman linked gum infections to cancers of the mouth, colon, stomach, anus, and rectum. "I am of the opinion that oral sepsis is by far the commonest predisposing cause of malignant disease," he wrote. He reported a case of rheumatoid arthritis not once but "twice cured by the removal of septic teeth."[12]

Physicians ordered extractions, tonsillectomies, and the removal of other suspect organs for the treatment of disorders ranging from hiccups to madness—for arthritis, angina, cancer, endocarditis, pancreatitis, melancholia, phobias, insomnia, hypertension, Hodgkin's disease, polio, ulcers, dementia, and flu.

Vaccines were sometimes concocted and administered in concert with dental extractions in the belief that they would counter the effect of the germs that were released from the roots of the teeth.[13]

The English writer Virginia Woolf was preparing for such an ordeal in May 1922 when she wrote to her friend Janet Case. "The dr. now thinks that my influenza germs may have collected at the roots of 3 teeth. So I'm having them out, and preparing for the escape of microbes by having 65 million dead ones injected into my arm daily. It sounds to me to be too vague to be very hopeful—

but one must, I suppose, do what they say," she wrote.[14] After collapsing at a party in 1925, Woolf wrote an essay entitled "On Being Ill" that opened with an account of awakening in a dental office after an extraction. She likened the feeling to a kind of after-death experience: "We have a tooth out and come to the surface in the dentist's arm-chair and confuse his 'Rinse the mouth—rinse the mouth' with the greeting of the Deity stooping from the floor of Heaven to welcome us."[15] In spite of such measures, she experienced mental and physical maladies until her life ended in suicide sixteen years later.

Meanwhile, in the United States, the physician Charles Mayo, of the Mayo Foundation in Rochester, Minnesota, expounded on the importance of the focal theory. "I have always had a brotherly feeling for the dentist," he began, in a talk delivered to the Dental Society of the State of New York. "Years ago, I used to like to 'pull' teeth myself. Among other things, no matter what the disease, I always felt if I could get the old snags out of the mouth part of the cure would be accomplished," he said.

Mayo acknowledged that some of his patients had complained about being left toothless. But he was convinced that the oral cavity was the seat of most illness. "In children the tonsils and mouth probably carry 80 percent of the infective diseases that cause so much trouble in later life," he noted in his talk, which was followed by "numerous lantern slides showing the foci of infection about the teeth that were the cause of systemic disturbances and diseases."[16]

"Total clearance," the removal of all the teeth, remained widely recommended.

Henry Cotton, the superintendent of the Trenton State Hospital in New Jersey, was convinced that dental infections were to blame for the mental illnesses suffered by his patients. "As early as 1916, Cotton had begun to attack and remove the most obvious site of infection, the teeth: unerupted and impacted teeth; teeth with infected roots and abscesses, decayed or carious teeth, apparently healthy teeth with periodontitis, poorly filled teeth, sclerotic teeth, teeth with crowns. When many of his patients stubbornly refused to recover, he was undeterred, redoubling his efforts to locate the underlying focal sepsis he felt certain was there. Tonsils and sinuses were soon joined by spleens and stomachs," wrote Andrew Scull, a historian of psychiatry who authored a book about Cotton. Cotton's own two sons committed suicide, even after their father insisted on having their teeth removed as protection against focal sepsis, Scull observed.[17]

In the face of the mass extractions, dentist and dental x-ray innovator C. Edmund Kells stood up for tooth preservation. In an address in 1920 before a national dental meeting held in his hometown, New Orleans, Kells called the focal theory "the crime of the age" and denounced the sacrifice of teeth "on the altar of ignorance." He demonstrated the usefulness of his x-ray machine in examining teeth and the power it gave dentists to offer second opinions and to resist the orders of physicians to extract teeth needlessly. Kells urged "exodontists" to "refuse to operate upon physicians' instructions." And he contended "that the time has come when each medical college should have a regular graduate dentist upon its staff to teach its medical students what they should know about the oral cavity."[18]

But it could be difficult for dentists to defy physicians. The two professions not only distrusted each other—they inhabited separate worlds. The tensions and lack of communication hurt patients, concluded the respected biological chemist William J. Gies, in his major 1926 report on dental education in the United States and Canada for the Carnegie Foundation. The low regard in which many physicians held dentists, and the separate ways the two professions were trained, added to the problem, Gies believed.

For his report, Gies visited and critiqued every dental college in North America; by then there were forty-three in the United States alone. He found a number of the dental institutions were nothing but poorly run trade schools. "The biological ignorance of many dentists, owing to deficient education in the medical sciences and in the requirements of oral medicine, often accounts for the disrespect of physicians for the views of dentists, and frequently makes dental contributions to consultations on the health of patients unreliable."[19] Gies was also troubled by the entrenched disdain for dentistry he found among medical professionals. "Even research in dental fields is regarded, in important schools of medicine, as something inferior," wrote Gies, who himself had been deeply immersed in the study of oral disease at Columbia University.

Gies firmly believed that dentistry should be considered an essential part of the health care system. He called for the reform of dental education, for closer ties between dental and medical schools and between the two professions.

"Dentists and physicians should be able to cooperate intimately and effectively—they should stand on a plane of intellectual equality," Gies noted in a speech to the American Dental Association. "Dentistry can no longer be accepted as mere tooth technology."[20]

Others questioned how far the focal theorists would take their extreme approach to battling disease. "If this craze for violent removal goes on, it will come to pass that we will have a gutless, glandless, toothless and I am not sure that we may not have, thanks to false psychology and surgery, a witless race," warned a speaker at a meeting of the Philadelphia County Medical Society.[21]

The mass extractions and surgeries continued through the 1930s. As microbiology advanced, however, the research underlying the focal theory was held up for closer scrutiny. Proponents of the theory lacked the evidence of controlled clinical studies to back up their claims. Efforts to replicate their findings failed. After witnessing years of extractions and tonsillectomies, New York physicians Russell L. Cecil and Murray Angevine used their own research to debunk claims that the removal of teeth and tonsils could cure rheumatoid arthritis. "Comparatively rare in the private practice is the sight of a tonsil, either normal or diseased. How beautifully the teeth and gums are cared for! How unusual is the discovery of a neglected case of sinusitis! And yet we still have rheumatoid arthritis with us."[22]

Untold millions of teeth had been extracted, and the diseases the extractions were intended to cure persisted.

The era of focal theory ended as it began, with addresses and papers. The growing availability of antibiotics in the 1940s offered new tools for fighting infections. The Gies report led to reforms in the dental education system. Substandard dental schools were in some cases closed, in other cases improved.

But Gies's calls for closer ties between dental schools and medical schools met with resistance. Many dentists rejected the idea. In 1945, an effort to integrate the faculties of the dental and medical schools at Gies's own institution, Columbia University, was strongly opposed by the dental faculty. The dentists' act of defiance was applauded by the editors of the *Journal of the American Dental Association*. "The views of the majority of dentists in the country cannot be misunderstood on the question of autonomy. The profession has fought for, secured and maintained its autonomy in education and practice for too many decades to submit now to arbitrary domination and imperialism by any group," they wrote.[23]

Today, nearly all American dental and medical schools remain organizationally separate.

Even the urgencies of World War II offered no excuse for integrating dentistry with medicine, some dental leaders argued. When the U.S. Department of Defense placed military dental officers under the command of medical officers, some dentists registered deep disapproval. "Whatever lowers dentistry in the public eye affects the life of every dentist. If dentists in the Army and Navy cannot have authority over the affairs of their own Corps and are dominated by the Medical Corps, it does not take long until soldiers and sailors observe and realize this fact," noted an editorial in the publication *Oral Hygiene*. "Many of the officers in the Dental Corps have expressed the opinion that unless the American Dental Association is able to accomplish suitable correction to give autonomy to the Dental Corps the future of the association is in jeopardy."[24]

In 1940, the dental profession marked its one hundredth anniversary in Baltimore with a national conference. There were displays featuring images of Chapin Harris and his colleague Horace Hayden, and memorabilia from the world's first college of dentistry. There was a haloed statue of Apollonia, the patron saint of dentists and toothache sufferers, holding her forceps. (The third-century martyr was said to have been tortured before being burned.)

The event got wide media coverage. But the news about the state of oral health in America was not good. "More than 90 percent of the children in this country suffer from the most common ailment of mankind," American Dental Association president Arthur Merritt told radio listeners in a program broadcast by NBC. Among adults, gum disease was also rampant. "Neglect is the biggest menace to mouth health," Merritt warned. He urged people to visit the dentist. "No condition is so bad that modern dental science cannot help it."

But the help of dental science was simply not available to everyone, public health dentist Abel Wolman observed, in a paper delivered in conjunction with the event.

"Today less than 20 percent of the population of this country has adequate care of the teeth under professional direction," he noted. The cost of care was out of reach for many Americans, particularly the one-third of the country's families living on less than $1,000 a year. A publicly subsidized system of care would help, he said. So would stronger disease prevention efforts. But dentistry remained largely focused on perfecting procedural skills, Wolman asserted. "In the process of attaining mechanical perfection, the dentist has of course provided the United States with a superior type of dental care, even though by this imbalance, the broader application of dentistry to public health protection has been greatly delayed, if not even prevented."[25]

Dental leaders of the time acknowledged that millions of Americans lacked dental care. But they fought hard against federal proposals to meet the widespread need. They fought to preserve the autonomy of their profession.

After World War II, when congressional lawmakers took up a discussion of the idea of including dental benefits in a national health care program, a delegation of representatives from the American Dental Association traveled to Capitol Hill to testify against such a plan. It would be impractical and unrealistic, Harold Hillenbrand, editor of the *Journal of the American Dental Association*, told the lawmakers. There were not enough dentists to provide care for all Americans and not enough money to pay for the care. "Cruel as it may sound, it is not possible for all adults to get all the dental care they need at the present time . . . many people have been neglecting their teeth for generations. We feel that rather than undertake an impossible task for such adults, we should undertake the more possible program of preventing and controlling dental diseases in children."[26]

Dental organizations would remain firmly opposed to nationalized health care. They would continue to oppose such efforts to expand dental care, offering the strenuous defenses of the private practice system we still have with us today.

The focal theory is remembered at scientific conferences as a cautionary tale. Still, Willoughby Miller's "chemico-parasitic" theory of tooth decay did shed new light on the disease known as caries. His studies on dental plaque are credited with inspiring the invention of the modern toothbrush, and his work helped engender a movement that for a while brought oral hygiene lessons and services to public schools. Children across the country would learn to brush. They would memorize the slogan "A Clean Tooth Never Decays."[27]

The oral cavity is a dark cabinet full of wonders. It comprises many and varied environments, washed by healing fluid, lined by shining purple mucosa. It is inhabited by organisms as numerous as the citizens of earth. More than six hundred species of bacteria live there, some as yet to be named. The mouth sustains life. The digestive process begins there. Its glands and ducts produce disease-fighting saliva and lymph.

Scientists are pondering the riddles of the teeth, the mysteries of the mouth, the correspondences between oral health and overall health. The super-organism known as the human body is inhabited by 100 trillion microbes. Within it, the mouth has its own intricate ecological niches: the pockets of the gums, the plaque of the teeth, the walls of the cheeks, the surface of the tongue, the hard palate, the soft palate, the tonsils, the saliva. These habitats are rich with microflora that flourish and die, cooperate and compete, and even travel, through subtle mechanisms that are still only beginning to be understood.

Just as in the days of van Leeuwenhoek, the sight of those animalcules can thrill and dazzle. Up on the screen at a distinguished international gathering of dental researchers in Boston in 2015, Gary Borisy offered a new glimpse of them. Spectral imaging techniques revealed vivid configurations alive in the darkness. Hedgehog-like hemispheres with purple spikes. Surreal knitting baskets full of tangled yarn. The shapes were actually clusters of common oral flora, *Streptococcus* and *Corynebacterium*, *Porphyromonas* and *Fusobacterium*, *Capnocytophaga* and *Leptotrichia*, living in communities.[28]

There was something aquatic about them, a reminder of their wet wilderness habitat. And it was no coincidence that these particular animalcules were scraped from the teeth of healthy young workers at the Marine Biological Laboratory in Woods Hole, Massachusetts. Borisy himself worked at the marine lab before he came to the Forysth Institute, a preeminent independent oral health research institute in Cambridge, Massachusetts. With him, he brought insights and methods used to study marine ecosystems to the exploration of the human oral microbiome.

"The microbes form partnerships. They trade nutrients. They need oxygen, they need anchorage," Borisy explained. "If we want to understand how the community is functioning, we don't just look at individual organisms . . . we need to know who is next to who, and who is next to what."

A far more complex picture of the microbial factors at work in health and disease is emerging, thanks to breakthroughs in imaging, genetic mapping, and informatics.

On a systemic scale, the findings are reshaping everything from ideas about antibiotic use to childbirth practices. They are impacting ideas about tooth decay and gum disease too. Tooth decay and periodontal disease are now understood to be driven not by single pathogens, but instead by what leading researchers describe as "consortia of organisms in a biofilm."[29] In health, the oral microflora may abide in a state of "dynamic balance" within a biofilm such as dental plaque. Or the balance may shift, offering opportunistic bacteria a chance at dominance. Their rise comes at the expense of other flora associated with healthy teeth and gums. The imbalance can open the way for disaster on a microbial scale.

"Are dental diseases examples of ecological catastrophes?" asked British researcher PD Marsh in a prizewinning lecture delivered in 2001 at an international meeting of microbiologists. In terms of oral health, the question reflected the kind of thinking that has helped usher in the twenty-first century.[30]

The idea of the mouth as an ecosystem, as vital and vulnerable as a coral reef, has continued to gain credence. Many factors can affect the oral environment. Hundreds of common medications reduce the flow of saliva and consequently rob the teeth of protection against decay. Sugar consumption favors acid-loving and decay-causing bacteria. Poor oral hygiene practices can promote the overgrowth of detrimental microbes. Parents may inadvertently transmit cariogenic bacteria to their babies when they share spoons or attempt to clean a dropped pacifier by placing it in their own mouths. During a ten-second French kiss, partners exchange an average of 80 million bacteria, found Dutch researchers, collecting saliva samples from human couples visiting the Royal Artis Zoo on a summer afternoon.[31]

The mouth is connected to the rest of the body—yet the connections are not yet fully understood. Bacteria are associated with gum disease, but scientists are not sure whether they play a causal role in the disease or grow in the pockets of the gums as a result of the breakdown of tissue due to another cause.[32]

Gum disease in itself can be debilitating and studies suggest it could be linked to conditions beyond the mouth that burden millions of Americans. Yet those links are far from being fully understood. Systemic maladies reveal themselves in lesions of the oral mucosa, in antibodies in the saliva.

Oral microbes have turned up in the cardiovascular and gastrointestinal systems, in the joints. But the implications of these microbial journeys are not clear. Scientists continue to debate whether their presence in these distant sites suggests that the organisms play a causal role in systemic conditions such as arthritis, diabetes, cardiovascular disease, and obesity.

The old focal theory furor of the early twentieth century may have been put to rest. But the mysteries of the ways oral diseases may relate to systemic diseases have not been.

The questions are leading to heated debates. They are also, in at least a few cases, breaking down the long-institutionalized boundaries between medical and dental research.

Is there a connection between periodontal disease and rheumatoid arthritis? The question brought researchers Jeffrey Payne and Ted Mikuls together; they may not have met otherwise. Though both were teaching at the University of Nebraska, they were working on campuses that were sixty miles apart. And more than miles divided them. They were separated by history and training.

Payne, a dentist specializing in periodontology, diseases of the gums, was based at the university's college of dentistry in Lincoln. Mikuls, a physician specializing in rheumatology, diseases of the soft tissues and joints, was working at the university medical center and at the Veterans Affairs hospital an hour's drive away in Omaha. The two were introduced by a fellow faculty member in 2004. What evolved was a collaboration that has spanned more than a decade and has offered new insights into possible associations between two diseases that, while often studied separately, have many characteristics—and victims—in common.

Periodontitis and rheumatoid arthritis are both chronic inflammatory diseases. And while periodontitis destroys the soft and hard tissues around the teeth, rheumatoid arthritis takes a similar toll upon the cartilage and bone in joints. When faced with an infection, the body's immune system mobilizes a defense, in the form of inflammation-heightening proteins. These proteins are critical in fighting disease. But the inflammatory response can be a double-edged sword. When inflammation becomes chronic, it can destroy tissue and bone, and set off what has been described as a cascade of downstream effects. Payne and Mikuls both suspect that gum disease and rheumatoid arthritis might initiate or aggravate one another through the mechanisms of inflammation. Researchers are still a long way from being able to demonstrate that treating periodontal disease would help alleviate or prevent the suffering caused by rheumatoid arthritis. But such interprofessional collaborations hold promise in exploring oral-systemic links, said Payne. "The tendency is to separate the mouth from the rest of the body, but when you think of reducing the inflammation and the potential systemic risk, it is something that both fields should be looking at," said Payne. "And integrating the care of patients better."

Yet there are challenges to working across professional boundaries, in caring for patients and in doing research. Though interest is growing, the current clinical system does not yet offer much support to efforts to integrate care.

The mouth may be part of the body, but physicians are trained to look past the teeth and gums. "Medical training is pretty much from the tonsils south," Payne observed and Mikuls readily concurred. "I'm a rheumatologist," Mikuls noted. "I have fifteen-minute time slots with patients. I don't have a dental chair in my office. I'm not going to start doing full periodontal exams. What I am getting at in my facetious, mean way is there are a lot of resources involved in doing that and it's not standard practice. It would take a leap at this point to get to that, although that may be what is needed."

Building upon past research has also been complicated by another disjoint between the two professions: the fact that dentistry lags behind medicine in the area of disease diagnosis. While the diagnostic criteria for rheumatoid arthritis have been accepted since the 1980s, a number of different definitions for periodontitis have been used by researchers over the years. What is more: dentistry has historically lacked a commonly accepted system of diagnostic terms. "All of our codes are procedural," Payne noted. Treatment codes have long been used in dentistry for billing purposes and for keeping patient records, but the long absence of a standardized diagnostic coding system for dental conditions has inhibited the understanding of the workings of oral disease, some researchers have said.

"We're behind medicine a lot," said Joel White, an applied dental scientist and professor at the University of California, San Francisco (UCSF) School of Dentistry.

"Back in the days of the bubonic plague, medicine captured why people die. We don't capture why teeth die. We are centuries behind." A standardized vocabulary of diagnostic terminology could help dentists in providing care and tracking clinical outcomes, said White, a member of an international working group dedicated to piloting such a system.

A uniform, commonly accepted diagnostic coding system would represent a major shift of emphasis in dentistry, "a move from treatment-centric to diagnostic-centric" care, said Netherlands-born UCSF dentist Elsbeth Kalenderian, who spearheaded a dental coding initiative as a professor at Harvard.[33] Efforts are now under way to put such a system into place. The system would represent a blend of features drawn from Kalenderian's model, the World Health Organization's International Classification of Disease (ICD), and a system developed by the American Dental Association.

The integration of medical and dental records will become increasingly important as researchers such as Robert Genco, from the University of Buffalo, continue with their work. Over the past three decades, Genco has focused upon periodontal disease and its relationships with wider health conditions. His research began in the early 1980s in a trailer clinic on the Gila River Indian Community in Arizona where he studied two diseases rampant among the people there: periodontal disease and type 2 diabetes. "Are people more likely to have periodontal disease if they also have diabetes?" Genco and his colleagues asked themselves, as they followed 3,600 of the Pima people over time. "The answer is overwhelmingly yes," Genco said, summing up their findings. Their conclusion, that periodontal disease is a complication of diabetes, has since been borne out by a number of other studies. The idea is slowly entering the mainstream. Some insurers have begun to conclude that periodontal care pays off in lower-risk scores and medical costs for patients coping with diseases such as diabetes.[34]

Meanwhile, Genco has pressed on with more studies on the oral-systemic workings of disease. He believes the prevalence of gum disease and diabetes in the Pima community both stem from obesity, which began to plague the tribe after the people adopted a modern diet in the postwar era. "In order to survive in the desert, it seems that their thrifty genes may have evolved to carefully conserve fat through times of drought and famine," Genco explained in an essay for a special issue of *Scientific American*. "After World War II, when the tribe changed from their traditional diet to an American one, their fat intake rose from about 15 percent to a whopping 40 percent of calories—and their genetic evolution backfired."

Years of study have led Genco and his team to a sense that obesity, periodontal disease, and diabetes are all "syndemically" bound by inflammation. Other researchers are more conservative in their assessments. The diseases are deeply complex. But the clues of biology will eventually bring oral health into the larger understanding of health, and dental care into the wider health care system, Genco has predicted. The gap between oral health care providers and medical care providers will need to be bridged, he said in an interview. "We all have the same common basic sciences. We all train in a similar fashion. But still the professions are separate. We don't look too much at the rest of the body and the physicians don't look at the mouth." Science has become a leading force in integration, Genco explained. "It's getting us to look together at the patient as a whole. And in particular in diabetes. Where the interaction is so intimate. A patient with diabetes is at risk for periodontal disease. Once the diabetic patient has periodontal disease their diabetes gets worse. So it's a two-way street. So physicians and dentists really have to integrate in their management of the patient. So it is bringing the professions together. Putting the mouth into the body."

To the nineteenth-century German pathologist Rudolf Virchow, the germ theory always seemed an insufficient explanation for widespread disease. At the heart of the epidemic, he found not just germs but poverty—and politics. "Medicine is a social science, and politics is nothing more than medicine on a grand scale," wrote Virchow, the father of social medicine.

Through centuries of religion and science, the mouth has endured in its particularity. Dreaded, revered, a seat of identity, survival, contagion, and power, the mouth right now is also a contested territory. In the year 2000, it was America's top public health official, the surgeon general of the United States, who reframed dental disease as oral disease and oral disease as a public health crisis.

David Satcher's message came in the form of a plain green book with the anchor and caduceus, the seal of the U.S. Public Health Service, printed on the cover. In *Oral Health in America: A Report of the Surgeon General*, Satcher warned that from cavities to gum disease to oral cancers, a "silent epidemic" was raging in America.

"Those who suffer the worst oral health are found among the poor of all ages, with poor children and poor older Americans particularly vulnerable," his report noted. "Members of racial and ethnic minority groups also experience a disproportionate level of oral health problems." The report surveyed the biology of oral health and disease and the wider determinants too: environmental and genetic factors, health behaviors, economic and social factors. The lack of dental insurance and money to pay for dental care, poor diets, tobacco use, a shortage of dentists working in poor communities, and a lack of health literacy all contributed to the crisis, Satcher concluded in the report, the government's first-ever comprehensive study of the nation's oral health. "Oral health means much more than healthy teeth," stressed Satcher. He called the mouth "a mirror of health and disease," "a sentinel or early warning system," "an accessible model for the study of other tissues and organs," and "a potential source of pathology affecting other systems and organs."

Oral Health in America ended with a call to action: an appeal for increased research, the removal of barriers to care, the raising of awareness about the importance of oral health among average citizens, lawmakers, and health care providers, and the building of an American health care system "that meets the oral health needs of all Americans and integrates oral health effectively into overall health." Advocates for oral health seized upon the report as a rallying point. They went on to highlight dental deaths and stir long-simmering struggles over the use of dental auxiliaries to expand care. Some, but not all of them, were dentists. Their approach came as a new challenge to organized dentistry. The biological and political understanding of oral health has continued to evolve.

Meanwhile, in the world beneath our noses, oral microbes thrive and struggle and unexplainably wander. The teeth bear silent witness to our human condition. They are lost and they are found again. They say that we traveled, we suffered, we invented, we lived.

The discovery of a cache of forty-seven human teeth in a Chinese cave, probably more than eighty thousand years old, has provided new evidence that *Homo sapiens* journeyed out of Africa tens of thousands of years earlier than was previously believed. The teeth that belonged to those early migrants carry evidence of their diets, their illnesses, their culture, their possible encounters with their contemporaries, the Neanderthals, their dispersal routes into Europe.[35] And in a decayed fourteen-thousand-year-old wisdom tooth found in northern Italy, researchers recently announced they had discovered the earliest known evidence of dentistry. The cavitated third molar belonged to a young man who lived during the Late Upper Paleolithic Era, a period when people were painting on cave walls and developing early tools. Images from inside the decayed lesion, obtained using spectron microscopy, disclosed a pattern of chipping apparently made with a tiny stone pick.[36]

Part II

THE DENTAL ART

5

The Birth of American Dentistry

CHAPIN HARRIS RODE THROUGH THE NIGHT. BEHIND HIM LAY GEN-
erations of honest tooth pullers and wandering quacks. Before him
lay the new profession he was inventing. In America, in the days
before the Civil War, most dentists were itinerants, like Harris, riding from town to town. Their work took them to worlds unseen
by other travelers. They set up their temporary offices in homes,
factories, inns, and taverns. They brought out their dreaded instruments. They scraped, they drilled, they extracted. They plugged
with gold, amalgams of tin and mercury, molten lead. For pain
they proffered leeches and arsenic, nutgalls and mustard seed, lau-
danum and vinegar. They were feared and often disparaged. There
was no formal training. Anyone who called himself a dentist was
one. Chapin Harris called himself a dentist.

On this night, in 1831 or 1832, Harris hurried to the bedside of
a physician who lived in the countryside, thirty miles from Baltimore. Harris found the doctor with his jaw locked shut by infection, burning with fever. Two weeks before, the physician, who

Harris called "Dr. E." in his writings, had begun feeling pain in his lower-left wisdom tooth. He had called a fellow medical man who "had pronounced its extraction impracticable."

But over the following days the pain intensified. Swallowing became difficult, then breathing. Bloodletting and cathartics proved useless. A practitioner with the deftness, skill, and strength to remove the abscessed tooth was needed. When Harris arrived, a wooden wedge was used to pry open the mouth of Dr. E. "sufficiently to permit the extraction of the offending tooth."

"The cause, that had occasioned his sufferings, having been thus removed; I left him, and was soon after informed that he had perfectly recovered," Harris recalled. With the story, he offered an ancient piece of healer's wisdom.

"Ever since the days of Hippocrates, it has been considered an axiom of medicine, that the first step to be taken in the treatment of disease, is the removal of all the primary causes," Harris wrote.

Harris was born in 1806 in Onondaga, New York. He moved to Ohio at the age of seventeen, and after receiving some preliminary training, perhaps from his older brother, he began to practice the dental art. In his mid-twenties, he traveled in the South and Southwest. In 1838, Harris spent a month in the river town of Littleton, North Carolina, where "he did over 4,000 dollars worth of dental work in an office room 12 by 16 feet. He had no dental chair or head rest but sat in a chair and put his foot on a stool, the patients sitting on the floor, resting their heads on his knee," according to a biographical review, published in a dental journal in 1905.[1]

After he saw his last patient of the day, Harris turned to his writing, often working until long past midnight. "He was a laborious student and followed the practice of writing far into the morning after days of ceaseless labor and fatigue to the end of his life," the article reported.

In 1838 Harris was completing a book, *The Dental Art*, first printed in Baltimore the following year. Throughout the text Harris used anecdotes and case studies, such as the story of Dr. E., to teach lessons, illustrate principles. He wrote of the chicanery of charlatans, with their nostrums and promises, and the labors of earnest healers. He explored the riddles of oral disease, using stories of the patients he himself had seen and reports passed on to him by other practitioners. The young gentleman with tumefaction of the gums. The gentleman of great respectability with swellings accompanied by great pain and inconvenience. The lady whose "splintered" jaw Harris wrote of helping to repair, after a stagecoach overturned on the road between Washington and Baltimore. "The wounds of her face, having been properly dressed, the detached portion of the jaw was carefully adjusted and secured by a ligature." For her there were bloodlettings, and more than a month of washings, five or six times a day with tincture of myrrh. At the end of it, though, she was mended.

"She perfectly recovered," Harris wrote. Patience. Patience and vigilance.

Most harrowing were the stories used to illustrate the crucial nature of the teeth, the urgency of their care, their vital connection to the body.

"Miss W., a maiden lady of about 50 years old, in comfortable circumstances and for the most part, addicted to sedentary occupations had suffered much from a pain in her right cheek."

Miss W. consulted a physician. "He found but a single tooth, one of the second molares, in the superior maxillary of the affected side, and that was in a semi-decayed state. The gums above the tooth and . . . on either side of the tooth were much swollen and of a livid redness."

She was reluctant to have the ruined tooth drawn out. "The immediate extraction of the tooth was, however, thought advisable." She conceded. Yet even after the abscessed tooth was gone, the pain persisted.

The germ theory had not yet shed light upon the workings of infection. And Miss W.'s physician did not use the word *infection* to describe what he saw. But the infection from the tooth had migrated to the antrum maxillare, the upper sinus. A perforation was made into the cavity of the sinus. A silver spoonful of foul discharge was released, Harris recounted. The physician decided to treat the "affection" but faced difficulties "reaching the disease with remedies." The opening into the antrum was enlarged. "The usual antiseptic and detergents were locally applied, while tonics and a generous diet were prescribed to sustain the patient's general health."

Those measures failed. On May 26 "the patient was found in a perfect state of apoplexy, the disease having penetrated the bone constituting the basis of the cranium, and seized upon the brain itself."

For Miss W. all was lost, Harris wrote. "On the 30th of the same month she expired, and was thus released, by death, from the most horrible disease that can be conceived, but which had its origin in nothing more extraordinary than a neglected carious tooth."

Harris wondered and worked. He kept on riding and studying. Insatiably curious, a voracious reader, "not satisfied with the meager amount of knowledge he possessed, he secured the books of Delabarre, Fox, Hunter and others," recounted Harris's biographical review, referring to the leading French and British dental practitioners of those times.[2] In Europe, the mechanical skills of dentistry had been transmitted through an apprenticeship system that dated back to the Middle Ages. But by early in the eighteenth century, led by the French surgeon-dentist Pierre Fauchard, a few practitioners had begun to incorporate scientific principles into their work.

Fauchard used a microscope to debunk the age-old belief that tooth decay was caused by gnawing worms. He worked to expose quackery and insisted that medical information should be shared among colleagues. In nineteenth-century England, Joseph Fox also rose into the elite ranks of the healers. Fox worked as a dental surgeon at London's Guy's Hospital. A series of lectures he gave there formed the basis of his books, first published in London in 1803 and 1806. The writings became a touchstone for Harris, who edited, annotated, and published them in an American edition.[3]

There was a quiet authority in Fox's observations and in the scores of richly detailed plates; they summed up in English what was known or believed about the world inside the human mouth. "The teeth are formed in a manner peculiar to themselves, differing from the mode observed in the formation of bones in general," wrote Fox.

Fox traced the sensations in the teeth to the fifth pair of cranial nerves, the trigeminals, which, through their three branches to the eyes and jaws, signal feelings such as pain to the brain. He documented the development of the teeth from their fetal beginnings as granular papilla, rising from primitive dental grooves to their gradual hardening within the alveolar sockets of the jaws. He outlined the emergence and shedding of the twenty primary teeth, the succession of the thirty-two permanent teeth. Fox catalogued the shapes and functions of the incisors, cuspids, bicuspids, and molars, the chemical composition of their enamel and roots, the earthy composition of their tartar.

Fox suspected that decay was caused by the consumption of hot and cold food. He described the ravages of caries at the turn of the nineteenth century. Small children were not exempt from the pain and disfigurement. "In two or three cases I have seen every tooth in a diseased state at so early a period as three years," Fox wrote. "The little patients are generally dreadfully afflicted, and their rest being disturbed and their being unable to masticate food with comfort their health is often much impaired."

Fox also warned of charlatans who would take advantage of pain for their own profit. The newspapers of those days were filled with ads for patent medicines promising miracle cures and painless relief for everything from cancer to tooth decay. In fact, few maladies were viewed with more dread than diseases of the teeth.

"There is scarcely any pain to which the human body is subject, that is so much under the influence of the passions of fear or hope, as the toothache," observed Fox. The sheer awfulness of the pain made sufferers uniquely vulnerable to exploitation, Fox observed. "Empirics are not wanting who take advantage of this circumstance, and pretend to cure toothache by certain charms and nostrums. Indeed at the moment they can often appear to be successful, from the passions of fear or hope causing a temporary suspension of pain."

The quacks may have lacked interest in science. But science held dangers of its own. In the late eighteenth century, the famed Scottish-born surgeon John Hunter set off a rage for tooth transplantation that endured for decades on both sides of the Atlantic. Animal experiments led Hunter to conclude that teeth possessed a "living principal" that made them "capable of uniting with any part of the body." Hunter reported the successful transplantation of the bud of a human tooth into a rooster's comb in 1778 and began performing human-to-human tooth transplants. He found a ready demand for the procedure. With the rise of medicines, foods, and drinks containing processed sugar, decay was running rampant particularly among the affluent. The rich wanted new teeth. The desperately poor provided a source. They lined up to sell their teeth.

"The best remedy is to have several people ready, whose Teeth in appearance are fit: for if the first will not answer, the second may," Hunter advised.[4] The operations were not always successful, even Hunter acknowledged. "I am persuaded this operation has failed, from a tooth being forced in too tight."

Indeed some of the transplants were disasters, with recipients developing oral infections and sometimes contracting syphilis. Fox condemned tooth transplants warning of "disagreeable and alarming symptoms." And Harris, in an annotation added to the American edition of Fox's book, agreed.

"To say nothing of the turpitude and cruelty of thus mutilating and disfiguring one person for the gratification of another, the operation itself is one which is very painful and sometimes even dangerous," Harris warned.

The pathos inherent in the idea of the poor giving up their teeth to satisfy the rich was not lost on the popular imagination. One such transaction was explored in a short story, "An Event in the

Life of a Dentist," that appeared in a periodical of the day. The tale turned upon the decision of a lovely and destitute woman to sell her teeth in order to ease her father's dying days. The dentist, Dr. Nippers, spotted the humble and dignified Louisa in a millinery shop: "What most particularly attracted him were her fine teeth, the most beautiful he had ever seen."

After hearing the young woman offering some of her exquisite needlework to the proprietor for a mere pittance, he approached her.

"My pretty girl, have you nothing more to sell?"

"Nothing more, sir."

"You do not know how rich you are," continued the stranger, "let me make you a fortune by purchasing some of your teeth."[5]

Over the long nights he labored over his own book, *The Dental Art*, Harris worked to distill the lessons he had learned so far in his journey as a practitioner. He drew upon his studies of the dental masters of France and England, the observations of American colleagues, and what his own eyes and hands had taught him about dentistry. *The Dental Art*, published in Baltimore in 1839, became the world's first college dental textbook and would endure as the most popular dental book of its time. It was renamed and reprinted in thirteen editions over the next seventy-four years.

It was the product of an ambitious and tireless mind.

In its pages, Harris wondered at the beauty of the primary teeth: "little germs, sparkling with whiteness." He preached of the importance of keeping the teeth clean. He recommended toothpicks made of goose quills to remove particles of food, and regular brushing with a dentifrice of powdered orris root, chalk, and pumice. "Proper attention to the cleanliness of these organs contributes more to their health and preservation than is generally supposed."

He wrote of the scourge of tooth decay. While some believed inflammation caused it, and that teeth rotted from the inside out, Harris was convinced decay worked from the outside in, beginning with a small opaque or dark spot on the enamel. "It always commences upon the outer surface of the tooth, usually under the enamel, and then proceeds towards the center, until it reaches the lining membrane." He suspected the process was caused by "the action of some solvent." He advocated for tooth preservation. For arresting the progress of decay he recommended drilling and plugging: "Vast numbers of teeth, by its means, have been rescued from the ravages of caries," he wrote. For drilling, there were flat, round, and cherry-headed drills with socket handles, and drills fitted into stocks and driven with a bow and string. For plugging some used tin or silver. Harris rejected those metals, contending they broke down too quickly. But lead was worse, he said, because of its "deleterious effects on the general system."

Metal amalgams, poured into teeth in a molten state, he wholeheartedly condemned, particularly one "composed principally of mercury and silver . . . known by the name of Royal Mineral Succedanium." Harris warned of charlatan dentists who "pretended to extraordinary skill" in the use of the stuff. Plugs made with it, in a few days time inevitably "loosened and dropped out." For restorations, Harris insisted on one substance, and one substance alone. "Gold is the only metal that should be used for plugging," he wrote.

There were leeches and tinctures to relieve the pain of complicated decay that caused the lining of the tooth to swell and suppurate. But often in those days, there was no way to save such teeth. For extraction, Harris reserved some of his most forceful words. "This operation is, generally, considered as of comparatively little importance, and yet, there are but few operations in surgery, that excite stronger feelings of horror and dread. . . . Persons have been known to be willing to suffer with odontalgia for weeks and months, rather than to have the offending tooth removed."

The widespread fears were well-founded. But they could be addressed by well-trained practitioners, Harris said. "The extraction of a tooth, if conducted by a skillful hand, is a safe and easy operation; but if attempted by the unskillful, may occasion the most frightful and dangerous consequences." He wrote of a blacksmith who "in attempting to extract one of the superior molar teeth, brought away a piece of the jaw, containing five other teeth, together with the floor and the posterior and anterior plates of the antrum."[6]

Baltimore, where Harris settled in the 1830s, was a place of stunning contrasts. It was a gothic, gaslit mecca of wealth and industry: the birthplace of the American railroad, a thriving port city, a center of commerce and trade. Yet there, too, was the misery of the city's almshouse and the shantytowns and hovels down by the harbor, teeming with indigents and poor workers. There were slaves as well, including Frederick Douglass, brought to Baltimore aboard a sloop sent down from a tobacco plantation north of the city.

"We arrived at Baltimore early on Sunday morning, landing at Smith's Wharf, not far from Bowley's Wharf," Douglass would remember in his famous autobiography.[7] Coming to the city along with a load of sheep bound for the slaughterhouse would be a turning point in Douglass's life. It was in the city that he gained his freedom and went to work at the wharf. It was there he learned to read and write.

Baltimore was a center of science and healing, home to the University of Maryland College of Medicine, opened in 1807 as the College of Medicine of Maryland. The school stood on Lombard Street, housed in cupolaed and columned Davidge Hall, which was modeled after the Pantheon in Rome. It boasted a fine library and a famous collection of anatomical specimens, an operating theater, laboratory, and teaching hospital. Decades before the germ theory, the brilliant John Crawford lectured there, suggesting disease was caused by "animacular life so minute as to escape observation."

A young man hoping to gain admission to medical college in those days often first worked as an apprentice in the home of a physician. "During the day he pounded out powders, washed bottles and made up pills in his master's laboratory; he accompanied the doctor on his rounds, watching him practice, handing him his instruments and running errands," noted a history of the University of Maryland. "As the boy's knowledge grew, he increasingly took a hand in the practice, extracting teeth, bleeding the patient or making a distant call on a case that did not seem serious."[8]

The doctors were on the brink of new insights into the workings of disease. Yet the origins of the epidemics of typhoid, yellow fever, malaria, and cholera that swept through Baltimore with regularity remained mysterious. Some people blamed the poisons of bad air. Others blamed the idle and wandering poor living in crowded and squalid housing by the harbor. Science itself was also feared and mistrusted. The founders of the medical college would long remember the night that an angry mob broke into the dissection laboratory and carried away the cadaver.

Just as grave robbers offered up corpses for medical study, some did an unsavory traffic in teeth as well. In the February 23, 1833, issue of the *Baltimore Saturday Visiter*, below the obituaries with their winged death heads and a listing of interments performed by the city health office, appeared two more small notices: one for a dentifrice that claimed to give "the teeth a beautiful whiteness" and the other, unsigned, under the headline "CAUTION."

"A correspondent requests to caution certain persons from being too bold in robbing graves for the sake of obtaining human teeth. He says a young lady of wealth and respectability recently died and left a notice, stating that no one need trouble themselves about her, as all her teeth had decayed long ere she left this world—and those she had been using, she had bequeathed to a friend."

Such an item may have fueled the fevered imagination of Edgar Allan Poe, who was living in Baltimore, sharing a small brick duplex with his aunt and his young cousin (and future wife).[9] It was about that time, in 1835, that one of Poe's earliest tales, "Berenice," was published: a horrific tale of a man's dental obsession.

The tormented narrator of the story, Egeus, who is engaged to his dying cousin, is transfixed by her luminous teeth. "They, they alone were present to the mental eye, and they, in their sole individuality, became the essence of my mental life." After the young woman is buried, her lover, in a frenzy, violates her grave. When he comes to his senses he discovers in his room a muddy spade and a fateful box: "In my tremor, it slipped from my hands, and fell heavily, and burst into pieces; and from it, with a rattling sound, there rolled out some instruments of dental surgery, intermingled with thirty-two small white and ivory-looking substances that were scattered to and fro about the floor."[10]

At the same time, Baltimore dentist Horace Hayden was moving among the city's elite circles of scholars, scientists, and artists. He was a member of the local literary society, the Delphian Club of Baltimore. He was president of the Maryland Academy of Sciences. Hayden was a polymath from an age about to be eclipsed by specialization.

Accounts of his life vary, but according to one, Hayden was born in 1769 to a Connecticut military family and began reading as a very small child. When he was fourteen, he voyaged to the West Indies as a cabin boy. When he was twenty-four, he moved to New York and worked as an architect.[11]

The beginnings of Hayden's dental studies were traced to a 1792 visit to the New York dentist John Greenwood, whose initials were engraved upon the dentures of George Washington.[12] After arriving in Baltimore about 1800, Hayden studied and practiced medicine and dentistry. When the British attacked Baltimore during the War of 1812, Hayden enlisted and served as an assistant surgeon.[13]

He worked in biology and geology as well. He wrote papers about silkworm culture and teething, and ulcerations of the tonsils. Outside the city of Baltimore, Hayden discovered a dark, crystalline mineral that was named in his honor: Haydenite. In 1820, he published the first general text on geology to be printed in the United States, a sweeping and ambitious survey of the structure of the globe and the terrain of the United States. In it, he refuted Neptunism, a popular theory of the day that held that all the rocks on the Earth's surface had been formed from the crystallization of minerals from early oceans.[14]

For a couple of years, before and after the publication of his geological text, Hayden attempted some lectures on dentistry at the medical college.[15] But the lessons were not unanimously well received.

"I was one of his class and found the lectures very speculative and unsatisfactory," recalled one of the students in a letter. "Certain it is, that those engaged in tooth pulling, filling and filing, which then seemed to be the sole business of the craft, took no interest in Dr. Hayden's attempt to enlighten them. Nevertheless he is entitled to credit for an effort, however unsuccessful, to give dentistry better claims to public confidence," the student wrote.[16]

The dental lectures languished. Hayden, could not formalize dental education on his own. It would take his partnership with Chapin Harris, four decades his junior, to do that. In the span of a year of sleepless nights and frenetic travel, the elderly polymath and the young specialist joined forces.

But theirs was a sometimes uneasy alliance. Harris believed dentistry needed a scientific journal. Hayden, on the other hand, balked at the idea, according to one account "alleging he had labored too hard and too long in the acquisition of professional knowledge to sow it broadcast through the land by means of a magazine."[17] Still, the two went to New York and, in 1839, at a meeting at the home of a colleague, found backers for the idea. The first issue of the *American Journal of Dental Science* was published in 1839. Harris would serve as the Baltimore editor for years.

Both men saw the need for a national professional organization. Hayden had tried several times in the past to start one—without success. But working with Harris and New York colleagues, the American Society of Dental Surgeons, hailed as the world's first national dental organization, was founded in 1840. Hayden was chosen as president.

Finally there was a need for professional training. Harris in his writings had suggested the possibility of establishing "professorships of dentistry in the Medical Schools." According to an enduring version of the story, Harris and Hayden approached the physicians of the College of Medicine at the University of Maryland with the idea of adding "dental instruction to their medical course." But the physicians, the story goes, rejected the proposition in a letter to Harris "giving as an excuse 'that the subject of dentistry was of little consequence, and thus justified their unfavorable action.'"

The physicians' rejection, now remembered as "the historic rebuff," was reported in a 1904 school history.[18] But their fateful letter to Harris has never been found. Some, over the years, have challenged the veracity of the creation story of the dental profession. "The truth is that no such attitude was ever assumed by medicine; no such derogatory opinion was ever expressed," wrote J. Ben Robinson, a longtime dean and devoted historian of the school.[19]

Whatever may have happened between the physicians and the dentists, Harris and Hayden did not succeed in establishing a dental department within the medical college at the University of Maryland. It was then, it has been said, that paths of American medicine and dentistry officially diverged. "Thus was begun a split which is not yet healed," observed sociologist Robert O'Shea. American dentistry did not evolve as a specialty of medicine but instead as "a separate and independent health service."

"The circumstances around the founding of the Baltimore school might be termed 'symbolic events'—actions that had great historic consequences themselves. As well as ones that portray enduring social relations," wrote O'Shea.[20]

It is certain that at the time the physicians were facing other demands and pressures. Maryland's medical college, which they had built with their own money, had just begun to emerge from a protracted legal battle between university regents and a state-appointed board of trustees. Epidemics continued to threaten the city and they were powerless to stop them. The progress of science was challenging their time-honored medical theories and treatments. Specialties were evolving. Quacks and charlatans promised miracle cures. Medicine was at a deeply unsettled place.

Harris and Hayden did not give up on their project. As O'Shea observed, the two men were following well-established precedent. Without formal education, dentistry would remain a humble trade, and dentists would never rise to privilege as professionals.

Harris went to New York and attempted to establish a "chair of dentistry" in a New York medical school. That effort also failed. But thirteen colleagues at a dinner Harris attended subscribed $100 each toward opening a dental school in Baltimore.[21] Harris returned to Baltimore and he and Hayden went to work in Hayden's office, spending their nights laying out plans for a new institution, the first of its kind in the world: an independent college of dental surgery. In the winter of 1839 to 1840, they gathered enough signatures from the residents of Baltimore to petition the state legislature for permission to incorporate a college of dental surgery in the city. The charter was granted. A bill passed by the legislature required professors to hold at least one four-month term per year and gave the faculty the authority to confer a Doctor of Dental Surgery degree upon any student who attended all the lectures for two terms.

In 1840, the Baltimore College of Dental Surgery opened, with much fanfare but without its own building. That first lecture was delivered in a Baptist church on Calvert Street. Classes were taught in the homes of the professors. The college president was Horace Hayden. Chapin Harris became the school's first dean and served as a professor of operative dentistry and dental prosthesis.

"Gentlemen—the profession for which you are preparing, is honorable; it is useful; it is one that will enable you to be serviceable to your fellows—to relieve much of human pain and mitigate many mortal woes," Harris told the first class of five students.[22]

At the first commencement, in 1841, the graduates were addressed by physician and professor of pathology Thomas E. Bond Jr.

> You have been taught that dental surgery is not a mere art, separate from, and independent of, general medicine; but that it is an important branch of the science of cure. Your knowledge has been based on extensive and accurate anatomical investigation. You have seen and traced out the exquisitely beautiful machinery by which the organism is everywhere knit together. . . . You have

been taught to regard the human body as a complete whole, united in all its parts.[23]

But the grand picture was regularly eclipsed by narrower concerns. In 1842, Harris and Hayden suffered an irreparable falling-out over conflicting papers outlining theories on diseases of the maxillary sinuses. Their bitter feud would play out in the pages of the dental journal they brought to life.

Horace Hayden died in 1844. He was eulogized not by Harris but by Bond, the professor of pathology. "He loved knowledge for its own sake, and studied nature from the force of that instinctive curiosity which is the animating principle of genius," Bond noted.[24]

Then, for more than a decade, the new profession closed in upon itself, torn by what came to be known as "the Amalgam War." The American Society of Dental Surgeons that Harris and Hayden founded forced members to sign a pledge to abstain from using the restorative material. Many refused. The pages of the dental journal were filled with arguments over the dangers and merits of mercury amalgam. The society collapsed in 1856.

During those same years, in the wider world, questions about the larger causes and patterns of disease were being explored. Vistas were opening. It was in 1848 that pathologist Rudolf Virchow traveled from Berlin to a depressed rural area of Prussian-controlled Upper Silesia to investigate an outbreak of typhus. His resulting report, describing the poverty and hunger of the landless victims, mostly members of the Polish minority, left a permanent imprint upon the epidemiological imagination. And it was in 1854 that London doctor John Snow traced the source of an epidemic of cholera to a contaminated pump at the corner of Broad and Cambridge streets. His mapping of the water sources of the victims led him to conclude the disease was waterborne, not caused by miasmas or the depravity of the poor. When followers of Snow and Virchow talked about removing the causes of disease, they spoke of microorganisms, but they also spoke of physical and social conditions in communities.

This was social medicine, the medicine of prevention, the science of public health. At the same time, the work of clinical medicine was continuing its shift to the localized study of individual organs and pathologies. Specialization, with all its promises and costs, was advancing. Medicine would incorporate and expand beyond surgery in its approaches to healing.

The dentists would take their own path. The dental department instituted at Harvard University in 1867 was formally associated with the medical school, but it would remain a rare example of such an alliance. Over the years, efforts to better integrate dental education into medical education would come and go. In his landmark 1926 critique of the dental system, the eminent William J. Gies would warn, "There is a growing need for dentists who will be not only dental engineers and dental surgeons but also dental physicians and dental sanitarians."

Reforms were made. But in essential ways, dentists and dental care would remain separate from America's larger health care system. Americans would need to negotiate this separate dental system to find oral health care services. The profession of dentistry would remain focused upon the surgical procedures needed to treat tooth decay and other symptoms of oral disease. Unlike physicians, who would maintain hospital affiliations, most dentists would build private practices for the delivery of their services. A separate financing system would grow up around their work. They would organize in order to defend the standards and licensing of their profession as well as their professional autonomy. Far fewer dentists would concern themselves with social medicine, researching wider patterns of disease, or the delivery of oral health across populations. Far fewer would work in laboratories, researching the microscopic causes and conditions underlying health and disease.

Chapin Harris died in 1860.

"Liberal to an extreme in life, Dr. Harris failed to leave his family well provided for after his death," the 1905 biographical review of Harris's life recounted. Fifty prominent dentists founded a "Harris Testimonial Fund" and appointed a committee to collect donations to sustain his family. "After canvassing this profession for some months, at much expense, the committee reported that nearly one thousand dollars had been subscribed but that about nine hundred dollars had been expended collecting it—the balance of $85 was sent, with a note to Mrs. Harris explaining it," the essay noted. Her reported response was "take back this beggarly gift, I spurn it."

Harris spent his career stressing the importance of the teeth to the entire body. But in the brief preface of his book *The Dental Art* he also acknowledged a narrower view. "The anatomy of the teeth is introduced, only so far as it is actually necessary, in order to enable the reader to fully understand the subject which he is treating," he wrote.

The book has long since been put aside. A fragile copy rests in the National Library of Medicine in Bethesda, Maryland. Its stories of pain and mystery, its lessons and riddles remain, locked like specimens in amber.

Since *The Dental Art* was written, countless millions of infected teeth have been extracted. Tooth decay, though largely preventable, has not yet been conquered. In fact, federal data show it remains the most prevalent chronic disease of American children and adults.[25] The scars and lesions remain. They are symptoms of an epidemic.

On January 11, 2007, about thirty miles from Baltimore, in a place that had been deep in the country and a day and a night's ride in Chapin Harris's day, a boy named Deamonte Driver, a normally energetic child, came home from school not feeling well.

"He kept complaining of a headache," his mother, Alyce Driver, said. His grandmother took him to Southern Maryland Hospital Center, not far from the fallow fields of semirural Brandywine where his grandparents' red and white house trailer stood in the patchy shade of a grove of trees. He was given medicines for headache, sinusitis, and a dental abscess, Alyce Driver said. The following day, a Thursday, Deamonte went back to school.

"That Friday he was worse," his mother said. "He couldn't talk." She brought him to Prince George's County Hospital Center, where Deamonte received a spinal tap and a CT scan.

"They said he had meningitis," said Alyce Driver. The child was rushed to Children's National Medical Center in Washington, D.C., where he underwent emergency brain surgery.

"They said the infection was on the left side of his brain," she said. "They had to remove a bone." On Saturday Deamonte started having seizures. "The infection came back," Alyce Driver said. "They had to go back in."

Deamonte required a second brain surgery and, this time, the abscessed tooth was removed. It was a molar on the upper-left side of his mouth, a so-called six-year molar, one of the first permanent teeth to erupt as the baby teeth are shed; there are four of them, two upper, two lower, strong, with deep roots and broad crowns: tools for living, but particularly vulnerable to decay. This tooth was ruined, infected to the core. Bacteria from the abscess had spread to the boy's brain, doctors said. Alyce Driver remembered a doctor telling her, "this kid is fighting for his life." Her world, which was fraught with struggle on the best of days, seemed to fall apart.

"I fell out," said Alyce Driver.

The extended family gathered around Deamonte's bed and appealed to heaven. "We prayed and prayed and prayed," recalled Alyce Driver. "We were all around the bed, my mom, my sister, my brother, my sister-in-law. Everybody but my father. He's not a hospital person." They called upon Jesus and asked him to save the boy. "He slept for two days straight. I said is my baby ever going to wake up?"

Finally Deamonte opened his eyes.

"It was amazing," his mother said. Keeping watch at her son's hospital bedside twelve days later, on January 24, 2007, the mother mused over the strange nightmare that started with one decayed tooth.

A thin scar ran across the top of Deamonte's head where doctors had opened his skull to treat his brain. He was still fragile. She worried about the next step, where Deamonte would stay when he had to leave the hospital. Alyce Driver was poor; in fact, she had been coping with homelessness since leaving a violent relationship. Deamonte had been in the care of her parents when he got sick. She had taken a construction course for women and had been filling out applications for jobs, but Deamonte's crisis had put a halt to her search for work. She could find no place to rent. She could not bring the fragile boy back to her parents' trailer. "There is just no space. My family is not quiet people. It's the front part of his brain that's damaged. Everything is sensitive."

Over the next days, Deamonte was up, moving slowly, getting physical therapy, trying to do some math homework to catch up with his seventh-grade class, begging to eat a cracker. Begging to play a game.

"I'd rather have him irking my nerves than wondering if I'd ever be irked again," said his mother ruefully, but with a new lightness in her voice. "I'm so happy he's doing better. I'm just gonna pray we can go somewhere where he's safe."

Finally, after more than two weeks and more than $250,000 worth of care at Children's, Deamonte was moved to another hospital, the Hospital for Sick Children, where he began an additional six weeks of medical treatment. The days passed quietly. Deamonte received physical and occupational therapy, did schoolwork, and enjoyed visits from his mother, his brothers, and teachers from his school. One of his teachers drove to see him, even though everyone knew she had lost her license.

"What are you doing up here?" he asked her, sounding like his old curious self. "You don't have a driver's license!" He posed for a picture, beaming with a little plush toy dog he was brought as a gift.

Yet Deamonte's eyes seemed to be weak, his mother said, and his complexion got darker. On Saturday, February 24, Deamonte refused to eat. But the boy seemed happy. He and his mother played cards and watched a show on television, lying together on his hospital bed. After she left him that evening, he called her.

"Make sure you pray before you go to sleep," he told her.

The next morning, Sunday, February 25, she got another call, this time from her mother. Deamonte was unresponsive. She found a ride back to the hospital.

"When I got there," Alyce Driver said, "my baby was gone."

6

Separate Lives

AFTER THE *WASHINGTON POST* CARRIED AN ACCOUNT OF DEAMONTE Driver's death, the news was picked up by other papers and Internet sites around the world. To many modern readers, the story seemed like a dreadful curiosity.

Chapin Harris had documented many awful deaths like Deamonte Driver's. They helped convince him of the need for a dental profession. By the twenty-first century, thanks to professional care and advances in antibiotics and water fluoridation, reports of death by dental infection were mercifully rare in America. But in Baltimore, Harris's modern successors, serving on the faculty of what had become the University of Maryland School of Dentistry, were not so surprised a child had died. They regularly saw the grave consequences of rampant oral disease. They knew that people with good jobs and dental benefits and the money to pay out-of-pocket for care had access to America's dental care system. But they also knew that people who were poor or working poor or underinsured or who relied upon Medicaid, or who had no benefits of any kind, were often shut out.

From Maryland's western tip in Appalachia to its isolated fishing communities along the Chesapeake Bay, some of these people eventually found their way to the clinic at the world's oldest dental college. The patients traveled for hours for low-cost appointments. They waited in predawn lines for treatment. Norman Tinanoff, Clemencia Vargas, and their colleagues at the school spent long days providing and overseeing care, teaching and researching. For years, they had been publishing papers warning of the epidemic of disease, the silent suffering of poor children and adults in the wealthy state, the shortage of dentists caring for them.

In one study of poor Maryland Head Start students across the state, Vargas, Tinanoff, and fellow researchers found more than half of the children, aged three to five, had untreated decay. Of those, a significant number were in pain. In the paper, published five years before Deamonte Driver's death, they warned that while most of the nation's Head Start children were poor enough to qualify for Medicaid "only 20 percent of Medicaid eligible children receive dental care."[1]

Beyond the system's most immediate shortcomings, they were convinced that dentistry's approach to addressing the epidemic was too narrow. Dentistry, in its separate world from medicine, had long been seen as a mechanical solution to tooth decay. But tooth decay was more than a mechanical failure. Tooth decay was the symptom of a complex, progressive disease that came with lifelong burdens and sometimes tragic consequences, particularly for the millions of Americans for whom care was out of reach.

Since Chapin Harris's day, the world's first dental college had evolved from a small proprietary school into a world-class institution. But the profession of dentistry had not evolved sufficiently to address this epidemic, said Tinanoff. He was seated at his desk in his office at the dental school, the light of the old city filtering in over his books and the African violets on the windowsill. He spoke of a profession focused upon procedures and restorations, upon drilling and filling cavities. Instead, he said, dentists should be addressing the underlying causes of disease.

"Dentistry has always been a surgical specialty. And that is where I think the mistake is now," he said. "I think it needs to get rid of the handpieces and approach this disease as a preventive system rather than a restorative one."

Tinanoff was a native son of the city of Baltimore, the first of his family to attend college, the son of two garment workers. His father had been a buttonhole maker and his mother had worked in a clothing factory. On the walls of his office, there were photographs that Tinanoff, an avid birdwatcher, had taken. In one picture, baby robins in a nest were lined up with their beaks open, like children waiting for dental care.

Tinanoff spoke of caring for children with tooth decay and infection so severe they required treatment in the operating room. The wait for time in the operating room could be long. In one case, Tinanoff learned that a child had died while on the waiting list. The case haunted him. "I can't be assured it was tooth-related. I didn't want to pursue it too much. You know. It's so painful."

He spoke of the importance of reaching out past the clinic to the neighborhoods of Baltimore, of bringing exams and preventive treatments to young children before the disease took hold of them. Challenges were daunting: raising the awareness of the importance of oral health in families coping with a host of severe needs, overcoming the low expectations and fear many poor patients had of the system and the fatalism they had about their teeth.

Yet such work was a long-standing passion for Tinanoff's colleague and fellow researcher Clemencia Vargas, an assistant professor at the school. Vargas, the daughter of a dentist and a social worker, began her own dental career in her native country, Colombia, packing a truck and embarking upon a mandatory rural service year, providing care in a poor village. "The need was huge," she recalled. "I thought it was fascinating."

Vargas went on to earn a PhD in sociology from Arizona State University. At the University of Maryland, she combined the skills:

teaching dental students about providing care to individual patients but also teaching them about public health, encouraging them to think about the social conditions that make communities vulnerable to disease. She led teams of dental students to poor schools and neighborhoods in and around Baltimore to screen children and get those in need of care to dentists, to provide preventive treatments and teach children about keeping their teeth healthy. And Vargas, who was deeply troubled by the idea of children suffering in resigned silence, urged her students to coach children to speak up if they were in pain—to advocate for themselves and for their own oral health.

She encouraged the dental students to think about their profession in a broader way as well—to consider the oral health needs of the entire community, not just the patients they might see in their offices. To some, Vargas could tell the idea was exciting. But for many others, she felt, the goal was to get out of dental school and start a successful private practice. She knew that, in America, locating a dental practice in a desirable community, selecting patients with insurance or the ability to pay for care out-of-pocket were the choices that made the best business sense for new dentists. Since the profession's beginnings, those choices had played a formative role in building the nation's enormous and successful private practice dental system. Yet dentists choosing where they would practice and who they would accept as their patients contributed to gaps in the system.

"We have these students being prepared with public funds. They are being educated with public funds. And they will go work in private offices and they will decide who they can see," said Vargas. "There is a point that I make and it is very special. Dentists cannot turn away anybody for any reason. Unless the patient doesn't have money. Basically you can't turn away someone for ethnicity, race, sexual orientation, medical or HIV status. The dentist has to see the person or work on a referral. But if the person doesn't have money. That's the difference. That's bad."

According to the American Dental Association's Principles of Ethics and Code of Professional Conduct, "Dentists shall not refuse to accept patients into their practice or deny dental service to patients because of the patient's race, creed, color, sex or national origin." Still, the code allows latitude in patient selection. It states that "dentists, in serving the public, may exercise reasonable discretion in selecting patients for their practices."[2]

"There is a lot of power," said Vargas. "And a tremendous amount of need. So what I say is that we have a very serious social problem that we are trying to solve with private means. And that doesn't match."

Others have raised similar concerns. The idea of dentists selecting patients seems to turn professional responsibility on its head, wrote Bruce Peltier, a professor of psychology and ethics at the University of the Pacific's Arthur A. Dugoni School of Dentistry. "The concept of careful patient selection does not seem to imply any duty to patients and their needs whatsoever. In fact, it actually seems to advocate abdication of any such duty," Peltier observed.[3] In the world of modern American dentistry, the boundaries between caregivers and salespeople, customers and patients have become blurred, Peltier suggested. The costs and competition that go along with running successful private dental practices have contributed to "an irreconcilable tension between selling and caring," Peltier and a colleague, Lola Giusti, wrote.[4]

But the system has remained the same.

It was a clear, cold day in January 1964 when President Lyndon B. Johnson went to Capitol Hill with a request for the creation of sweeping federal health care programs for the old and the young. Johnson began his address by invoking the words of Thomas Jefferson: "Without health, there is no happiness. An attention to health, then, should take the place of every other object." He praised medical advances that had conquered smallpox and nearly eliminated polio, that had drastically reduced deaths from influenza and tuberculosis.

But he argued against complacency. He spoke of older Americans, left without insurance upon retirement. He asked Congress to agree to expand the Roosevelt-era Social Security program to finance the cost of basic health services for elders. "In this way, the specter of catastrophic hospital bills can be lifted from the lives of our older citizens," Johnson said.

But he did not stop there. He asked for a health care program for poor children as well. "America's tradition of compassion for the aged is matched by our traditional devotion to our most priceless resource of all—our young." He spoke particularly of the millions with chronic illness and mental impairments. And he did not overlook the sorry state of children's teeth. "At age fifteen, the average child has more than ten decayed teeth," Johnson noted.

"There is much to do if we are to make available the medical and dental services our rising generation needs. Nowhere are the needs greater than for the 15 million children of families who live in poverty." Johnson spoke of the acute shortage of doctors and dentists and the need for new medical and dental schools, for federal investment in aging hospitals and clinics, of the importance of federal support aimed at integrating medical specialties into community-based group practices designed to offer comprehensive care. "Further delay will only compound our problems and deny our people the health and happiness that could be theirs."

Those were not Johnson's last words on the subject of health. The following month, he was back before Congress with a special address. America's infant mortality rates were higher than those of nine other nations. Thousands of sick citizens lacked care for treatable illnesses. One-third of elders seeking old-age assistance did so due to poor health. "For many others, serious illness wipes out savings and carries their families into poverty," Johnson warned. "For these people, old age can be a dark corridor of fear."

Johnson urged the passage of the King-Anderson Medicare bill. But dental leaders expressed doubts about the legislation. Like the leaders of organized medicine, they harbored long-standing fears about socialized medicine.

"Students of political prose might be pleased with the President's message, which is replete with short, punchy, emotional sentences about the health status of the aged, such as the reference to old age as 'a dark corridor of fear,'" noted an editorial in the March 1964 *Journal of the American Dental Association.* "Students of logic and fact will find considerably less to cheer about."

The editorial questioned the entire premise behind Medicare. And it raised the specter of government control of medical and dental services. "No notice is taken of the vast body of evidence showing that the aged health care problem is transitional in nature. No notice is taken of the past experiences in this and other countries with national treatment programs, where a deterioration of the quality of health care followed swiftly and inevitably," the piece noted. "These coming weeks are going to be a critical time in this struggle to defeat the King-Anderson bill. No Congressman, particularly in an election year, is indifferent to the views of his constituents. Each dentist should take note of this fact."[5]

In the 1964 elections, however, Democratic Medicare supporters won crucial seats in the House and Senate. In his 1965 health address, Johnson not only renewed his push for the passage of Medicare, he spoke more about his ideas for a companion health care program for the poor. It would become known as Medicaid.

Medicaid was created through the expansion of the Kerr-Mills program established by Congress in 1960 to provide aid to "medically-needy" seniors in participating states. To qualify, elders were required to pass a means test showing they were not poor enough to qualify for public assistance but too poor to pay their medical expenses. Organized dentistry had supported Kerr-Mills in its old form. But the expansion, aimed at covering poor children, came as a surprise. Neither Medicare nor Medicaid took market-based approaches to the delivery of health care services. They were social contracts, entitlements to care.

"In the broad panorama of history I am convinced that we are standing on a major dividing line of civilization," Syracuse oral surgeon David J. Kennedy warned in 1966 at a legislative hearing in Albany. "If we proceed with the Medicare Law as it is presently implemented, we have marched forward blindly into the true socialistic state."

"Our citizens will no longer have the courage or initiative to protest further inroads into their freedom," added Kennedy, the president of the Onondaga County Dental Society and the New York State Society of Oral Surgeons.[6]

As it turned out, dental benefits held a tenuous place in both programs. Medicare did not include routine dental care for seniors—and still does not. The program covers only a narrow range of procedures deemed medically necessary. Medicaid did not include a guarantee of dental benefits either in its original form. A children's entitlement to dental services was added to Medicaid in 1968, with the enactment of the Early and Periodic Screening, Diagnosis and Treatment Program (EPSDT), an initiative guaranteeing timely and medically necessary care for many common and preventable childhood illnesses, including dental decay. The federal government left it up to the states whether to cover dental care for poor adults.

In its size and scope, Medicaid has been called "the workhorse of the American health care system."[7] The program steps in where private initiatives seldom go. It serves people who are in crisis, and people who are poor, who would otherwise lack access to care.

But most dentists have continued to avoid it and do not accept patients whose bills are paid by Medicaid. They complain of the bureaucratic barriers of participating in the program. Many say the frustrations of dealing with poor Medicaid patients are overwhelming, that they frequently miss appointments. They don't value oral health, they say. They don't take care of their teeth. Dentists often stress that the overhead costs of operating their offices are high and that they lose money treating Medicaid patients. On average, Medicaid pays only half of what private insurance benefits pays for services to children, but reimbursement rates vary state to state, according to the American Dental Association.[8] Estimates about how many dentists participate in Medicaid also vary by state. In many states, most dentists treated few or no Medicaid patients, a 2010 federal survey concluded.[9]

While the ADA determined that in 2014, 42 percent of dentists had registered as Medicaid providers on the nation's Insure Kids Now database, the percentage of dentists available to treat poor beneficiaries has been a perennial concern. In 2013, only 35 percent of private practice dentists reported treating any patients on public assistance, down from 44 percent in 1990, a separate ADA survey of dental practices found.[10]

The social gulf between dentists and poor patients is manifested in ways that may compound the challenges of delivering care. It can be hard for better-off people to understand the barriers the poor face in accessing health care services. Transience and difficulties with telephones and transportation are common. Workers at low-wage jobs don't always have the option of taking time off for care. Maintaining oral health and getting timely dental care, no matter how important, can be eclipsed by other urgent needs. Parents may have lacked regular care themselves. The dental experiences they did have may have been very bad ones.

The power of the dentist can be terrifying, noted James Freed, a public health dentist, researcher, and retired professor from the University of California, Los Angeles. "It's a loss of control. That you are down here and they are up there. And they can do anything and you don't want to put yourself in that position."

Then there are the judgments, the sense that when the dentist asks, "How often do you brush your teeth?" a patient knows, "Whatever your answer is, you know it isn't enough." For dentists who spend their lives thinking about oral health, there can be frustration with patients, Freed said. The dentist may be thinking, "Why don't you take better care of yourself? Here I am working every day to try and make you better. It is driving me crazy." It can sometimes be hard to hide those kinds of feelings.

Yet something as basic as instilling tooth-brushing skills in children can be compromised by a mother's poor mental health, research has shown. Among mothers who had confidence in their ability to make sure their child's teeth were brushed, children brushed more frequently, concluded researchers in Detroit. Mothers who were tired, busy, or depressed were the least confident that they could take care of their children's oral health needs.[11]

In a series of focus groups, a team of researchers from the University of North Carolina School of Public Health explored the experiences, attitudes, and perceptions of racially and ethnically diverse parents and guardians who had sought dental care for their Medicaid-beneficiary children. Many of the parents reported that they faced daunting and sometimes humiliating challenges in navigating the system. "Searching for providers, arranging an appointment where choices were severely limited and finding transportation left caregivers describing themselves as discouraged and exhausted," wrote the researchers.

The participants reported that in some cases, the dentists seemed reluctant to see or touch their children because "they are dirty." Members of the focus groups complained even more about office staff, reporting that dental receptionists made negative comments about their Medicaid status, handling their benefit cards with disdain and treating them differently than other patients.

"You have to hold back your tears," said one mother.[12]

Those were the families who got appointments. In Illinois, a team of research assistants posed as the mother of a fictitious child with a broken front tooth. They phoned eighty-five Illinois dental practices twice, a month apart, in an attempt to determine whether a child's Medicaid status affected a parent's ability to get a dental appointment. In 170 paired calls, a total of 36.5 percent of the Medicaid children obtained an appointment, compared with 95.4 percent of privately insured children.[13]

A projected shortage of dentists threatens to make access to care even more difficult in poor and isolated areas, the U.S. Department of Health and Human Services Health Resources and Services Administration (HRSA) has suggested. The agency collects data and maps shortage areas for medical, mental, and dental health providers. In 2016, the map of America's dental care health professional shortage areas was pocked with roughly five thousand dark spots—communities home to roughly 49 million Americans classified as "lacking basic access to dental care."[14] It would take approximately seven thousand dentists to fill the need for care in those places, HRSA reported in 2015.

And the professional shortage problem is expected to grow in the coming decade, according to the agency's projections. Figuring in retirements and new graduates, and assuming that workforce participation patterns remain the same, the number of dentists active in the workforce is expected to increase by 6 percent to 202,600 in 2025, the agency has calculated. But at the same time, the demand for dentists is expected to grow by 10 percent. The shortages are expected to hit some states—and some populations—harder than others and to weigh most heavily upon California, Florida, and New York. Unmet demand for care "will likely exacerbate access problems for underserved populations who forgo basic oral health care because of lack of proximity to a provider, inability to pay for care, and limited oral health literacy," the federal report observed.

The authors found a bright spot in a growing surplus of dental hygienists that might be harnessed to help address increased needs. "Across the country, states are grappling with ways to expand access to dental care," they noted. "For example, Minnesota and Maine are exploring ways to expand the reach of dentists by providing additional training to dental hygienists."[15]

The tone of the report was neutral. Measures such as those in Minnesota and Maine and most recently in Vermont have opened the way for hygienists with additional training to provide expanded services, including drilling and extracting teeth. But they have been strongly opposed by organized dentistry for years. Far more modest steps have been fought in some states.

Dental leaders insist that HRSA's reports of current and future dentist shortages are misguided. The government agency relies upon "simplistic population-to-provider ratios" that do not capture the true picture of provider adequacy, Marko Vujicic, chief

economist for the American Dental Association's Health Policy
Institute, has written. Dentists across the country report they have
time on their hands to see more patients.

"Nationally, this is more than one of three dentists," noted Vujicic. "Second, there is compelling evidence to show that the main
barriers to dental care are overwhelmingly financial and are not
related to the availability of providers. . . . In the current situation,
adding additional dental care providers to the market is unlikely
to address the most critical issues concerning access to dental care.
Rather, the evidence strongly suggests that policy makers ought
to focus on solutions that address the demand-side constraints the
U.S. population faces—especially low-income Americans—in
accessing dental care."[16]

There are enough dentists, Vujicic and others say. There are just
not enough people in some places who are willing and able to pay
for their services to sustain demand.

States and the federal government had wide latitude over the
years to fund and organize dental programs for the poor, the
underserved, and for the customers buying benefits on the insurance marketplaces set up under the Patient Protection and Affordable Care Act. In this capacity, government plays an important role
in the dental marketplace. But dental care is often overlooked, and
underfunded, the dental leaders say.

Still, they point to signs of progress in some areas. Thanks to a
number of factors, including Medicaid reforms and expansion and
states' innovative efforts to expand access to dental care, more children have been seen in recent years. Between 2000 and 2012, the
percentage of Medicaid children getting at least one dental service
increased from 29 percent to 48 percent, a series of federal reports
on Medicaid performance found. Yet dental care has remained far
scarcer than medical care for poor children. About nine out of ten
Medicaid babies and children visited primary care providers in
recent years, according to the 2016 federal reports.[17]

Meanwhile, adult dental visits have been in a state of decline. Just
over one-third of working-age adults visited a dentist in 2012.[18]

One in five working-age adults said they could not afford needed dental care, a large national study found.[19] Slightly fewer than two-thirds of Americans—roughly 205 million—had private or public dental coverage at the end of 2014. Another 114 million Americans had none.[20]

The American Dental Association has long lobbied for higher Medicaid reimbursement rates and reduced red tape as ways of attracting more dentists to serve the poor. The organization has worked for more spending on dental care and research, arguing that dental health is often given second-tier status in government programs. The 2010 Patient Protection and Affordable Care Act did include children's dental benefits among essential health benefits, but a subsequent rule did not require parents to buy them. Marketplaces were not required to offer adult dental benefits, though by 2016 nearly all had incorporated them.

The health care reform law strongly encouraged states to expand Medicaid programs. But dental benefits for adults are not included in all state programs. They are often cut in times of financial austerity as a cost states decide they cannot afford to bear. Dental leaders call for more funding for public dental programs. Yet at the same time they have fought to preserve their professional autonomy and the private practice system. They have fought the introduction of midlevel dental providers, sometimes likened to nurse practitioners, who advocates say could bring down the costs of many dental services and disperse them more widely.

People may need care, but if they have no public or private insurance or money to pay for care, if they do not understand the importance of oral health, if they defer even routine preventive dental services or do not value them, they do not drive demand for care. It is a problem an additional supply of providers will not solve, dental leaders contend.

"It's like looking at oil change facilities. If people can't afford to get their oil changed, if you put more oil change facilities in that neighborhood thinking that will help, if it doesn't change the price to the recipient, its not going to change their ability to get their oil changed," explained Jonathan Shenkin, a Maine dentist who served in 2015 as vice president of the American Dental Association.

Shenkin said that he himself grew up poor. His family sometimes relied upon Medicaid. He said he takes Medicaid patients. Yet, even in Maine, where the Medicaid system is considered a very good one, it is very hard to work with, he said. "Every day I question why I take Medicaid. Because of frustration with the system," said Shenkin.

Raising Medicaid rates has helped some states attract more dentists to serve the poor. But in other states, the economies of getting dental care to the poor still don't work out, particularly in sparsely populated, rural areas, Shenkin said.

"It's all because dentistry is a business. It doesn't matter if it is a federally qualified health center or a dentist in private practice or an independent practice dental hygienist," said Shenkin. "You need people to come to your office to be able to bill to keep your doors open. To put your lights on. To pay your loans. Et cetera."

In recent years, America's dentists have done well financially. "Dentists Now Get Paid More Per Hour Than Doctors," read the headline over an article announcing the findings contained in a 2010 study comparing the growth of earnings among America's health care professionals.[21] For the study, researchers from Harvard University and the Rand Corporation employed a formula that used over two decades' worth of U.S. Census Bureau data to measure differences in earnings among thousands of health professionals: physicians, dentists, pharmacists, medical auxiliaries, and health care and insurance executives. During the years from 1996 to 2010, the researchers determined that dentists' average hourly wage increased from $64.30 to $69.60, putting them ahead of health professionals including physicians, whose earnings increased from $65.40 to $67.30 over the same time period.

In 2014, according to the calculations of the American Dental Association, the average annual net income for general practitioner dentists who did not own their own practices stood at $134,020.

General practitioner dentists who owned their practices averaged $183,340. Dental specialists made an average of $322,200 that year.[22]

According to the U.S. Bureau of Labor Statistics the median pay for dentists stood at $76.11 an hour in 2015, working out to an annual salary of roughly $158,000 a year.[23]

A family of three living in poverty in 2015 had an annual income of $20,090.

Thanks to the marketplace, most affluent communities in America have enough dentists. In fact, in some of these places, dentists are locked in fierce competition for patients. In a convention center hotel by Baltimore's Inner Harbor, a couple of blocks from Calvert Street where Chapin Harris addressed those first five dental students in a Baptist church with a rose window, there was on this summer day in 2015 a ballroom full of dentists and their staffs gathered for a two-day seminar with a well-known dental marketing guru.

"Write this down," Roger Levin commanded the practitioners. "Somebody else wants what you have."

Levin worked the crowd in a sleek blue suit, mic pinned to his rose-colored tie. His teeth were dazzling. He was the son and grandson of dentists. He knew from an early age that he too would be a dentist. He got his degree from the University of Maryland dental school. He soon realized he was more interested in the business of dentistry than in carrying on the family practice. In 1985, at the dawn of the modern cosmetic dentistry boom, he founded the Levin Group, which now advertises itself as the world's largest dental consulting firm, with offices in Baltimore, Phoenix, and Marseille, France. Levin travels the world delivering dozens of seminars each year. For these two days, though, he was close to home, in Baltimore.

"It all started in the 1980s. Veneers were invented," he told the crowd. "Today we are running real businesses."

His grandfather got out of dental school in the 1920s, and stories of the era when dentistry was a collegial profession were handed down in the Levin family. Back in the old days, when a new dentist was starting out, the established practitioners got together to support him, even sending patients his way.

"Now we still get together," Levin joked. "But we hire an assassin!"

Levin built a career around teaching strategies designed to defend his client dentists against the encroachment of others. "Marketing protects you against new competition," he warned. But, he added, dental school does not prepare dentists for the complex challenge. Many approach it simplistically.

"Putting your name on a toothbrush is not an internal marketing program," he cautioned the dentists during the course of the seminar. Patients should like their dentist well enough to recommend him or her to their friends, Levin insisted. Creating a practice that is appealing is the key to making patients want to do this. It's a formidable challenge, he acknowledged. Many people hate going to the dentist.

"People like to have fun. Contests are fun. Dentistry is not fun. We do root canals. The two scariest words on the planet, Sarah," said Levin, who over the course of the two-day seminar would display an uncanny ability to remember the names of people in the large room and include them in his sentences. Levin, a disciple of Dale Carnegie, invoked *How to Win Friends and Influence People* as a kind of scripture. Overcoming fear and resistance requires specialized skills. So does hanging on to patients.

"Make your practice more important in their lives, Sharon, than just a recall interval." Success doesn't happen by accident.

"The game of productivity is a very complicated game," Levin warned his fellows. The complexities must be mastered through persuasiveness and discipline. Salesmanship has its own language.

"By tomorrow at twelve o'clock we will be in control of our patients," he predicted. Up on the screen, animated darts hit bullseyes, emphasizing his points. "Value scripting: write it down. The ability to influence patients."

All too often, dentists have laxly marketed, missing opportunities to sell procedures, Levin contended. "The average practice is grossing $650,000. At $650,000 you can make a living. At $750,000 you can make a living. There is nothing wrong with that, Ron. You can do $1 million a year in four days a week. It is absolutely doable for general dentists."

His fellow dentists underdiagnose legitimate problems and overlook treatable conditions, he said. Levin recommended a multistage dental exam for each patient: the pockets of the gums and surfaces of the teeth should be thoroughly explored for signs of disease; a cosmetic exam might disclose potential for improving the appearance of the teeth. "People will spend money on cosmetics. Even in the Great Depression, women bought lipstick. We have to create awareness."

An implant exam could reveal the potential for replacement teeth. "Mrs. Jones. You owe it to yourself to find out how dental implants can improve the quality of your life. Stop explaining they are made of titanium. They are biocompatible. They don't care. The product the company is selling is rarely what the customer is buying. Nobody buys a vacuum cleaner. You buy a clean floor." Then there is the orthodontic exam that may reveal a case for straightening.

In terms of payment, up-front is to be strongly encouraged. Levin recommended offering a discount if the patient paid in full before the treatment began. For those who lack the means, there are options, including medical credit cards.

"Let me review our four wonderful payment options. *Wonderful* is a power word. Power words create energy. And then we can select the one that is most convenient for you."

The patient is required to settle the bill before the work is finished, Levin stressed. "Mr. Jones is here. We collect his money before the final treatment. What are you going to do? Rip that crown out of his mouth? Give that denture to another patient? We have scripting. It's very positive. We reschedule the patient."

The front office staff must learn to educate patients about the importance of keeping their appointments, he noted. "Write this down. A last-minute cancellation is a no-show. And you have just been royally screwed."

The program went briskly for the entire day. By the end Levin still seemed to have more energy than anyone else in the room.

The same was true the next morning. It was a humid early Saturday and outside the convention center, in Baltimore harbor, a tall ship rode at anchor, ghostly in the morning fog. A few tourists were already wandering toward the Hard Rock Cafe and the aquarium by the water where Frederick Douglass arrived from a plantation to the north, more than a century ago. Close by too on Sharp Street, dental instruments and supplies were offered for sale in the days of Chapin Harris and advertised in the world's first dental journal, which Harris faithfully edited for years. "Extracting Forceps, as improved by Professor C.A. Harris. The Plugging instrument invented by Professor H.H. Hayden together with a large assortment of Stockton's Incorruptible Teeth."

And right on time, Levin was back, as perfectly turned out as the day before, this morning in a gray suit, a blue- and white-striped shirt, a yellow print tie, glinting cuff links and watch. The first order of business was "Coffee with Roger," a session where dentists were permitted to ask questions. In response, Levin offered thoughts on "case presentation" and the effective use of intraoral cameras for showing patients what is going on inside their mouths. "We're dentists. We like toys," he noted. Still, such devices don't hold the secret to success. "Intraoral cameras don't sell treatments. Doctors sell treatments. It's our selling skills, our case presentation skills."

Someone asked about the wisdom of taking on a partner.

"Some of you don't make good partners," Levin warned. "Look at your kindergarten report card. Some of you don't play well with others."

A female dentist, Mfon Umoren, with Medicaid patients in Prince George's County asked Levin for his thoughts on practices accepting Medicaid.

"We have many practices that take Medicaid," Levin began. "It's great that some people take Medicaid to help the people who have needs." But Levin went on to warn the audience about Medicaid patients. "They tend to miss appointments," he said. "They take over your entire reception room. Some things from your reception room go home with them. Some stuff disappears. Hand towels disappear. If you have a basket of lovely things in your restroom, they take things home." In one case Levin said he heard that a toilet seat was carried away.

He said that rules about lateness and missed appointments need to be firmly stressed from the outset with Medicaid patients. "We are very nice to them. But we have to manage them differently. We use words we would never use with our fee-for-service patients. We value Medicaid. The only way we play a little gray is sequestering the hours of Medicaid patients. If people come in, they want to be with people like themselves."

Then it was back to the ballroom.

"Scripting is a science," said Levin. "Power words—write this down—are words that create energy."

"*Great. Wonderful. Terrific. Outstanding. Unbelievable.* Power words create energy. Energy creates trust.

"I will be on an airplane to London tonight. Put your seat belt on. Put your tray table up. Your seat back up. People like to be commanded.

"Mrs. Jones. Why don't we take care of your remaining balance right now? Command statements are always at the end of the script.

"With patients you need to command them.

"Mrs. Jones, we should do this root canal as soon as possible.

"Eighty-one percent of dental appointments are single-tooth treatments. We are talking to patients. Not selling."

Then there was the problem of wasted time.

"Scheduling. Everything is about time management. If you stop to do a hygiene check in the middle of a root canal, Sanjiv, there is a new product. It's called gauze. It stops the bleeding while you do a hygiene check."

Patients should be more closely scheduled, he said. "How many of you are on fifteen-minute time units? Ten-minute units give you thirteen more days of productivity a year. If we save you ten minutes an hour that increases doctor productivity thirty-two days a year. At four days a week that's two more months a year."

At midday, the workshop started winding down. "We end with our hygiene-maximizing system. It's very powerful," Levin promised. Hygienists with the right skills can "identify, educate, and motivate" the patient, Levin explained. He illustrated his point by dramatizing an exchange between a hygienist and dentist.

"There is a patient in hygiene very hot, rich, and motivated who wants veneers. Get in there now," the hygienist told the dentist.

"I want six of those upper veneers that Vicki told me about," the patient told the dentist.

"Close the case," counseled Levin. "Hygienists are not allowed to diagnose. What's the dentist's role in all this? Not to screw it up."

He ended the day with the story of a dental practice the Levin Group helped improve. The dentist had a staff of seven and $920,000 in annual production. The dentist wanted to retire, but the practice was too disorganized for him to take on a partner and make the transition, Levin explained.

"It was a nice practice. Chaotic but a nice practice," said Levin. The verbal skills of the front office were weak. The hygiene department needed new techniques to sell patients on the value of hygiene visits. Patients were turning larger cases down due to inadequate financing options. Thanks to time studies, full verbal skill training, and new patient orientation offered by the Levin Group, production was increased to $2.17 million, Levin told the crowd.

"Without great systems, you can't have great customer service," noted the dental marketing guru. "Like the Ritz-Carlton, it's all about an amazing experience." Then he was off to London.

7

Adventurers and Auxiliaries

As he worked to organize dentistry in the nineteenth century, Chapin Harris saw it as his mission to set up protections for
his new profession. For thousands of years, healers had carefully
guarded the real and reputed powers and skills regarded as the
source of their authority, their privileged place in society. In talks
and writings Harris warned of the threat posed by indigent huck-
sters who regularly arrived in cities and towns, pandering suspect
amalgams and remedies.

"Dentistry has been an open field, without any of the salutary
enclosures of legislation to protect it from the depredations of any
adventurer who might choose to prowl through the community,"
Harris told fellow members of the American Society of Dental Surgeons, gathered in July 1843 in Baltimore for their fourth annual
meeting.[1]

He exhorted his fellow dentists to work for the passage of laws in
their states "guarding the community from the injuries and decep-
tions that are annually practised upon it by ignorant pretenders

to dental knowledge, whose acquaintance with the principles of dental surgery is too limited and superficial to enable them to pass an examination before a body of men competent to judge of the qualifications necessary to be possessed by those who practice in this department of surgery."

Educational standards, licensing, and health regulations eventually helped limit the dangers posed by the kind of charlatans that most concerned Harris. The threat from those wandering adventurers has diminished. Now, some dentists are more worried about the ambitions of the hygienists who work for them in their offices, cleaning teeth, treating gums, exposing x-rays, applying fluoride and sealants, educating patients.

The vast majority of America's approximately two hundred thousand dental hygienists are women. They have typically spent up to three years earning the associate's degree they need to practice. Their training emphasizes disease prevention. More than half work part time. They earn about $34 an hour, according to the Bureau of Labor Statistics. They work under the supervision of dentists who hold doctoral degrees. Most work in private dental offices.

But many of the first dental hygienists spent much of their time in the field. They worked among schoolchildren. They brought dental services to encamped soldiers. Over the years, at moments when the urgency of the unmet need for dental care has been highlighted in some dramatic way, during the Progressive Era, at the end of World War II, throughout the deliberations and establishment of the enormous federal health programs of the 1960s, there have been calls for the expanded use of trained dental auxiliaries to deliver economical care to people whom the system has not reached—to elders in nursing homes, poor children, and adults. It happened again, in recent years, with the publication of the surgeon general's *Oral Health in America* report and with the passage of the Patient Protection and Affordable Care Act during the Obama administration. It is happening now.

Organized dentistry has a long history of opposing these efforts.

In the world of medicine, analogous battles over professional autonomy were waged when nurse practitioners and physicians' assistants came on the scene. They met wide resistance from medical groups in their early days, according to the authors of *Advancing Oral Health in America*, a report by the prestigious Institute of Medicine.

Physicians contended safety was the issue. "Concerns have been raised in other fields when new types of practitioners were being developed or when existing professionals sought to extend their scopes of practice," the Institute of Medicine observed. Yet over the years, the nurses have proven themselves.

"Professional tensions typically center around the quality of care provided by individuals with less training but in many cases, evidence has not supported this," the authors of the report wrote. "Advance practice nurses are often involved in high-risk procedures such as childbirth and the administration of anesthesia, yet the evidence base continues to grow that the quality of their care is similar to that of physicians."[2]

Today, in terms of professional independence, America's four million nurses are far ahead of dental hygienists. They enjoy strength in numbers. They are also more likely to be working in the larger world of the health care system, in hospitals, clinics, and health centers. In contrast, the typical hygienist continues to work in a private dental office, in a dental operatory roughly ten feet by eleven feet in size. Sometimes there is a window. Sometimes there is not, said Arizona dental hygienist Jill Rethman, who in 2015 served as president of the American Dental Hygienists' Association. "Eight hours a day, a lot of times with no view, literally and figuratively. You are isolated. And insulated."

Some dental hygienists continue to challenge their isolation and push for change. Their fight can mean confronting the powerful professionals they work for and depend upon for their livelihood. The advances they have made have been, in some cases, very hard-won.

—m—

Alfred C. Fones, who established the first successful dental hygiene school in the United States, had already seen a lot of dentistry when he got out of dental school in 1890. It had been fifty years since the Baltimore College of Dental Surgery, the world's first, had opened. His father, Civilion Fones, had earned his degree from the school and had gone on to build up a busy practice in the thriving port city of Bridgeport, Connecticut. Civilion Fones was a successful man, a professional and civic leader. At various times he served as the president of the local and state dental society, as a city councilman, alderman, and mayor.

But Civilion Fones's chosen profession was a challenging one. It was common to put in "ten hours a day at the chair," wrote dentist George Wood Clapp, a colleague of the younger Fones, reflecting upon those days. "The most conscientious practitioners wore out their eyes and their backs reaming root canals and putting in treatments.

"Huge fillings of amalgam were placed and sometime gold-foil fillings were hammered in, bit by bit, at a tremendous expense of vital force by both patients and operators," recounted Clapp.[3]

Dentists suffered from eyestrain and eye trauma from flying tooth fragments.[4] They inhaled the medicaments they used in their work: the ether, the chloroform, the vapor of mercury. They experienced x-ray burns. They contracted tuberculosis from their patients. The germs, bad breath, and fear the patients brought with them to the office were part of the dentist's daily life. The patients had much to dread. The dental treatments they received were often painful and the failure rate for restorations was very high.[5]

"The results of such methods of practice were not such as to justify any high opinion of dentistry or of dentists as servants of health," Clapp wrote. Still, when Alfred Fones got out of dental school, he joined his father's practice. He had been working for nearly a decade when, in 1899, he attended a talk and workshop at a meeting of the Northeastern Dental Association. It would change the course of his career—and the American oral health care system.

Today, public health leaders around the world talk about targeting the "upstream" causes of disease and social problems to prevent the broad "downstream" effects. They work to abate harmful pathogens and lead from water supplies to prevent the suffering and costly consequences of widespread disease and disability. They vaccinate against illnesses such as polio and diphtheria that once maimed and killed millions. When Alfred Fones was starting out, these ideas, and many more, were just dawning.

America was changing fast. Immigrants were arriving in waves. Cities were growing. Technology was offering new possibilities. Thinkers in many fields were wrestling with the growing complexities of life.

Yet there was a kind of optimism during those years remembered now as the Progressive Era—a sense that the challenges of an increasingly mechanized and diverse society could be met with improved education, efficiency, and hygiene. There was a lesson for dentistry in that, Alfred Fones would decide.

The workshop he attended focused not upon the surgical treatment or extraction of decayed teeth but upon preventing oral disease in the first place. The regime, developed by a Philadelphia dentist, D.D. Smith, centered upon the thorough removal of bacteria-laden plaque or "tartar" from the surfaces of the teeth. Patients were required to return to the office for regular treatments. They were also instructed in how to brush and clean their own teeth and how to follow a correct diet at home. Even before the germ theory, some dentists had suggested such practices might reduce disease.

But Smith, at least to Alfred Fones's ears, was the first to work out a practical oral hygiene–based system of preventive care for use in dental offices. "D.D. Smith was truly the father of dental prophylaxis," Fones would write.[6]

Excited, Alfred Fones returned to work. He tried Smith's methods in his own office and used them for four years. He reported that the health of his patients' teeth and gums got better. "Under the influence of the prophylactic treatments the health of the whole mouth improved," recounted Clapp. Patients' gums appeared far healthier and their teeth less prone to decay. "Here was salvation for the patient and release from drudgery for the dentist."

But the work was time-consuming. In 1905, Alfred Fones decided to train his cousin and chairside assistant Irene Newman in the preventive techniques so she could help employ them in their office. Meanwhile, the oral hygiene movement was catching on in other places as well. In Germany the first school-based dental clinics were being established. So were ideas about training new dental auxiliaries to deliver preventive care.

Alfred Fones found inspiration in the writings of C.M. Wright, a Cincinnati dentist who in a 1902 paper called "Plea for a Sub-Speciality in Dentistry" envisioned the training of "women of education and refinement for work of an honorable and useful kind."[7] Wright promised the field of special practice would "revolutionize dentistry—place it upon a still higher plane."

"The operation suggested is more in line with preventive medicine with all that this implies, than any other in the scope of prophylaxis that I can think of, such as boiled drinking-water, ventilation, sanitary plumbing, physical exercise, diet and bathing," Wright wrote in his "plea."

"We have set the men on pedestals who have been able to cut out a carious spot on a tooth, extend and form a cavity so that a clean surface of gold may take the place of enamel . . . shall we not commend and honor the specialist who patiently and regularly operates for the prevention of this and other diseases by intelligent and systematic care of the entire mouth? This is a fundamental idea of dentistry agreed by all and yet neglected."

Some Ohio dentists were troubled by Wright's ideas. They sought assurances that these newly trained practitioners would not begin to practice dentistry themselves. Wright attempted to ease their worries. The system was designed to ensure the women would remain auxiliaries, he told his colleagues.

"The fact that these women must be largely dependent upon the recognition and recommendation of the dentists for their employment, seems to me a barrier against invasion, and a protection against infringement," wrote Wright, who served on the faculty of the Ohio College of Dental Surgery, the historic Cincinnati dental school founded just five years after Baltimore's.

Wright's special one-year course, designed to train women as dental nurses and assistants and offered during the 1910–11 school year, included didactic and clinical training in anatomy, operative techniques, anesthetics, prophylaxis, dental medicine, and diagnosis. The Ohio program was discontinued after just three sessions, however, and its graduates were never allowed to practice as dental nurses. The dentists were suspected of shutting it down.

"There was strong and bitter opposition to this training course by Ohio dentists and it is reasonable to assume that this opposition was the reason the program was discontinued in 1914," noted Wilma Motley in an official history of the American Dental Hygienists' Association.[8]

But in Connecticut, Alfred Fones got farther. Like his father, who died in 1907, Alfred Fones was a professional and civic leader, serving for a time on the city's school board. It was in Bridgeport's crowded public schools that Fones confronted the epidemic of tooth decay and exposed it. He rallied dental colleagues to the cause of prevention. He wrote articles and mounted an all-out campaign for a dental program in the schools. To make his point, he brought schoolchildren with him to meetings with city officials, to help illustrate the human toll of oral disease. Like a kind of evangelist, he preached the wages of infection.

"The most conspicuous defect of the child is the unsanitary condition of its mouth," Fones wrote. "Like a pigpen or garbage drain slowly seeping its poison into the brook, which, flowing into the reservoir, contaminates the water supply of a city, so do the products of abscesses and decayed teeth with decomposing food slowly but surely poison the human system. Such mouths breed disease."[9]

The work of prevention needed to start with children. And to reach everyone, it needed to be done systematically. Millions of young patients across America needed dental hygiene services. Millions needed instruction on how to care for their teeth at home. The nation's dentists needed well-trained auxiliaries to help them.

"A busy practitioner cannot comfortably do this work alone, unless he limits the number of patients to comparatively few. He must have aid, and I believe the ideal assistant for this work to be a woman. A man is not content to limit himself to this one specialty while a woman is willing to confine her energy to this one form of treatment," Fones wrote.

In 1913, Fones opened his dental hygiene school. It was located in his handsome brick office building at 10 Washington Avenue in Bridgeport. The facilities were carefully designed, organized for order and cleanliness. In their six-month course, the students were instructed in instrument sterilization, tooth cleaning, and nutrition. They learned how to teach small children to care for their teeth. They were lectured by leading dental educators from Harvard and other schools.

"November 17, 1913 thirty-three women, including school teachers, trained nurses, experienced dental assistants and the wives of three practicing dentists began the course and, June 5, 1914, twenty seven were graduated as dental hygienists," Fones reported. The first graduate of the hygiene school, the first hygienist licensed in the state of Connecticut, was Fones's cousin and faithful chairside assistant, Irene Newman.

Fones convinced the state legislature to allow the hygienists to work in the state. And he convinced the city school system to "hire ten of his first graduates to daily inspect and prophylactically treat the teeth, and to instruct the entire first- and second-grade student body in methods of self-care."[10] Armed with portable chairs and instruments, the women went to work in 1914.

Over three years, Fones trained a total of ninety-seven hygienists. Some found jobs in private practices, while others were placed in a growing system of school dental clinics. In some cases, their skills took them beyond private dental offices and schools. One of Fones's graduates was hired to serve as resident hygienist at New Haven

Hospital. Another found work at an industrial dental clinic serving the employees of the Yale & Towne Lock Company of Stamford.

World War I brought dramatic change to Bridgeport. The city served as a munitions center for the war effort and young military men flooded into town. In 1917, hygienists cleaned and examined the teeth of the soldiers, distributed toothbrushes, provided oral health lessons, and referred those in need of additional care to local dentists. More European immigrants arrived in the city as well. The schools were crowded with transient families, many of them non-English speakers. Teachers and principals were distracted and overstretched.

Fones acknowledged that he could not have picked a more challenging time to proceed with his school hygiene program. Still at the end of five years, he had successful outcomes to show for the effort. Cavities were reduced by one-third across the schools where hygienists had been working, and school performance had improved, Fones reported. During the same period, the city saw a drop in diphtheria, measles, and scarlet fever and weathered a great postwar flu epidemic better than most other cities.[11] A local health official credited the school dental hygienists with "raising the sanitary intelligence of the community—which is, after all, the object for which modern health workers are striving," Fones wrote in his report.

Over the next decade, dental hygiene programs steadily spread to other states. "Today there are ten training schools in this country for dental hygienists and 26 states have amended their laws to permit women to practice this profession," reported the *Bridgeport Telegram* in a 1927 article, marking the naming of Fones to a prestigious award by the New York State Dental Society.[12] The public embraced the dental hygiene model. Local newspapers reported rates of tooth decay in schools, like standardized test scores are covered today, and illustrated stories showed hygienists caring for children. "Dental Hygiene Workers Are Kept Busy on Playgrounds of City" read the headline over a front-page photo feature run by the *Evening News* in Harrisburg, Pennsylvania.[13]

The dentists who were involved in the school clinics during that era found them sources of professional pride. "In the 1920s, the public school became to dentistry what the hospital had long been to medicine—a place to demonstrate charitable spirit and professional obligation and thereby establish 'social credit,'" observed the authors of a report on public school dentistry prepared by the Rand Corporation for the Robert Wood Johnson Foundation.[14] "The progress of school dentistry in the early twentieth century was thus integral to organized dentistry's desire to sell itself—both to the public at large and to organized medicine—as a true *health profession*, inferior to none."

But among some professional leaders, concerns about dental hygienists and the hygiene movement were growing. After World War I, the Progressive Era that kindled such programs gave way to a far more conservative national mood. Fears greeted the arrival of continuing waves of immigrants, as well as the spread of communism in other parts of the world. In America, medical and dental groups began to militate against the idea of state medicine.

In his president's address before the 1919 meeting of the Pennsylvania State Dental Society, Walter A. Spencer spoke gravely of "oral hygiene propaganda" that "has produced more demand for dental work than the supply of dentists can adequately meet."[15] And in a paper delivered at the same meeting, Massachusetts dentist Thomas J. Barrett issued a stern warning, linking the dental hygienist model to socialized medicine.

"Does anyone believe that you could train and equip at the present-day low standard of educational requirements a sufficient number of dental hygienists to give personal care to the teeth of all children of this great state, to say nothing of national needs, and all of this to be at public expense? That is a thought 'made in Germany,' and much resembles paternalism and German 'kulture' and not at all likely in this or any other state," said Barrett. The auxiliaries were poised to take the dentists' business, he said in his talk entitled "A New Species of Dentist: Do We Want It?"

"The propagandist is forceful in outlining the advantages that oral hygiene has in relation to tooth decay, and he goes so far along this line that he takes away from the skilled, educated and experienced dentist everything but the mechanical tools and turns all else over to the hygienist."[16]

His address was followed by fierce debate. A few rose to question his logic. But many other dentists joined Barrett in denouncing the dental auxiliary as a threat to the profession. "It looks to me as though it is like a great many evils," noted one attendee. "If you can license and control them it would be all right but most evils that are licensed cannot be controlled."[17] Dentists' worries about control continued to grow.

In his 1926 survey of the North American dental education system, William J. Gies wrote of the powerful potential for dental hygienists in delivering "preventive dentistry to children." But he also acknowledged that many dentists saw these new oral health professionals as a threat. "There is a widespread fear among dentists that dental hygienists will be inclined to violate their obligations, and independently to extend their practice beyond the statutory confines," Gies wrote.

The learned expert dismissed the concerns as unrealistic. "There appears to be no more real danger that dental hygienists will pretend to be dentists than there is that dentists will assume the role of physicians."[18]

Amid the national mood of conservatism and fears of communism that followed World War I, the American Medical Association launched a campaign against "state medicine." School health clinics began to close. In the wake of the Great Depression, as liberal leaders including President Franklin Delano Roosevelt called for the institution of a national health insurance program, leaders of organized dentistry joined organized medicine in the fight against government-led health care.

"State dentistry is wrong in principle and would be disastrous in practice," predicted one editorial in the *Journal of the American Dental Association*. "It is going to be difficult to down this monster of exploitation of the dental profession, and unless we are alert, we shall have fastened on us a system of dental practice that will not only bring ruin to our individual practitioners, but will also result in inefficient service to the people," warned another.

With the dwindling of school clinics, dental hygienists went to work in private dental offices. But the unmet medical and dental needs of America's young would come back to haunt the nation during the following decade.

In 1943 the skies of the world were dark with war, but millions of America's fighting-aged youths were unfit for service. In the days since the surprise attack on Pearl Harbor on December 7, 1941, military recruiters had concluded that as many as a third of the young men called up were not healthy enough to serve. Mental illness, tuberculosis, venereal disease, and tooth decay were rampant among them. In the first draft alone, two hundred thousand of the million men examined had been disqualified for dental defects. In the U.S. Capitol, hearings were convened before a subcommittee of the Senate Committee on Education and Labor, presided over by Florida senator Claude Pepper. Witness after witness testified as congressional leaders attempted to learn more about the crisis, including the needs of legions of "dental cripples" discovered by military recruiters.

Worries endured about the status of the nation's health, and the inadequacy of the dental workforce to reach all Americans. Concerns helped drive continued efforts to expand health care to the masses through government initiatives and workforce innovations. In Washington, members of Congress set to work on legislation that would create a national health insurance plan. In 1946, the legislation under discussion by the U.S. Senate was known as the Wagner-Murray-Dingell Bill, number S1606.

Leaders of the American Dental Association (ADA) who came to Washington to testify before the Senate Committee on Education and Labor registered their disapproval. Any plan to include dental services in such a program was unrealistic, they contended. "Because of the limited number of dentists, it is impossible to carry out any program that promises complete dental care to both children and adults," they warned.[19] The ADA called instead for far less sweeping measures: federally funded research into disease prevention and grants for community-level pilot programs for young people.

The dental leaders were questioned by a sponsor of the bill.

"Now you recognize that there is a grave shortage of practicing dentists in this country and that with the present force of dental practitioners, it would be impossible to give the American people full and complete dental care?" the committee chairman, Senator James Murray of Montana, asked.

"That is right, Senator," responded Carl Flagstad, chair of the ADA's committee on legislation.

"Of course," responded Murray, "the fact is that the dental practitioners have been kept busy with people who are able to pay adequately for the treatment they receive, but if dental care was opened freely to the American people, of course, there would not be sufficient dentists to take care of them all."

"That is right," said Flagstad.[20] The leaders of organized dentistry acknowledged the shortage of dentists when they resisted federal efforts to expand care during the postwar years. Yet they just as adamantly opposed plans to train additional dental workers to meet those needs.

In the late 1940s a program designed to teach dental auxiliaries to drill and fill baby teeth was launched at Boston's Forsyth Dental Infirmary. The project, supervised and approved by the state of Massachusetts and funded by the U.S. Children's Bureau, offered two years of additional training to a dozen hygienists interested in working in the schools. Dental leaders reacted with wrath.

"More than 300 Massachusetts dentists crowded into a State House hearing room yesterday to demand repeal of a bill permitting dental hygienists to fill children's teeth in school clinics," the *Berkshire County Eagle* in Pittsfield, Massachusetts, reported.[21] "In demanding repeal of the bill yesterday, spokesmen for the dental profession described it as 'an opening wedge for socialized medicine.' The hygienists' two-year training, they argued, could not possibly be equivalent to the six years dentists are required to study before practicing."

But among public health officials, concerns about the shortage of dental care only grew over the decade that followed. In 1961, the Commission on the Survey of Dentistry in the United States recommended broadening the duties of dental hygienists to help meet the need. Men had long been prohibited from training as hygienists out of fear that they would be more likely than female hygienists to pose competition to dentists. The panel called for the removal of the legal and educational restrictions against male hygienists.[22]

With the launching of Medicare and Medicaid programs in 1965, demand for a wide range of health care services burgeoned overnight. In medicine, nurse practitioners and physicians' assistants emerged to respond to the growing demand for care, staffing clinics, particularly in underserved and rural communities.

To dentist and innovator Ralph Lobene, dental hygienists with expanded skills could likewise broaden access to dental care, making it cheaper and more widely available. Under Lobene's leadership, a new Forsyth experiment—"Project Rotunda"—was set into motion in the early 1970s. In a specially constructed circular clinic at Forsyth's Boston research center, a select group of hygienists were trained to drill and fill teeth. The clinic's spokelike configuration gave patients privacy while allowing instructors to oversee the hygienists' work. The project was intended to explore "one approach toward meeting the most formidable challenge that dentistry faces in the next decades: delivering high-quality oral health care to the entire population—approximately twice the number of Americans who now annually receive at least minimal dental therapy," Lobene wrote.[23]

He made no secret of his exasperation with the existing dental system in America. "The outdated philosophy that this health service is a privilege to be enjoyed only by people affluent enough to afford it has long been tacitly accepted by the dental profession. As a result, American dentistry's manpower, educational facilities, and styles of practice are geared to meet the needs of, at best, half the population," he noted.

Again, dental leaders mobilized to quash the project. The Massachusetts state board of dental examiners obtained a ruling from the state attorney general concluding that the program was in technical violation of the state's dental practice act. `

"Dr. John Horack, chairman of the state board, said Forsyth officials and their supporters 'want a free rein to do whatever they deem possible,'" the *Lowell Sun* reported on January 2, 1974. Horack said he was opposed to hygienists drilling and filling teeth.

"The chairman also indicated the board action may have been taken as a protective measure for members of the profession," the newspaper reported.

"They say that it [the program] would provide care to more people, but up at the board we are told dentists aren't busy," Horack said.

Lobene's findings were released. The hygienists demonstrated their advanced training. Newspapers across the country picked up a *United Press International* article, using a variety of headlines, many of which made the dentists look bad: "Hygienists' Work Has the Dentists Uptight," "Hygienists Out-Perform Dentists," and "Dentists Make More Mistakes."

But the project was doomed. Looking back on the effort Lobene observed that, as the medical profession evolved, patients had come to accept physicians' decisions to delegate routine medical services. "Within the American dental profession, however, acceptance of the concept of delegating irreversible procedures such as routine restorative work is still not high," he wrote. "One reason suggested is that many dentists may not feel as secure about their professional image as physicians do."[24]

In the wake of lobbying in statehouses, and pitched battles with dental boards across the country, dental hygienists say they have made progress since those days. In more than a dozen states, hygienists can now bill Medicaid directly for their services. As of

2016, a total of thirty-nine states, termed "direct access" states by the American Dental Hygienists' Association, allow hygienists to provide care in at least one practice setting to patients who have not first been seen by a dentist.

The situation varies widely by state. In California, hygienists with advanced licenses are allowed to work under the remote supervision of dentists to perform a wide variety of procedures, including treating cavities with low-cost temporary restorations. The minimally invasive approach to treating decay does not require anesthetic or drilling. The soft decayed area of the tooth is instead scooped out with a hand instrument and then coated with a glass ionomer sealant that contains fluoride, which arrests the progress of the decay. The approach, called by various names including Interim Therapeutic Restoration (ITR), was first developed by a Dutch dentist for use in field clinics. It has been promoted for more than two decades by the World Health Organization as an effective treatment for tooth decay in many settings. American dentists have been slow to adopt it.

In Colorado, where only one-third of dentists were treating Medicaid patients in one recent year, and where eight counties were classified as "dental deserts," hygienists also gained significant independence. In 2015 Delta Dental Foundation, the philanthropic arm of the insurance giant Delta Dental, committed more than $3 million to set up sixteen dental offices within medical clinics in the state. Each clinic was staffed with a dental hygienist.

Yet in Georgia in 2016, a bill was killed that would have allowed dental hygienists to clean teeth in nursing homes and school clinics without a dentist present. It was strongly opposed by dentists in the state. "I've never seen such hostility" toward a piece of legislation, state representative Sharon Cooper, a Marietta Republican who chaired the House Health and Human Services Committee, was quoted as saying.[25]

For more than a century, experiments by innovators and studies and reports produced by nonprofits, learned academies, universities, and federal agencies have continued to suggest that dental hygienists, particularly with additional training, could be more widely used to help address the unmet dental needs of millions of Americans. Hygienist leaders agree.

"For too long, oral health care services have been tied to the private, fee-for-service dental office where so few vulnerable populations in particular but many others have trouble accessing," said Karen Sealander, a Washington lobbyist for the American Dental Hygienists' Association. "We need to open up additional access points and we really need to integrate oral health into primary care. We could see a hygienist working with an ob-gyn. Seeing pregnant women, working with a pediatrician. Seeing children, counseling mothers and caregivers and kids old enough to be counseled in self-care oral hygiene and providing clinical services there as part of a preventive visit. That puts the hygienist in this primary care setting."

In private conversations dentists have acknowledged they believe a bigger role for hygienists is inevitable, said Sealander. She said she was convinced it would make sense. "Why shouldn't you be able to go to a CVS MinuteClinic and get your shingles vaccine and inoculate your teeth against tooth decay with sealants and fluoride? I mean we know how to inoculate against tooth decay. But we don't make it easy for people to do."

Hygienists, joined by grassroots organizations and in some cases supported by federal watchdogs, continue to press for change. Hygienist Tammi Byrd's efforts in South Carolina turned into a decade-long odyssey that nearly ruined her.

A poised and fit woman with a deep faith, Byrd had worked for years with other local hygiene leaders to get a state law changed that would allow them to visit children in schools. Untreated oral disease was a longtime problem in the state, and Byrd was not the only one to be troubled by it.

All the way back in 1980, members of a state General Assembly review panel were concerned enough about the problem to ask the state board of dentistry to "consider the expansion of dental hygienists' functions and the lessening of restrictions on the supervision of dental hygienists in order to increase the availability of dental services in South Carolina."

Some counties in the state had only one dentist, the reviewers observed. Changing regulations to free up dental hygienists to work in underserved areas "would allow a wider segment of the population an opportunity to receive preventive services and instructions," the reviewers wrote. "Such patients as those in nursing homes, elderly shut-ins, and the indigent could receive services otherwise not available, and the public health and welfare would be better served."

Some states were allowing hygienists to do such public health work, the reviewers noted. But in South Carolina, regulations restricted hygienists from working in such settings unless a dentist had examined the patients first. The problem was, there weren't many dentists focused on examining the patients.

Medicaid health screenings identified tooth decay as "the number one health problem among South Carolina school children." Yet a preschool health assessment indicated that only 13 percent of children entering poor schools in the 1997 school year had received a preventive dental service, a team of researchers from the Medical University of South Carolina reported.[26]

The hygienists continued to press for more responsibilities and the dental leaders in the state continued to resist. "We had been trying to get legislation passed," Byrd recalled. "Trying to get stuff done."

Their drive for change appeared pretty hopeless. It seemed the legislation would never be passed. Then in 1999, Byrd had an epiphany. She said it came to her as she was preparing a Bible study lesson for a group of teenagers at her church the following evening. The Bible lesson was to focus on something called a "God-Sized Project," she explained. Such a project is "bigger than you are. It's something that costs more money than what you have. It's something that you don't have the power to control." She pondered the material. Suddenly the words of the lesson hit home. Her hygiene campaign was like that.

"God took a two-by-four and hit me on the head and said, 'You have never given me the project,'" she recalled. "I told him it was his. And to open the doors."

It was not long until the impasse finally began to dissolve. State lawmakers working with dental leaders started taking steps intended to help address the lack of care. Medicaid paperwork was streamlined and reimbursement rates for Medicaid dental procedures were raised. The state dental association launched an aggressive campaign to attract more dentists to the Medicaid program and some new providers did sign up.[27] Then, in 2000, the state General Assembly approved the legislation Tammi Byrd had spent so many years working and praying for.

"March of 2000," said Tammi Byrd. "Our law had passed."

The legislation removed the requirement that the children be examined by a dentist before hygienists could offer cleanings and protective sealants in the schools. It lifted the requirement that a dentist provide written permission for the procedures.

"This new law removes a regulation that hindered access to dental care," announced the state's governor, Jim Hodges, when he signed the legislation. "Thanks to this legislation, parents won't have to pull their children out of school to go to the dentist and seniors will have access to dental care in their retirement homes."

As written, the new law would allow "dental hygienists to offer preventative dental care in places such as schools, nursing homes, public health clinics, hospitals and charitable institutions," the governor's office explained in a statement. "Dentists rarely practice full-time in these settings."[28]

But big questions remained. Where would these hygienists come from? Who would organize the services? Byrd quickly realized that the victory might turn out to be a hollow one. The state itself had no team of hygienists ready to go out and do the work. Byrd faced this new dilemma. She had a good life: a solid marriage, a growing daughter, a wonderful church. Her work in a successful private dental practice yielded a steady paycheck. The schedule at the dental office was even arranged to afford the staff regular four-day weekends. Byrd spent hers enjoying competitive water skiing with her family.

The change in the state law of South Carolina seemed to Byrd to have come as an answer to her prayer. Now she wondered what God expected from her in return. She asked heaven for answers. "I prayed about it and I prayed about it and I prayed about it," she said.

She concluded that God wanted her to get care to the children who were going without it. There were 250,000 of them. She could not do it alone. She reminded God she did not know how to run a business. "But he kept laying it on my heart. Laying it on my heart. Laying it on my heart. And so I went to my husband and said, 'I know this is gonna sound crazy, but I think I want to quit my job. I want to mortgage our house. And I want to start a business. I want to put hygienists in schools and start seeing kids.'"

When she explained the idea to her husband, Jim, his first reaction was to laugh. But then he went outside and came back in. He was much graver when he spoke.

"You are serious about this, aren't you?" he asked.

"And I said, 'Yeah, I am. I am serious about this.'"

She applied for a loan from the Small Business Administration. She quit her job in October 2000, noting the date, Friday the thirteenth.

"December twenty-eighth we finally got funding. We got our loan secured and we borrowed a quarter of a million dollars." She used her house and her secondhand car as collateral. She ordered the equipment she would need to send hygienists into the schools. "I thought the legislation was God-sized. This is waaaay bigger than what I thought. You know they say he wants to take you places where you have never been. Well he sure did."

She called her company Health Promotion Specialists. The hygienists would visit participating schools and examine the children at no charge to their families. They would send a letter home with each child. With the parents' permission they would provide cleanings, fluoride treatments, and protective sealants, billing Medicaid or private insurance or the parents directly. If the hygienist saw signs of decay she would advise a follow-up visit with a dentist, Byrd explained.

Byrd based her plans on the idea that her company would be directly reimbursed by Medicaid for the hygienists' services. "We need to be reimbursed for our services because if we can't be reimbursed for what we are doing we can't work. I mean the reality of volunteering is it's not sustainable." Not every state allowed hygienists to bill Medicaid for their work; in fact, most state dental boards required that a dentist needed to submit the bills to Medicaid. But Byrd had consulted the state Medicaid provider manual and saw nothing about a requirement in South Carolina that hygienists work through a dentist to submit their bills.

She had consulted Sam Griswold, the director of the state Department of Human Services, and had a letter from him stating his eagerness to work with her program. "I am pleased to offer the support of the Department of Health and Human Services (DHHS) in your effort to increase access to oral health care for the children through the Health Promotion Specialists Public/Private Partnership Project," Griswold wrote back to her.[29] "My staff is currently working on the methodology for Medicaid reimbursement for registered dental hygienists for providing preventive services. . . . The DHHS is looking forward to working with the registered dental hygienists to make oral health more accessible to the Medicaid population."

But at the South Carolina Dental Association, the organization representing the state's dentists, alarm bells were ringing. "The Hygienists Are Coming! The Hygienists Are Coming!" read a headline in the October 2000 issue of the *South Carolina Dental Association (SCDA) Bulletin*. The accompanying editorial warned of recent activities by members of the state hygienists' association. "They seem to be asking for approval and assignment of insurance provider numbers. This would be a critical key to independent practice because it authorizes insurance companies to pay hygienists directly!" noted the editorial, which concluded, "This posture is an offensive move toward private practice."

A meeting was set up at Griswold's office to discuss the project. Byrd expected to be seeing Griswold, and maybe a couple representatives from the state dental association.

"When I pull up, there are all these Suburbans. Like seven or eight Suburbans parked on the street and I'm thinking, 'Is the president in town or something?' I mean there are all these big huge SUVs everywhere. And then these doors start opening, and all these dentists start pouring out of all of these SUVs."

The dentists at the meeting threatened legal action, she said. SCDA executive director Hal Zorn reported the same in the November 2000 issue of the bulletin: "Based on its attorney's guidance the (SCDA) Board has directed President Charles Millwood and myself to seek an immediate injunction should the S.C. Department of Health and Human Services—or any other agency for that matter—attempt to pay a hygienist directly for work performed under general supervision."

A quarter of a million Medicaid children were going without dental care in the state, experts had reported. In his article, Zorn suggested the problem did not lie with dental providers, but with parents.

"There are thousands of students in South Carolina's public schools who do not have access to dental care. This is not because the dentists, hygienists and assistants of the dental team are not interested in their needs. It can be something as simple as the parents not placing any emphasis whatsoever on the oral needs of their children," Zorn wrote. "I have been told of one child in Allendale County who needed a root canal. The mother did not bring the child to two scheduled appoints [sic] in a row and then showed up and demanded that the tooth be pulled 'because she was sick and tired or hearing the child whine and complain.'"

Byrd left the meeting with the dentists shaken and worried. She had quit her job, mortgaged her house, taken out a loan. It was too late to turn back. She had to go forward. "It was going to take too long to fight this legal battle to get reimbursed," she said. "I had to figure out how to get a dentist working with me that will let us get paid." Given the controversy, she did not have an easy time finding one, but eventually a dentist based in Hilton Head agreed to help.

She moved forward with plans to start in three or four school districts with three or four hygienists. "January 2001 I hired a couple of hygienists. We started seeing kids," she recalled.

In February, state senator John Drummond, who had worked to change the law, had a chance to see a hygienist checking the teeth of the children in his hometown elementary school. "I hope they do it in every school in South Carolina," he told a reporter from the local newspaper.[30]

And the program took off, Byrd said. "From January to April the word got out about our program. And every school district wanted it."

Byrd ordered more supplies and hired more hygienists. When schools in a new county asked for the program, she found a hygienist in that area to start working for her. She borrowed more money. She started billing Medicaid. But the reimbursements were slow in coming. She had some desperate moments, waiting to hand out her first paychecks. She herself wouldn't get paid for two and a half years, she said. But she pressed forward. By the end of the school year, the hygienists had screened over nineteen thousand children in more than two dozen districts across South Carolina and had provided cleanings, sealants, and fluoride treatments to four thousand of them.[31]

June came. The state legislature that had passed the legislation allowing the hygienists to go into the schools and provide care to children without first being seen by a dentist went into recess.

On June 15, the South Carolina Dental Association sent out a letter to school officials across the state. The letter assured school officials that state dentists were working to address "the access to oral health crisis which existed here in the Palmetto State." As a result of reforms to the state Medicaid program dentists had treated an additional sixty thousand children so far that year, they wrote.

But their letter went on to warn of "another impending crisis here in South Carolina which will directly affect the oral health of the children of this state."

The letter put Tammi Byrd and Health Promotion Specialists at the center of that new crisis. Her company was not cooperating with local dentists, the letter said. In some cases, the children were already "patients of record of local dentists," the letter said. But when the hygienists treated the children in the school, the children became the "patients of record" of the Health Promotion Specialists' supervising dentist whose office was in Hilton Head. "When a child has a toothache on the weekend or during class is the school going to transport the child to Hilton Head to see the dentist?" the letter asked.

"Well guess what?" recalled Byrd. "A bunch of school districts started sending us back our MOA—our letter of understanding that we have to work with them. Started sending that back with a letter stating, 'We had no idea this was that controversial. We're gonna have to put this on hold for now.' And they had that dental letter stapled to it."

Then, while the state legislature was in recess, the dental board moved forward with plans to reimpose the requirement that a dentist examine the children before the hygienists treated them. It was the same requirement the legislature had removed.

State legislator Gilda Cobb-Hunter, who had supported the change in the law that removed the requirement for an examination by a dentist, got wind of the plan. She fired off a July 11 letter to the board. "I have learned that the South Carolina Board of Dentistry has drafted plans to file, under the guise of emergency regulations, a highly restrictive requirement," she wrote. The measure would "destroy the legislative intent" of the act the governor had signed.

The board of dentistry pushed ahead with the emergency regulation anyway.

"The need for immediate action is required in order to protect patients in this State from further injury resulting from the performance of procedures by dental hygienists without prior examination and determination by a licensed dentist," the document read. "The Board has received initial complaints of professional misconduct and has determined that without this regulation, dental hygienists are in a position to apply topical fluoride and perform the application of sealants and oral prophylaxis before a proper diagnosis of cavities and other serious dental health conditions have been properly assessed by a dentist."

"They drew up an emergency regulation," Byrd recounted. "And they were able to put it in because the statute says if lives are in extreme danger when the legislature is not in session, that you can pass an emergency regulation to protect the citizens of the state."

Dental board officials told the press that the board had acted in order to safeguard public health. "The dental group says it is only protecting children by seeing that dentists, not lesser-trained hygienists, diagnose problems," reported the Associated Press. Cleaning teeth could pose health risks to some children, particularly those with heart conditions, dental officials warned. Some might need an antibiotic before a cleaning. "It's not unusual at all. We see people every day that we have to pre-medicate," board president Charles Maxwell told the AP.[32]

In the same article, a school official defended the hygiene program. "We have had in our health room, children who come in and cry with toothaches. Well, they are not learning anything in the classroom if they're in pain," principal Sue Hendrix said.

Byrd spoke too. "Dentistry has always been delivered in a private office if the patients got there," she told the AP. "But the reality is a lot of patients never got there."

South Carolina's leading newspaper, *The State*, criticized the dental board's move in an editorial. "It's frustrating when arbitrary rules seem to stand in the way of helping thousands of South Carolina's children," noted the piece. "Many poor children in our state are not receiving routine, preventive dental care. According to the state Department of Human Services, 65 percent of the children in

South Carolina who are eligible for Medicaid did not see a dentist last year, meaning some 250,000 were without care," the authors wrote.

The editors acknowledged the dentists' arguments. "The dentists believe the best care for children's teeth comes from a regular relationship with a community dentist, not periodic visits from an itinerant service." But, they added, "It's a crying shame to think that the desire to provide the best possible health care could prevent some children from getting any preventive dental care at all."

Byrd and her lawyer went before an administrative law judge to try to stop the board from enforcing the examination requirement. They were told they needed to seek a hearing. They were granted one—in October. The dental board's emergency regulation would remain in effect for six months.

"My personal opinion is if they could financially kill us from July until January then we would disappear," said Byrd. "And nobody else would ever try to do this again."

Late that summer, Byrd sued the state dental board and dental association. She charged the groups "banded together to prevent hygienists from delivering preventative dental care so that the dentists can gain this service for themselves."

But in the meantime, she had to abide by the regulation. "We hired two dentists," she said. "We had to lay off half of our hygienists."

The fall semester was terrifying for Byrd. Some of the districts had been scared off, but the program was still operating in thirteen districts. Byrd kept thirteen hygienists. The dentists made the rounds examining children, but while waiting for the exams, half the hygienists remained idle. They saw thousands fewer children that year. The Internal Revenue Service was asking for a quarterly payment and she was broke. It looked like she was going to lose her family's home. One night, she laid down on the floor of her office and cried. She told God she didn't even know what to pray for.

Finally, she got up and went out to her car to drive home. A worship song came on the radio, with lyrics that called out to God in the darkness. "It goes, 'There's a mountain in the way and a lock on the door. Either move. Or move me.'"

Byrd said she felt a sudden sense of calm settle over her. "I said, 'Okay, God. I'm thankful. I'm not sure why.' And I had this peace. It's gonna be okay."

As her company fell deeper and deeper into debt, Byrd sought help from the American Dental Hygienists' Association. The organization contacted the Federal Trade Commission (FTC) and the government watchdog agency launched an investigation. Meanwhile, Byrd kept visiting school boards, trying to reassure members and regain trust. And board members kept asking, "Didn't we get a letter from the dental association saying this was substandard care?"

"And I'm saying, 'Yeah. But it's not.'"

She worked on. There was no other way. In September 2003 Byrd was driving her mortgaged Toyota Camry when her cell phone rang. A reporter was calling from the *State* newspaper. He told her he had received a press release from the Federal Trade Commission saying that the South Carolina Board of Dentistry was being charged with constraint of trade.

"Can you give me a comment?" he asked her. Byrd told the reporter she needed to read the document before she spoke with him. Then she hung up the phone and tried to gather her composure.

In the complaint, the Federal Trade Commission spelled out its charges: that the South Carolina State Board of Dentistry, "which consists almost entirely of practicing dentists, restrained competition in the provision of preventive dental care services by unreasonably restricting the delivery of dental cleanings, sealants and topical fluoride treatments in school settings by licensed dental hygienists." The FTC noted that though the state General Assembly had passed legislation in 2000 eliminating a statutory requirement that a dentist examine each child before a hygienist could provide services "the Board in 2001 re-imposed the very examination requirement that the legislature had eliminated, and extended it to the application of topical fluoride in school settings as well.

"The effect of the board's action was to deprive thousands of school children—particularly economically disadvantaged children—of the benefits of preventive oral health care services," the complaint charged. "The Board's anticompetitive action, undertaken by self-interested industry participants with economic interests at stake, was contrary to state policy," the FTC concluded. Any benefits it offered were outweighed by its "harmful effects on competition and consumers."

The state dental board challenged the complaint. It sent letters to hygienists working with Byrd's program warning them they might be "practicing dentistry without a license." The dental board fought the FTC all the way to the U.S. Supreme Court. But the nation's highest court refused to hear the case and the charges stuck.

In 2007 the case was settled. The South Carolina State Board of Dentistry was ordered to announce to all dentists, hygienists, and school superintendents throughout the state that it supported the policy allowing hygienists to treat children in public health settings without first being examined by a dentist.

The FTC announced it would monitor the dental board's conduct for another ten years. "As this case reflects, state regulatory boards that restrict competition in ways not contemplated by state law are subject to antitrust laws," noted Jeffrey Schmidt, the director of the FTC's Bureau of Competition, in a statement. "This case is important because it protects access to preventive dental services for children—especially those from low-income families—in schools."

The years have passed and Byrd's program is rebuilding. She and the hygienists have seen tens of thousands of children. She has given up competitive water skiing in favor of practicing yoga and teaching it at a local gym. She still prays. And she still fights.

"I'm getting ready to stir the pot again," she warned with a rueful laugh.

On a trip to Massachusetts, she took a weekend course at the Forsyth Institute, the former home of the controversial Project

Rotunda. Byrd's class focused on Atraumatic Restorative Technique, a variation of the minimally invasive treatment for cavities that specially trained hygienists in California have begun providing. Byrd and the other participants were taught how to prepare and coat decayed surfaces of teeth with a glass ionomer sealant containing fluoride that works to arrest the progress of disease. The method has been found useful in treating young, fearful, or disabled patients, and those awaiting traditional restorations. Research has shown its safety and long-term effectiveness.[33]

"Hygienists can place temporary restorations. This is considered primary preventive care that's reversible," said Byrd. Still, she was building a coalition, in case state dental leaders started militating.

"I read an article the other day," she said. "Dentistry has built a Mercedes. And it's beautiful. It's gorgeous. It works well. But guess what. They don't want anybody to build a good ol' Ultima or Camry. And a lot of people can't afford the Mercedes. They need the Ultima, the Prius, and the Camry. And dental hygienists are ready to do that," she said. "Take this ample supply of hygienists we have, that are not being utilized to the top of our license or at all, and use us to serve these populations who are not getting care."

8

The System

By framing dental workforce questions as marketplace issues, the Federal Trade Commission has lent its formidable voice to debates roiling dental boards and legislatures in states across the nation. In addition to its work in South Carolina, the agency challenged dental leaders in Louisiana who lobbied to shut down a mobile practice delivering care to children in schools. It advocated for independent-practice hygienists in Maine. Yet some dental groups continue to defy the powerful agency. They insist they are not acting out of self-interest. They say they are protecting Americans from second-class care.

In 2016, the FTC waded into the debate in Georgia—a state with roughly 150 federally designated dental professional shortage areas. Dental hygienists were fighting for legislation that would have allowed them to provide basic preventive care in nursing homes, schools, and public health clinics without a dentist being present to offer "direct supervision." The FTC wrote in support of Georgia House Bill 684, reminding state officials that only 27 percent of state residents were getting dental services. The measure would lead "to increased access and more cost-effective care, especially for Georgia's most vulnerable populations," the agency noted.

Advocates were heartened and hopeful that the legislation would pass. Amendments were added at the request of the Georgia Dental Association (GDA) and the bill continued to move through the legislative process. But when it reached the House Rules Committee, it died a sudden death. Advocates charged that the state dental association had worked behind the scenes to get it killed.

In a statement, GDA executive director Frank Capaldo provided a familiar explanation. He said that, ultimately, dental leaders turned against the bill out of concern for patients. "Why did the Georgia Dental Association, after making suggestions for numerous amendments, change its support on Georgia House Bill 684 when it reached the House Rules Committee? Simple! At the end of the day our member dentists could not compromise their first order of ethical care, to do no harm—as would have inevitably resulted from patients believing that a cleaning was the same as an exam. Yes, the passage of HB 684 would have benefited many dental practices financially who could have deployed unsupervised hygienists to provide cleanings to Medicaid patients. Instead, to their selfless credit, dentists chose the safety of the most vulnerable citizens of Georgia over themselves," Capaldo noted.

The highest-profile faceoff between the FTC and the dentists in recent memory had nothing to do with the efforts of licensed oral health professionals to deliver preventive dental services to poor schoolchildren or suffering nursing home residents. The fight concerned something on the opposite side of the dental coin—retailers who were opening up teeth-whitening booths in suburban spas and shopping centers.

Teeth can be stained by foods, drink, tobacco use, and aging. Bleaching treatments consist of applying peroxide-containing preparations, which employ chemical action to lighten the enamel and dentin layers of the teeth. Teeth whitening commands a multi-billion-dollar share of America's market for cosmetic dental goods and services.[1] Do-it-yourself teeth-whitening kits are sold in pharmacies. No prescription is needed. The kits are as easy to obtain as toothpaste. Beauty salons and mall kiosks offer teeth whitening in some places.

But bleaching treatments have also become a steady source of income for dentists. Dental organizations have challenged salon operators and others offering teeth whitening. They have argued that these non-dentists are practicing dentistry without a license. They contend that these vendors could be putting customers at risk. In Georgia, Trisha Eck, owner of Tooth Fairies Teeth Whitening, told Fox News in 2014 that she closed down her business after a state dental board investigator determined her business was an unlicensed dental practice. "He comes from the dental board and he's telling me he can shut me down. He can fine me; I could face prison time," Eck said. "That's a little intimidating."

In other cases, the vendors have received threatening letters from dental boards. In recent years, dental boards in at least twenty-five states have taken steps to shut down the establishments, according to a libertarian think tank that has supported the non-dentists.[2]

The teeth-whitening battle in the state of North Carolina had been brewing for more than a decade when, in 2014, it finally reached the U.S. Supreme Court. By that time, the state dental board had sent out at least forty-seven official cease-and-desist letters to non-dentist teeth-whitening service providers and product manufacturers. The letters often warned the recipients that the unlicensed practice of dentistry was a crime. The American Dental Association backed the North Carolina dental board in court. Meanwhile, raising safety concerns, the ADA petitioned the U.S. Food and Drug Administration asking the federal agency to tighten the regulation of the peroxide-containing tooth-whitening preparations. The FDA, which regards the products as cosmetics, denied the request. The Federal Trade Commission also rejected the dentists' safety arguments. In its case, the FTC held that the North Carolina state dental board "illegally thwarted competition by working to bar non-dentist providers of teeth-whitening goods and services from selling their products to consumers."

In October 2014, during an intense hour of arguments, the nine justices of the U.S. Supreme Court delved into whether the state dental board overstepped federal antitrust laws in sending out the threatening cease-and-desist letters to the operators of the teeth-whitening businesses. Arguing before the court on behalf of the FTC, Deputy Solicitor General L. Malcolm Stewart asserted that the six practicing dentists who served on North Carolina's eight-member dental board had an "evident self-interest" in controlling the market.

But an attorney for the state dental board countered that the dentists' actions were not subject to federal antitrust laws. The members of the dental board were acting as an agency of the state. As members of the dental profession the dentists on the board were the best-qualified individuals to regulate the practice of their profession in the state. "The benefits of expertise outweigh the risks of conflict of interest," argued the attorney, Hashim M. Mooppan.

Justice Ruth Bader Ginsburg seemed troubled by the assertion that the dental board merited special protection as an agency of the state. A lower court had ruled that the dental board had sent out the cease-and-desist letters without state oversight. "Why should there be an antitrust exemption for conduct that is not authorized by state law?" she asked. "The objection here was that this board was issuing a whole bunch of cease-and-desist orders. They had no authority to do that. No authority at all."

In the end, the nation's highest court ruled against the dentists and for the operators of the teeth-whitening businesses. "After receiving complaints from other dentists about the non-dentists' cheaper services, the Board's dentist members—some of whom offered whitening services—acted to expel the dentists' competitors from the market," the majority of justices agreed. "In so doing the Board relied upon cease-and-desist letters threatening criminal liability, rather than any of the powers at its disposal that would invoke oversight by a politically accountable official."[3]

The court found it was legal for the vendors to offer their teeth-whitening services.

In the nineteenth century, America's dentists and doctors organized to protect the marketplace for their services. They successfully asserted that as professionals, they were not involved in commerce, and therefore they could not restrain it. For more than a century, they enjoyed what sometimes has been described as a monopoly over a significant share of the health care market.

That control was dealt a blow in 1975 from the U.S. Supreme Court decision in the case of *Goldfarb v. Virginia State Bar*. The highest court found that members of learned professions were not exempt from antitrust laws. And the ruling was consonant with a larger sea-change sweeping over America—a philosophical shift away from government and professional regulation and toward free-market principles and consumer choice. Empowered, the Federal Trade Commission began investigating and prosecuting anti-competitive behavior in the health care marketplace.[4] The FTC acted quickly to see that longtime restrictions against medical and dental advertising were lifted with an aim of promoting wider consumer access to services at lower costs. In 1982, the U.S. Supreme Court upheld the FTC's legal challenge of the American Medical Association's prohibition on advertising. As part of a contingent agreement, the American Dental Association was bound not to interfere with advertising except to regulate any that was "false and misleading."[5] The agency went on to issue comments to state legislatures and professional boards across the country meant to protect competition between dentists and non-dentists for some services.

"Innovation in dental care delivery improves competition, which can bring higher quality care at lower costs to consumers. Society and the economy benefit when consumers have more access to basic services. Innovation and improvement that expands safe access to dental care helps by lowering cost and providing better health and safety outcomes," noted Gustav P. Chiarello, an attorney adviser to the agency, in a presentation highlighting the FTC's work in the area of dental regulation.[6]

Beyond fights over hygienists and teeth-whitening shops, the FTC has assumed a role in the epic debate over dental therapists. It is hard to find a cause that has more upset the leaders of organized dentistry. The dental therapist model has been employed for decades in countries around the world. The technically trained providers work as part of larger dentist-headed teams. They often serve as "dental extenders," leaving the dental clinic or office to bring care out into the field—to schools, geriatric centers, and village clinics where patients might otherwise lack access. They are cheaper and faster to train than dentists. They typically undergo an intensive two- or three-year course of study that focuses upon biomedical sciences, motor skills, and clinical dental training. Under their licenses, they can perform a range of procedures including drilling teeth and even some extractions—procedures that have traditionally been carried out only by dentists.

In the United States, groups representing dental hygienists, tribal communities, and grassroots organizations have embraced the dental therapist model. The cause has also found support from philanthropies including the Pew Charitable Trusts, the W.K. Kellogg Foundation, the Robert Wood Johnson Foundation, and the Rasmuson Foundation—organizations that see as part of their mission the promotion of wider access to all types of health care. The groups have issued studies and reports supporting the safety and cost-efficiency of the dental-extender model, findings that have been just as consistently challenged by the dental organizations.

But since the days of the Forsyth experiments, when a handful of hygienists were taught expanded skills, the struggle to find ways to get cheaper care to more people by teaching non-dentists to perform such procedures has continued. The American Dental Association insists that services it terms "irreversible surgical procedures" should only be performed by a dentist. Organized dentistry has used its formidable financial and lobbying power to fight dental therapists.

Advocates credit the timely intervention of the FTC with helping to advance the model. In 2013, the federal agency used its authority to weigh in on proposed accreditation standards for dental therapy training programs being considered by the body responsible for overseeing dental education in the United States—the Commission on Dental Accreditation (CODA). The FTC's communication with CODA was hailed by advocates as an influential public endorsement of the dental therapist model.

"Expanding the supply of dental therapists by facilitating the creation of new dental therapy training programs is likely to increase the availability of basic dental services, enhance competition, reduce costs, and expand access to dental care, especially for underserved populations," the FTC noted.[7]

Ultimately, in 2015, CODA adopted official standards enabling programs designed to educate midlevel dental providers to apply for accreditation. The move was celebrated as a milestone by the backers of dental therapists. "It's a pretty big deal," said David Jordan, leader of a dental access project for Community Catalyst, a national nonprofit consumer advocacy group. Jordan said implementation of the standards would provide guidance to policy makers in at least ten states considering the idea of putting dental therapists to work.

The American Dental Association was far less pleased. "The ADA, while fully supporting CODA and its role in assuring high-quality standards for dental education, remains firmly opposed to allowing non-dentists to perform surgical procedures," the organization said in a statement.[8]

In keeping with their privileged place in society, the learned professions are expected to act in the best interest of their communities, to put the common good above personal gain. In this spirit, dental organizations, including the American Dental Association and its affiliates, state dental associations, have strongly supported community water fluoridation programs nationwide. The programs have been credited with dramatically reducing tooth decay over the past two generations. The ADA publishes a respected peer-reviewed journal and maintains facilities and laboratories for testing and developing dental products and materials. It supports research on health policy and encourages volunteerism among its more than 157,000 member dentists with annual "Give Kids a Smile" events and free Mission of Mercy clinics.

ADA leaders themselves have acknowledged the lack of care in many places, the costs of emergency room visits, the plight of elders who cannot get to the dentist. They insist that the problems can be solved. They ask for additional federal and state spending on dental services. They are promoting a new model of their own, a community dental health coordinator, trained to help get patients to existing dentists. They contend that the shortcomings of the current system can be traced back to the failure of the nation to place a priority upon oral health.

In 2012, the W.K. Kellogg Foundation issued a voluminous compilation of available research on dental therapists working in fifty-four countries, from New Zealand to Canada. The philanthropy determined the practitioners had been "providing quality preventative and restorative services to patients for nearly 100 years."

The American Dental Association dismissed the paper as "a 460-page advocacy document intended to support a predetermined conclusion." In a statement on the Kellogg paper, the organization went on to acknowledge the need for some kind of change. The solution to America's dental problems would not lie in dental therapists, the group insisted. "The nation will never drill, fill and extract its way out of what amounts to a public health crisis among some populations. Throwing more 'treaters' into the mix amounts to digging a hole in an ocean of disease." The ADA called for "a fundamental shift in oral health from a model of surgical intervention to one of disease prevention, because virtually all dental disease is preventable."

Ultimately, the blame for the crisis lay not with dentists, or with a lack of access to care, the group said. "Underlying the extent of untreated disease is a societal failure to understand and value oral health. When the nation decides to put its resources into preventive measures like community water fluoridation; first dental visits by age 1; oral health education, assessment and sealant programs in schools; better integration with the medical community; and realistic funding of care for those in greatest need, it will have made a dramatic step toward ending untreated oral disease. Absent these things, dental therapists will not have an appreciable positive effect on the public's oral health. And if such measures are put in place, the debate over therapists will be moot. They will not be needed."[9]

As the battle has worn on, dental leaders have continued to speak out. They have exerted their formidable clout in statehouses across the country and on Capitol Hill. The ADA boasts a rich war chest for campaign contributions and lobbying and a staff of legislative and policy experts in Washington, D.C. The organization was designated one recent election year as a "heavy hitter" on Capitol Hill by the Center for Responsive Politics. The nonpartisan group, which tracks political spending, determined that the ADA's lobbying expenditures regularly exceed $2 million a year.

In the months leading up to the final passage of the Obama administration's health care reform law, the Patient Protection and Affordable Care Act, ADA leaders sent out an update to members with talking points for meeting with lawmakers. They urged dentist members to let their lawmakers know that dentists would be opposed to any plan that "required health care providers to participate," that "directly or indirectly dictated fees for the private market," or that "would lead to a government-run health system."

While praising the emphasis upon prevention and public health, the ADA criticized proposals that failed to provide additional funding for Medicaid dental programs. The group advocated for the passage of a bill called the Essential Oral Health Care Act that offered grants to support the purchase of equipment for charity clinics and that would make the rates paid by Medicaid for dental services consistent with market rates.[10] At a 2009 Washington Leadership Conference, the ADA pushed for dental Medicaid coverage for all adults living at or below the federal poverty level.

"Medicaid promises 'coverage' to millions of our neediest

citizens," the organization said in a statement. Yet inadequate funding betrays the program's goals, it added. "In many states, reimbursement lags so far below reasonable fees that dentists cannot afford to participate in Medicaid without losing money on every procedure."

The Patient Protection and Affordable Care Act (ACA) was signed by President Barack Obama in March 2010. As in the massive federal health reform efforts that came before it, dental care was treated separately, and only partially and imperfectly integrated into the program.

While dental coverage for children was included in the law's essential health benefit package, the law did not require that dental benefits be universally embedded into insurance packages for sale in state and federal marketplaces. It did not require people shopping on the marketplaces to buy dental coverage for themselves or their children. Because dental benefits were sold separately from the required packages, they did not receive the same subsidies as other health care coverage. The law did offer strong incentives for states to expand Medicaid. By early 2016, more than 15 million new beneficiaries had been added, mostly in states that expanded Medicaid.

But the Patient Protection and Affordable Care Act also left millions of Americans without dental benefits. And those who obtained them through Medicaid expansions in many cases faced the same challenges that had been experienced by millions of previous beneficiaries; in many areas, Medicaid dentists were very hard to find. In an acknowledgment of that problem, the health care reform law supported a number of pilot initiatives intended to help states explore ways to provide health care services more efficiently and at a lower cost. One initiative, the Alternative Dental Health Care Provider Demonstration Project, aimed to offer a total of fifteen states grants of roughly $4 million each to set up pilot programs for models such as dental therapists. As lawmakers considered funding for the fiscal year 2011, more than sixty public health, consumer, and oral health groups came out in praise of the measure.

The American Dental Association, joined by other organizations representing dentists, including the Academy of General Dentistry and the American Academy of Pediatric Dentistry, pressed lawmakers to block funding. "The American Dental Association writes to state its opposition to funding of the Alternative Dental Health Care Provider Demonstration Project," noted the group's president at the time, Raymond Gist, and executive director Kathleen O'Loughlin in a March 8, 2011, letter to leaders of the Senate Labor, Health and Human Services, Education and Related Agencies Subcommittee.

With five new dental schools opening in the years since 2000 and others being discussed, "the dentist workforce is growing," the ADA leaders assured members of Congress. "There is no evidence to support the economic feasibility of midlevel providers such as dental therapists who are trained to perform irreversible, surgical procedures."[11]

The funding for the pilot programs was blocked. Yet out of urgency and with a measure of defiance, dental therapists have begun delivering services anyway. A lawsuit by the American Dental Association and the Alaska Dental Society did not stop dental health aide therapists, or DHATs, from going to work in Alaskan tribal areas, on remote islands, and in bush villages. Variations on the dental therapist model have also been adopted in the states of Minnesota and Maine and, most recently, in Vermont. States including Massachusetts, Kansas, Michigan, New Mexico, and Ohio are in the process of weighing legislation, pilot programs, and other measures to authorize dental therapists.

Additional tribal communities have also embraced the model as a way of addressing rampant oral disease.

In early 2016, leaders of the Swinomish Indian Tribal Council in Skagit County, Washington, spurned federal restrictions and state licensing laws and announced they were putting a dental therapist to work in their clinic. Oregon approved a pilot program allowing two tribes to hire midlevel providers soon after.

The advocates of dental therapists say they will go where dentists will not go and solve problems organized dentistry will not solve.

In spite of vast changes to their lives over the past three centuries, Alaska Natives have fought to hold on to their ancient traditions, their dances and ceremonies, their hunting and fishing that embody both survival and prayer. Increasing reliance upon Western diets, however, has exacerbated problems with tooth decay. Soda pop arrives by the crate load to villages that are unreachable except by plane or boat or snowmobile. Public water supplies and other community sources of fluoridated water are rare. People drink melted snow. The perennially underfunded Indian Health Service has had chronic difficulty hiring dentists to serve in remote communities. Even if they come, they often leave. Alaska Native children suffer from tooth decay that has been estimated at rates more than twice as high as other American children. In Alaska, complete tooth loss by the age of twenty is not uncommon.[12]

Wrapped in icy mist, the village of Angoon is perched upon a spit of land east of Sitka, surrounded by slate blue water. Beyond the village, there are mountains, deeply furred by forests. Since ancient times, the people have called the place the "Brown Bear's Fort" and the bears still outnumber the humans. Pieces of Angoon's story are scattered along the narrow roads. There is a tiny wooden Russian Orthodox church and a row of tall wooden poles, crowned with ancestral totems, fish, and bears. There is a small power station and the Alaska Native Brotherhood Hall and wooden homes, one crumbling into the sea. There is a dump on the edge of the village where eagles casually feed.

And there is a modern clinic where, beyond the lighted windows, on this morning DHAT Brian James, clad in dark blue scrubs, was at work. He had the compact build, thick black hair, and dark, twinkling eyes of his Tlingit people. He greeted his next patient, Reggie Nelson, a local elder who came to the clinic a couple of months before to have a hopelessly decayed tooth removed. Nelson was back for some restorative work.

"It looks like we have one more filling to do," said James. He gave Nelson a shot of anesthetic and they chatted about fishing. When James was ready to begin he said, "You feel anything sore or sharp, you raise your left hand and we'll stop."

Then James did the thing that had stirred battles in courtrooms and the halls of Congress. He took out a dental handpiece, with its burred bit. As it whirred, he carefully removed the decay from Nelson's molar. Then he placed a filling in the elder's tooth.

When James decided to become a DHAT, there was no place in the United States for him to train. He and the other seven of the first Alaskan DHATs were sent by their tribes to New Zealand to learn their skills. The tribes were within their rights to set up the DHAT program, the Alaska state attorney general decided in 2005. Though state and federal dental groups opposed dental therapists, federal laws relating to the provision of Indian health care trumped the state dental practice act, the attorney general said.

Dental groups sued anyway. They sought support in the court of public opinion as well. One full-page advertisement placed by the Alaska Dental Society featured a snarling bear: "2nd class dental care for Alaska Natives deserves a ferocious reaction," read the headline over the ad. "No Alaskan should face irreversible dental surgery by an unlicensed dental therapist with no dental degree."[13]

When James completed his training, he returned to Alaska to begin his work, even as the lawsuit by the ADA and the state dental society naming him and the other DHATs continued to threaten to shut down the program. In 2007, the case was settled. The claims of the dental groups against the Alaska Native Tribal Health Consortium were dismissed by the state Superior Court, allowing the DHATs to continue to work legally in tribal areas. James was licensed through the federal Indian Health and Welfare Act's Community Health Aide Program, an initiative that got started in the 1950s as an emergency response to a tuberculosis epidemic that was devastating Alaskan tribal villages. With professional medical care out of reach, village residents were singled out for the training they needed to provide lifesaving care and medication to their neighbors.[14]

Community health aides had managed to dispense other basic health care services in hundreds of villages across Alaska, but they lacked the training to address the epidemic of dental problems. "Although village clinics provide essential medical care, in many instances villagers must travel hundreds of miles by bush plane or boat to obtain dental care," reported researchers. They estimated that well over half the children had untreated tooth decay and that gum disease was plaguing many elders.[15]

Since James received his training, a focused two-year training program for DHATs has been established in Alaska. The students learn to provide basic restorative procedures as well as preventive care and community education about oral health. They also serve an additional four hundred hours as preceptors to the dentists who oversee their work, often remotely, reviewing x-rays and patient records via computer and discussing cases by phone or e-mail.

When the elder's filling was done, James bathed the patient's teeth and gums with an iodine solution to fight the decay process. He followed up with a fluoride rinse to help strengthen the enamel. "I'll try to save the teeth I have left," said the elder, softly. "I'm seventy. I've got maybe ten more years."

Maybe much longer, James suggested with a smile. "My grandma lived to be ninety-five, or ninety-seven." He shrugged and chuckled. No one knew exactly how old his grandma was. After he finished, the young Tlingit and the elder lingered in the doorway of the clinic, placing one another in the ancient tribal order, using the names of the clans that have helped define the collective identity of their people, that have guided their potlatches and rituals for generations.

"I'm Big Eagle Nest House," said Nelson. James said he was from Cohoe House.

"Do you participate in the dance festival?" asked Nelson.

"I dance with the Noow Tlein Dancers," answered James, naming a prestigious group performing in the big Sealaska biannual celebration in Juneau.

As he was leaving the clinic, the elder was smiling. "If you have any trouble, you let us know," James told him. "We will be here 'til Friday." On Friday, he and his assistant would take the float-plane back to Sitka. They would return to the clinic in Angoon for another week next month.

Alaska is such a unique place. Maybe the new model needed to take shape in a place like Alaska, suggested Kenneth Bolin, a Texas dentist, sitting in the Tundra Restaurant in Bethel, population six thousand five hundred, the largest community in western Alaska, four hundred miles from Anchorage, forty miles from the Bering Sea, reachable only by air or water.

Private practice dental care "does not reward prevention," Bolin mused. There is no incentive for dentists to locate in poor communities "because there is no business model," he observed. But in Alaska's tribal communities, unlike in many other poor places, the care is paid for with Indian Health Service funds and provided in tribal clinics. "Here, because care is more centrally provided, there is a payment mechanism to pay for these folks to do prevention," said Bolin, who was in Bethel to teach second-year DHATs working in the local clinic. "There is not in the private sector."

In recent years, Alaska Native and American Indian communities have gained increasing power to shape and pay for their own health initiatives, based upon their own perception of need, to take back their own health, their own teeth. Alaska Natives have struggled for and won a measure of federal recognition of their claims on their ancestral world. Most Native Alaskans have remained on their traditional lands and do not live on reservations. The Alaska Native Claims Settlement Act, signed into law in 1971, gave title to over 40 million acres of land to be divided among the people of about 220 Native villages and twelve regions within the state. Village and regional corporations were established to select the lands and manage the millions of dollars in payments and oil revenues received through the settlement.[16]

Life has remained very hard. Together with American Indians in other parts of the country, Alaska Natives constitute America's poorest ethnic group. About half are low-income and one-third live below the federal poverty line. Some progress has been made in recent years. But the familiar burdens of poverty are widespread: low high school graduation rates, high levels of alcoholism and other addiction, obesity, depression, diabetes—and rampant tooth decay.[17]

There is a small airport in Bethel and a general store selling everything from snow machines to milk at $9 a gallon, to animal pelts to skinning knives to bear bells, to fishing gear to household staples. The town also has a "huffing" clinic to serve people addicted to gasoline fumes and other inhalants, a domestic violence shelter, and a Yup'ik immersion school. Bethel is a delta town, a transportation and commercial center for southwestern Alaska. Out in the bush, out in the river villages, small wooden houses stand on stilts above the permafrost. Villages, such as Kwethluk, are not linked to Bethel by any road. In the winter, the trip is usually made by driving upon the frozen surface of the Kuskokwim River, past the skeletons of the summer fish camps strung along the icy riverbanks and a car hopelessly stranded in the ice. And a dog sled, speeding lightly, silently along.

There is a regional hospital in Bethel where people from the villages come for health care. The operating room has seen a steady stream of children requiring drastic reconstructive dental surgery. "There are four hundred children born to mothers on the delta. Each year we treat two hundred in the operating room for full mouth rehabilitation," said dentist Edwin Allgair, who was seated in a tiny cubicle, overseeing Bethel's busy fourteen-chair dental clinic. "Half the children born here are going to have severe early childhood caries. They will have to be put to sleep to be treated."

Beyond Allgair's desk, second-year DHATs were caring for patients. And from his computer and his telephone, he was supervising graduate DHATs working in places like Holy Cross, more than one hundred miles away. The clinic waiting room was crowded with patients, some who had come from Bethel and some who had made long journeys in from the villages, in need and in pain. Those in the worst shape would be seen first, he said.

"If you have a chipped tooth, you will wait while people with swollen faces and abscesses get taken care of," Allgair explained. The triage system could not reward people who sought timely care. It tended more toward crisis management, he said with a touch of weariness. "If we give an appointment to everyone, we are booked out ten months into the future."

But making appointments that far in the future did not work in a place with the inherent climate, travel, and poverty problems faced by Alaska Natives. Accepting appointments for only one or two days at a time did not work either, though. Patients would get their emergency needs met, but nothing else. "They weren't getting a treatment plan. They couldn't get follow-up care," Allgair said. Anyone in the market for a regular dental exam had to call and call, and often wait for months. Even with the slow addition of DHATs, the system was making up for years of lack.

Dental disease had the community in its grips. Allgair spoke of caries like any other epidemic, in biological terms. "The community has such a high bacterial load. With the little care available, it doesn't really lower the total bacterial exposure," Allgair said. The traditional Alaska Native custom of prechewing foods for babies, intended to nurture them, was spreading the disease even faster. "The kids are blessed with high loads of bacteria. It's not just a dental issue. High otitis media—with the kid swallowing pus all day it's not hard to see why he gets an earache. It's the same bacteria. *Strep mutans*."

Allgair acknowledged that for many Alaska Natives, dental disease, however grave, had long been overshadowed by the other problems weighing on people living in poverty, living through long winters, in isolation, in seasons of darkness, in communities plagued by alcoholism and depression. Some of these factors could be missed by a dentist. "We're dentists. We are focused on teeth."

But the hardships shape behavior that impacts oral health. Mothers and grandmothers sometimes dose babies with nicotine, or put soda in their bottles to keep them quiet, Allgair said. He said he learned to explore the social conditions driving the epidemic here by reminding himself to "keep asking why."

"Why do you put soda pop in his bottle?"

"To keep him quiet."

"Why is it important to keep him quiet?"

"Because if he cries when his uncles come in, they'll beat him." This was what a mother told him. He thought about it afterward.

"Being quiet has a higher survival value than having perfect teeth."

The mother had gone to the trouble of bundling the child up, bringing the child and a sibling on a plane from the village to the clinic in Bethel for a checkup. What could he say? "Thanks for bringing him, Mom. Here is some fluoride. Here are some health care tips. See if you can dilute the stuff in the bottle."

Allgair said he believed improving access to dental care in more villages would make a difference. "She is doing everything she can. If the therapist were there in the village, these are the parents who would be taking advantage of the care."

In Anchorage, in a clean, well-lit classroom with a row of lockers and desks and a window overlooking the Chugach Mountains, Mary Williard, a slender auburn-haired dentist, was teaching a half dozen first-year DHATs in her quiet way. The students started their studies just a few days before.

Williard was moving through a lesson about oral cancer at a brisk pace. "You are looking for lumps, bumps, swelling, color changes, texture changes. In these two years you are gonna know what normal looks like. You'll know normal really well."

The students looked pretty much like college students anywhere, but one was the mother of five. They had come from all over Alaska, far out on the Aleutian Island chain, the tundra, a village near the Arctic Circle. Some struggled with loneliness and homesickness. But they knew they would make a good living when they went back. They would also be different people.

"First we look. Then we touch. Palpate," Williard coached. The students got their mirrors from their lockers and practiced examining themselves. Feeling their own faces. "It's a nice, slow, firm deep pressure. Not hurting yourself, but feeling down to the bony structure. Controlled, slow movement. Coming up underneath the mandible."

Then Williard spoke to them about beginning to think of themselves as healers. Maintaining their own hands, for example, the hands they would use in their work. "There are a lot of changes in what you do, how you care for yourself personally to become a dental professional," she told them. "You are going to be pressing your fingers into people's skin." Long sharp nails or rough nails could hurt the patients, she warned. "In dental school, you cut your nails every Friday night. If you cut yourself you will be healed by Monday."

She went to dental school in Ohio. Coming to Alaska was doing something she believed in. She was no stranger to controversy. "Pull that lip out. Look, then palpate. Going to the upper lip. Pull it out far enough so you can see the depths of that tissue. The buccal vestibule up there. We look at the buccal mucosa. Then palpate. Pull the tongue out and feel it. Again, the tongue is soft and mooshy. It should have no hard lumps and bumps."

There was excitement among the students as they were allowed to put on their dark blue scrubs for the first time. They learned about infection control in the clinic, spraying and wiping down the chairs and all the other equipment. Then, shyly at first, they put on gloves and paired up to practice giving one another oral exams. They crossed that intimate boundary into that mysterious world—the mouth of another.

9

Color Lines

IN AMERICA, ACCESS TO HEALTH CARE HAS ALWAYS BEEN DIVIDED along racial lines. For many black and Hispanic Americans, gaining access to the system that dispenses dental care continues to pose formidable challenges.

Thanks to factors including water fluoridation and preventive care, tooth decay has decreased in modern times. But the predictions in the early 1980s that the disease called dental caries was near extinction turned out to be premature. Millions of Americans continue to suffer from tooth decay. And untreated decay, with its pain, disfigurement, and loss of function, inflicts a particularly heavy burden upon black and Hispanic children and adults.

Today, nearly one-quarter of preschool-aged American children have decay in their baby teeth, according to preliminary findings from the most recent National Health and Nutrition Examination Survey (NHANES), an enormous and ongoing federal health surveillance project. The disease is far more widespread in minority children.

While roughly one-third (31 percent) of white toddlers and primary school–aged children (aged two to eight) have decayed teeth, the disease afflicts closer to half of black and Hispanic children (44 percent of black children and 46 percent of Hispanic children). And minority children are twice as likely as white children to go without treatment for the decay, NHANES found.

By the time Americans reach adulthood, decay is almost universal. But access to treatment is not. An estimated 91 percent of working-age Americans have dental caries. While decay is about as common among minorities as whites, minorities are far less likely to get care for their decay. Less than a quarter of white Americans have untreated decay, while more than a third of Hispanic and more than 40 percent of black working-age adults have untreated decay, federal data reveal. Black elders are more likely to have lost all their teeth than white elders.[1]

In many parts of the country, health care, including dental care, was strictly segregated until the 1960s. Some Americans can still remember the segregated health care system in its least subtle form.

Physician David Satcher can remember. As surgeon general, he issued the groundbreaking *Oral Health in America* report in 2000. He has served as a leading advocate for addressing the racial disparities in dental care—and for integrating dental care into the larger health care system. As he has said over and over, "Oral health is integral to general health."

Satcher was born in 1941 and grew up on a farm outside Anniston, Alabama. The health care system that served the white residents of the community was closed to him and his black family.

"The hospital was segregated and for a long time it didn't admit blacks at all," he recalled in an interview. As a toddler, his life was nearly claimed by a case of whooping cough that was complicated by pneumonia. "I almost died at the age of two," he said. His mother performed mouth-to-mouth breathing to keep him alive, he said. "I owe a lot to my mother who basically at times breathed for me. She stayed up night after night."

The dental system was also segregated, Satcher recalled. Routine dental care was not known to the poor family. He was taken to Anniston's black dentist only once as a child. "I remember having an extreme toothache—having to get a tooth pulled."

The first dental checkup Satcher received occurred when he was going off to college in Atlanta. He graduated from Morehouse in 1963. It was only after Satcher left home that things began to slowly change in his state. In 1964, Title VI of the Civil Rights Act outlawed separate accommodations, including separate waiting rooms for medical and dental services. Racial signs were removed from clinic and hospital waiting rooms, entrances, drinking fountains, and restrooms.

But the old habits lingered in Alabama and elsewhere, a team of federal inspectors reported in 1966. "Some of the clinics which had achieved physical desegregation had failed to eliminate procedures which resulted in Negro and white clients being treated on different days. In Tuscaloosa, for example, where the county health department had eliminated the designation of immunization clinics as 'white' and 'colored,' Negroes continued to visit the clinic on 'their Tuesday,' the health officer reported."

During the years of segregation, dental care had been offered only to white residents of Selma through the Dallas County health program, the survey authors noted. Then early in the summer of 1965, "a Negro youngster went to the Dallas County Health Center in Selma, Alabama, and asked for someone to look at his teeth. An attendant gave him an appointment and when he returned a few days later, a dentist repaired his teeth. This marked the first time a Negro had been cared for at the Dallas County Dental Clinic," they wrote. "A few days later, several Negro children sought dental care at the clinic. At this point the county health officer adopted a new procedure for treating children and announced that dental care would be provided to school children on a school-by-school basis.

"Appointments were made through the schools and children were treated in their schools rather than at the clinic. Although

Negro children were included in the county dental program for the first time, the new procedure assured that the treatment would be largely on a segregated basis."[2]

Satcher has carried the record of separate and unequal dentistry in his own teeth. "I have had all kinds of dental problems," said Satcher. "I've paid the price for not getting oral health care as a child."

His report continues to be regarded as a clarion call for better dental care, particularly for the poor, the uninsured, the under-insured, and minority patients unreached by the current system. Satcher said he has been encouraged by the expansion of dental benefits to children through the Patient Protection and Affordable Care Act. He has found hope in signs of growing awareness of the importance of maintaining oral health as part of overall health; in the increasing willingness of medical professionals to provide pre-ventive fluoride treatments to children in their offices; and in the work of dental hygienists and dental therapists to bring care to poor and isolated schools and communities. "I think midlevel providers are important because they offer a service that is needed, and they offer services that are otherwise unavailable."

But Satcher said he remains frustrated with the nation's persistent oral health disparities. Caries is a multifactorial disease. Bacteria and diet play major roles in tooth decay. So do home hygiene hab-its and access to professional care. The complexities of poverty, with its social, emotional, and economic burdens, put millions of Americans, including a disproportionate number of minorities, at additional risk of decay.

The American health care system still needs to recognize and respond to this reality, said Satcher. The toll of tooth decay and other oral diseases may not end, as Satcher said, "until we have a health system that makes sure everybody has access." But, he noted, "I think universal access is still the thing America is not committed to."

Max Schoen would remember the moment for the rest of his career. He was a young dentist, just starting out in the days after World War II. He was leafing through a professional magazine when he saw the illustration. It was a design for a "model" dental office with separate waiting rooms for black and white patients. He looked at the design and thought about the patients waiting separately for the dentist, unseen by one another, divided by walls. He thought about the dentist with his separate waiting rooms for white patients and black patients. He wondered if the dentist used separate instruments for the white patients and the black patients. Then he thought about the white dentists who did not see black patients at all.[3]

He grew up in a Jewish family in Brooklyn during the Great Depression. His father, a physician, died of a heart attack when Max was still young.[4] Schoen went to dental school in California. He served in World War II. Now he was back and his country troubled him. He did not keep that fact a secret.

When Schoen was twenty-nine years old, he earned the distinction of being the first dentist to be called before the House Committee on Un-American Activities. It was on the morning of Friday, September 21, 1951, that Schoen arrived at the Federal Building in Los Angeles. He was sworn in and faced the congressional panel bent upon unearthing Communist Party activities in the city of Los Angeles and in the motion picture industry. Schoen was asked if he had distributed Communist Party literature at a meeting at a Unitarian Church. He was asked about his rumored work with the Hollywood West Side chapter of the Civil Rights Congress (CRC). The CRC greatly troubled the House Un-American Activities Committee. Members of the CRC worked for the right of Southern workers to unionize and defended blacks facing death sentences in high-profile cases.

The group had also taken up the cause of the Australian-born Harry Bridges, the president of the International Longshoremen's and Warehousemen's Union.[5] While many labor unions were racially segregated, the longshoremen were fully integrated at Bridges's insistence. Discrimination is "the weapon of the boss," Bridges said. He insisted on solidarity and coast-wide contracts that covered workers in ports from San Diego to Bellingham, Washington. When workers at one port struck, they all struck.

"A strike is a small revolution," Bridges would say.[6] Federal Bureau of Investigation chief J. Edgar Hoover was eager to have Bridges deported as a communist.

Schoen declined to answer the questions about the meeting at the Unitarian Church, or the work with the Civil Rights Congress. He cited the Fifth Amendment. Then committee member Clyde Doyle, a California congressman, asked the young dentist if he had been to Russia or any other Soviet country. Schoen said no. He had served in the Pacific during the war.

"This committee is assigned to investigate subversive people and propaganda," said Doyle. "We are investigating the Communist Party, for instance, of which we believe you are a member. How shall we go at it?"

Schoen suggested that if the committee was interested in investigating subversive activity, it should look into the continued existence of poll taxes that prevented Negroes and poor whites from voting in the South, as well as the "recent riots which took place in Cicero, Illinois, where a young Negro couple was by force and violence prohibited—or they were not able to occupy—an apartment which they had rented. This I believe to be an extreme subversion of the Constitution of the United States."

Doyle responded by bringing the inquiry back to communism. "I have deliberately given you a chance to give recommendations to this committee, and I am glad to see you are anxious to protect the rights of the minority, in other words, the Negroes and the Jewish people and the poor whites. But of course, that is the communist line, to appeal to that group, and we understand that. Now give us your thought on investigating the Communist Party, please."

Schoen, as he had done before, declined to answer. "This question relates to an organization which has appeared on your list and is considered subversive by this committee; therefore I refuse to answer on the basis of the Fifth Amendment."

"You," noted Doyle, "are not a very good sport, are you?"

"I don't think this is a sporting situation, actually," said Schoen.

Pennsylvania congressman Francis E. Walter, addressing Schoen as "Young Man," tried a gentler approach. He asked what Schoen was afraid of, why he declined to answer their questions if he had nothing to hide. "Nobody is on trial for anything. We are seeking information." Then Doyle urged the dentist to come to his senses. "I pray to God that you get on your knees and see if you can't clean up some of your thinking and get out of that subversive outfit and get over to the American line."

Michigan congressman Charles Potter asked Schoen how much he had earned the previous year. Schoen said he was a bad businessman but estimated he had probably earned $7,000.

"Under our form of government you have been able to meet a normal success in a very honored profession," Potter told him. "And you are part of an organization that would overthrow the very thing that has made you a successful man and given you an opportunity to enjoy a way of life that you otherwise wouldn't have enjoyed if you were part of a system behind the iron curtain. I say, Doctor, that you are a very ungrateful person and a very dangerous man."

The subcommittee chair, Congressman John S. Wood of Georgia, accused Schoen of taking shelter behind the very Constitution he sought to destroy.[7]

Then they let Schoen go back to his work. His mission turned out to be larger than running a private dental practice. Schoen would come to describe it as "actively espousing health care for all regardless of the ability to pay."[8] To further this goal, he committed a radical act. He invented dental insurance.

Efforts in Washington to amend the Social Security Act and to create a national system of health benefits had gotten under way in the mid-1930s, under President Franklin Delano Roosevelt. Such steps toward "state medicine" had been opposed by organized medicine and dentistry. After World War II, as fears about communism and socialism continued to flare, the prospects for national health care seemed dim. That was when the idea of private health insurance began taking root. Across the country, private employers began to offer medical coverage as a fringe benefit to attract and keep good workers. Dental benefits were not part of those early plans.

A couple of years after his appearance before the House Committee on Un-American Activities, Schoen learned that Harry Bridges's longshoremen's union was exploring the idea of offering dental benefits to the members of its West Coast chapter. The union had sought guidance from the University of California Los Angeles Institute of Industrial Relations. Schoen asked to be invited to the meetings.[9] The union had $750,000 in its trust fund to spend on the dental project. Leaders asked Schoen to figure out how far the money would go toward providing dental care. Schoen studied the costs and benefits for weeks. The challenges inherent in the design of efficient and cost-contained programs to serve groups of patients of all incomes, of all races, would engage him for the rest of his career.

Schoen concluded the longshoremen had enough money in their trust fund to offer comprehensive benefits to every eligible union child up to the age of fifteen. He suspected the answer would disappoint the longshoremen, that they would abandon the idea of the dental benefit plan. After all, some of them did not have children and the children of others were too old to be eligible.

"Much to my surprise, they thought it was an excellent idea both from a health and a political standpoint," Schoen noted. The union approved the plan. The plan called for a prepaid group practice in the Los Angeles harbor area that would provide the services. No such thing existed, so Schoen set one up—it was a pilot group practice, a racially integrated team of dentists who joined him in a salaried partnership. Schoen found a sympathetic architect and contractor to help remodel a store building into a ten-chair dental office in Harbor City. Another pilot group practice was established to serve union families in the San Francisco Bay area. In the pilot year, nearly 10,860 children were enrolled.

The providers in the group, including a range of dental specialists, hygienists, and assistants, all worked for salaries. The group practice offered care in return for a fixed, capitated payment for each beneficiary each month. The fee was paid by the union. The local leaders of organized dentistry were less than pleased by his model. One dentist who applied for a job with the group practice seemed so perfectly suited and eager to help that Schoen and his wife worried a little. "Bea and I were convinced he was a spy from either the dental association or the government," Schoen recalled. Schoen hired him anyway and he turned out to be sincere.

While he was working, a steady drumbeat of warnings sounded from the pages of the *Journal of the Southern California State Dental Association*. Subversive forces were bent upon destroying the profession, editors wrote. "We in the United States, suffer from a rash of Pale Pinks, Parlor Pinks on up through to Crimsons," noted a typical editorial. "Our particular interest here is the effects which are threatening our livelihoods in the practice of dentistry."[10]

Schoen's experiments with fee schedules and team approaches and salaried group practices were seen as deeply threatening by many of the dental leaders. His plans for extending care to underserved communities aroused suspicion. His ideas turned traditional fee-for-service private practice dental care on its head. The members of Schoen's group practice team worked for the same capitated rate whether the patients needed complicated restorations or routine hygiene care. Schoen calculated the rates the members would be paid using equations that took into account the cost of the providers' time and the projected needs of the populations of patients to be covered. Schoen hoped his model would shift the incentives away from restoring diseased teeth and toward disease prevention, recalled James Freed, a longtime colleague, sitting at the long, well-scrubbed dining table in his Los Angeles home.

"Max wanted to change dental practice. And his idea of capitation versus fee-for-service was that it would lead to a change in the way dentistry was practiced that would benefit the public's health," said Freed. The pilot was successful, Freed added. "They were really taking care of people. It was quality care."

The innovations drew the interest of federal health officials focused on finding ways to stretch health care dollars to meet wider needs. "In the group practice plans, services were provided by a limited number of dentists and dental specialists operating in a group setting. As the experiment progressed, the weaknesses and strength of the various plans began to reveal themselves and, through experimentation and improvisation, solutions and techniques evolved," concluded the authors of a government report on the project in its early years.[11]

At the same time, Schoen's work continued to attract the intense ire of conservative dental leaders in the state. "They hated his guts. They called him a communist," recalled Freed.

Schoen went on refining his model. Building upon Public Health Service programs in Woonsocket, Rhode Island, and Richmond, Virginia, Schoen and colleagues developed dental plans aimed at delivering efficient and cost-effective care to farmworkers, schools, state governments, and unions. After the passage of the Medicaid law in 1965, Schoen organized a pilot dental program to serve families at a neighborhood health center in Los Angeles.

He hoped to find an approach to getting care to the poor that was free of stigma. "The tried and true methods, even with variations, simply do not provide 'mainstream' dental care to the lower strata of our urban population," Schoen observed. He believed a group practice with a good reputation could attract patients from all races and classes. "A poverty patient cared for in a group practice environment can be treated in the same manner as anyone else," he wrote.[12]

The Los Angeles program, like his other group practice projects, was based not upon the fee-for-service model widely used in private practice dentistry, but upon prepaid services provided to the participating families at a fixed rate, in this case, $16.67 per month.

The costs were paid by Medicaid and nonprofit programs. As with his other programs, the dentists and other staff members in the group worked for salaries.

"Radical new approaches are needed to set the stage for a solution," Schoen told colleagues, members of the dental health section of the American Public Health Association who had gathered for a conference in 1969.[13] To make the capitated group practice system work, patients needed to stay with the practice long enough so that their initial need for expensive restorative care would be met and be replaced over time by less expensive preventive and maintenance care.

It was too radical for some of Schoen's fellow alumni at the University of Southern California (USC), though. The group practices amounted to "closed panels" that drew patients away from nonparticipating dentists, they contended. "Schoen's close identification with the closed panel mode of dental practice was a lightning rod to dental practice traditionalists in Southern California," wrote Clifton O. Dummett, a sympathetic minority faculty member at the University of Southern California dental school.[14]

Anger rose among the alumni when rumors surfaced that the school's dean, John Ingle, planned to appoint Schoen to the faculty as a professor of community dentistry and put him in charge of a program aimed at teaching students to run a model group practice that would operate on a capitated fee schedule. "Dr. Max Schoen is considered a 'red flag' to the faculty and alumni," wrote one member, Robert West, in the alumni association's newspaper, *Trodent*. "I'm just an old, naïve solo practitioner who still believes in the free enterprise system and freedom of choice."[15]

In the same issue, the president of the dental school's alumni association, Nickolas Chester, announced that the alumni association was prepared to withdraw its "support in a monetary and moral way" from the school if the plan went forward. "It is my hope that this controversial matter may be resolved at an early date," Chester wrote.[16] Not long afterward, Ingle, who had served as dean for eight years, announced he was resigning to become a senior staff officer at the Institute of Medicine in Washington, D.C. The dean told the school newspaper his departure was "unrelated to the controversy."[17]

Schoen served for a year as a part-time professor of community dentistry at USC.

Then he went east for a stint teaching dentistry at the State University of New York at Stony Brook. He returned to California in 1976, where he taught public health and preventive dentistry at the University of California in Los Angeles until he retired in 1987.

Over the years, as prepaid dental benefits became increasingly commercialized, Schoen continued to grapple with the challenges of public and private dental insurance models. He recognized that the capitated payment system, if abused, could reward undertreatment. He organized teams of quality-control reviewers to visit providers and study patient records to determine whether patients were receiving adequate care.

Not every provider measured up. State experiments with capitated Medicaid dental programs began offering troubling examples of patients going without care. Provider shortages also plagued Medicaid. As the program grew, Schoen worked to raise reimbursement rates so more providers would participate in the program. Yet when rates were raised, the biggest beneficiaries sometimes turned out to be "Medicaid mills"—practices designed to maximize profits rather than to serve the best interests of patients, a problem that persists.

"It was just a lifelong struggle," Freed recalled with a melancholy laugh. Still, Schoen continued his work. "I think he felt we could still do it right. There was still a chance."

As he neared retirement, Schoen looked back on his career with hope. "I believe we proved anew, with a number of different plans for both children and adults, that it was perfectly possible and economically feasible to get almost all of any given population, regardless of socioeconomic status, to make regular use of preventive and therapeutic dental services."

He continued to favor industrial and community-based models. He continued to favor the expanded use of hygienists and other auxiliaries to provide more care at lower cost. He never blamed the poor for failing to find their way to care: "Low use is not the victim's fault, but rather, that of society."[18] He described the enduring tension between the private interests of his profession and the wider dental needs of Americans as "almost the ultimate clash between dentists' long term liberty and the public's equity."[19]

And he reflected back upon the day long ago when, as a young dentist, he paused to ponder the plan for the segregated "model" clinic in the pages of the trade magazine. Years had passed since the signing of the Civil Rights Act. The walls between the black and white waiting rooms no longer appeared in the designs. Still, racial disparities in care, and in oral health, persisted:

> Today, such flagrant discrimination is both outlawed and considered unethical. However it has continued in many subtle ways. This limitation is easily accomplished by refusing to accept the fee schedules. This practice is not racial discrimination as such since Medicaid covers all racial groups and the majority of Medicaid patients are white. It is however, cultural discrimination. I have heard many dentists say that they do not like to treat "those kinds of people," although the reasons they give are ostensibly financial.[20]

Schoen denounced the cosmetic dentistry boom; he never gave up hoping for universal health care. He decried what he described as America's "non-system of private practice" dentistry. But those could have been brave words, his colleague Freed suggested. "Somebody said, 'If you don't think there is a system then just try to change it,'" noted Freed. "That's what Max did."

Schoen died on December 9, 1994, in Los Angeles, of a heart attack. At his memorial service, Freed spoke, recalling a story from mystical Judaism.

"The world is supported by thirty-six just people," Freed said. "And nobody knows who they are. But the world depends on them. It depends on these thirty-six people. And when one of them dies, somebody has to replace him. I said Max was one. Somebody has to replace Max.'"

Group dental practices are more common than they once were. But unlike physicians, the majority of dentists still own their practices and are sole proprietors.[21] "Dentistry has remained a 'cottage industry,' which has fought incorporation into larger systems of managed care and capitated payments that have permeated medical groups," observed dental workforce experts Elizabeth Mertz and Edward O'Neill in *Health Affairs*.[22]

Yet the third-party payment system Schoen pioneered has served as a democratizing agent, bringing quality-control measures and fee schedules to dentistry and making services more accessible to millions. Today, roughly two-thirds of Americans have some kind of dental coverage. In the marketplace for dental care, they enjoy an advantage over the one-third of Americans who have no coverage of any kind.

"Americans with dental benefits are more likely to go to the dentist, take their children to the dentist, receive restorative care and experience greater overall health," reported the National Association of Dental Plans, a trade group, which represents dental insurers, in 2015.[23] Science has largely agreed. The Institute of Medicine has found "strong evidence that dental coverage is positively tied to access to and use of oral health care." Those who lack benefits are more likely to belong to minority groups.

Plans vary widely. Private dental coverage provided as part of workplace benefit packages covered roughly 155 million Americans at the end of 2014. More than 50 million received dental benefits through public programs, including Medicaid and the Children's Health Insurance Program (CHIP) for the children of the working poor. Not all benefits have proven to be equally useful in the marketplace for dental services. Though progress in closing the gap has been made in very recent years in some states, beneficiaries of Medicaid and the Children's Health Insurance Program—including many minority children—remain more likely to go without the care they need than their privately insured counterparts. "At least in dental markets where well-insured or private-pay patients are common, Medicaid coverage alone will be insufficient to remove race-based disparities in dental utilization," concluded the authors of one major study of racial disparities in dental coverage and dental care.[24]

At the end of 2014, an estimated one-third of Americans lacked dental benefits of any kind. The group included millions of elderly Medicare beneficiaries. It also included nearly 68 million Americans under the age of sixty-five—more than twice the 32 million medically uninsured Americans of that age group, according to the National Association of Dental Plans. People without dental coverage of any kind are only half as likely to visit a dentist as people with private benefits, according to the American Dental Association.[25]

While dental and medical benefits are almost always sold separately, people who lack medical insurance have been typically more likely to lack dental insurance. But the lack of health insurance that long impacted minorities was showing some signs of being addressed under the Patient Protection and Affordable Care Act, early studies indicated. "In 2013, the year before most of the law's provisions for subsidized insurance took effect, non-elderly blacks were 47 percent more likely than whites to be uninsured. For American Indians, that figure was 93 percent; for Hispanics, 120 percent."[26] Those disparities have narrowed. Still, the coverage gap that leaves one-third of Americans without dental benefits has proven more complicated to bridge.

The health insurance marketplaces established under the 2010 health care reform law were required to offer children's dental benefits. But parents were not required to buy them. Offering adult dental coverage was not required by the law. In spite of those factors, the American Dental Association predicted that through the expansion of Medicaid and the Children's Health Insurance Program, and through the sale of private benefits under health care reform, nearly 9 million children could receive some kind of dental insurance by 2018. Adults, particularly young working adults, were purchasing dental benefits on state exchanges even though they were not required to, the ADA found.

"The Affordable Care Act has the potential to alter dental benefits coverage patterns," the authors of an ADA study concluded in 2015.[27] For patients, any kind of coverage can help defray the expense of services. Still, the cost of dental care represents a major barrier to millions. "According to national surveys, 42 percent of adults with tooth or mouth problems did not see a dentist in 2008 because they did not have dental insurance or could not afford the out-of-pocket payments," the Government Accountability Office (GAO) reported to Congress in 2013. "In 2011, 4 million children did not obtain needed dental care because their families could not afford it."

The out-of-pocket costs have continued to rise, the GAO found. Between 1996 and 2010, the annual out-of-pocket cost of dental care increased 21 percent, from $242 to $294 for people with private dental insurance. For those without dental coverage, the cost of care rose 32 percent. The average person without dental insurance paid $392 out-of-pocket for care in 1996. In 2010, the out-of-pocket cost stood at $518.[28]

The lack of dental coverage and the rising cost of care continue to contribute to disparities in oral health. "The bottom line is that as a nation we aren't where we want to be in ensuring that Americans have access to affordable dental care and have good oral health," said GAO official Katherine Iritani in an online discussion of the findings. "The federal government has done a lot in recent years to bring attention to access issues, particularly for the low-income children that are served by Medicaid and Children's Health Insurance Program. But more needs to be done. Access barriers are complex and more needs to be done."

—∽—

Dentistry remains an overwhelmingly white occupation. There have never been enough minority dentists. That problem has also contributed to racial disparities in care. While Robert Tanner Freeman became the first African American to receive a dental degree, from Harvard University's School of Dental Medicine in 1869, the doors of most American dental schools and dental societies would, for nearly a century, remain largely closed to blacks. Most of America's first formally trained black dentists attended two schools that were opened in the late nineteenth century by two historically black colleges—the Howard University College of Dentistry in Washington, D.C., and the Meharry Medical College School of Dentistry in Nashville.

But minority dentists remained rare and, partly as a result, dental care remained severely limited in many communities. In 1930, there were nearly 12 million blacks living in America, and fewer than two thousand black dentists.[29] The resulting shortage of care attracted the attention of Swedish economist Gunnar Myrdal in the early twentieth century.

"Large numbers of Negro patients turn to white dentists, in spite of the fact that, in the South at least, they are treated on a segregated basis, with separate instruments, in a separate chair," Myrdal wrote in *An American Dilemma*, a landmark study of 1930s race relations in America.[30] America's segregated dental system was just part of a larger and more complex divide that exacted an enormous human toll. "Discrimination increases Negro sickness and death both directly and indirectly and manifests itself both consciously and unconsciously," Myrdal wrote.

Black dentists, who were not welcome in many white dental associations, established their own professional organization in 1913. About thirty charter members, from Maryland, the District of Columbia, and Virginia gathered on a July day at a shoreline hotel in Buckroe Beach, Virginia, for the first meeting. In ensuing years, minority dentists from other states joined them. The group grew to become the National Dental Association.

In the Southern states, dental societies remained segregated long after groups for physicians, nurses, and pharmacists began accepting black members. "All available information indicates that at the present time not one state or county dental society is open to Negro dentists," wrote Howard University physician and researcher Paul B. Cornely in 1956. "Since Negro nurses and pharmacists are able to join their professional societies without going through their local units, and the doors have been opened to Negro physicians, the Negro dentist in the South remains the only member of a major health profession who is still barred from even joining his national organization, the American Dental Association."[31]

In 1958, the National Dental Association began pressing the American Dental Association to make state dental societies drop racially restrictive membership provisions.[32] Four years later, at its 1962 meeting in Miami, the ADA moved to strip voting powers from a dozen state societies who continued to refuse to admit black dentists as members. The State of Maryland Dental Society was one of the twelve to face ouster. The Maryland group agreed to change its practices.

Still, black dentists remained outside the state system in important ways. It was not until 1968 that a black dental surgeon became affiliated with the staff of a metropolitan general hospital in Maryland.[33] And it was not until 1968 that the University of Maryland dental school appointed its first black faculty member, Harvey Webb Jr.

In the 1970s, Webb wrote about the impact of the shortage of minority dentists upon the oral health of the nation. "A great disparity in the dentists to population ratio exists between whites and Blacks. There is one white dentist for less than 1,900 white patients, while one Black dentist must serve an average of 12,000 Black patients." The Maryland Board of Dental Examiners was one of thirty state agencies that remained all white in 1970, a report by the state commission on human relations found.[34]

Dental schools at Howard University and Meharry Medical College continued to account for the majority of black dental school enrollment until the 1970s, Webb observed. The dental school at the University of Maryland did not graduate its first "indentifiably Black" student until 1972, Webb wrote. "Purging deep seated biases from every phase of American life, including the dental profession, will be a far more difficult task than most people realize. But that is no excuse to do nothing."[35]

Today, minority dentists remain vastly outnumbered in their profession and in their communities. While more than 12 percent of America's population is black, fewer than 4 percent of America's dentists are black. Roughly the same figures hold true for Hispanics, noted the authors of the 2011 Institute of Medicine report *Advancing Oral Health in America.*

Diversity among health professionals improves access to care in underserved and minority communities, and minority providers put patients at ease and provide culturally sensitive services. Minority dental students are more likely than their white peers to aspire to serve minority patients, the report observed.

"Among dental students graduating in 2008, 80 percent of African American students and 75 percent of Hispanic students expected at least one quarter of their patients would be from underserved racial and ethic populations; nearly 37 percent of the African American students and 27 percent of the Hispanic students expected at least half their practice would come from these populations," noted the Institute of Medicine. "In comparison, only 43.5 percent of white students expected at least one quarter of their patients to come from underserved racial and ethnic populations, and only 6.5 percent expected at least half of their practice to be comprised from these populations."[36]

On July 26, 2013, the National Dental Association (NDA) gathered at a well-appointed new resort and conference center in Prince George's County, Maryland, to celebrate the organization's hundredth anniversary. There was an air force honor guard to post the colors and a video presentation recounting the history of the NDA.

"Our legacy is one of service, education, and civil rights," the group's president, Edward H. Chapelle, told the members who packed the ballroom.

The U.S. congresswoman Donna Edwards, a Maryland Democrat and African American, welcomed the dentists. She spoke of the importance of dental care. She spoke of the death of Deamonte Driver. She spoke of a member of her own family too. "My own brother was just twenty-six," she said. "A dental abscess claimed him," she continued. "It killed him within seventy-two hours." The congresswoman urged the dentists to continue their work "so no family has to suffer what Deamonte's family suffered. So no family has to suffer what my family suffered."

A troupe of young dancers performed. Then Maya Angelou, former poet laureate of the United States, made her way slowly to the stage. Her hair was silver. She wore dark glasses. She was born in 1928. She had less than another year to live.

She told a story from her famous memoir, *I Know Why the Caged Bird Sings*. It was a story of her childhood in Arkansas, of growing up in a segregated world. It was the story of a child with two rotten teeth and a blinding toothache. She told it the way she had written it in her book: How her grandmother Annie took her to the white dentist in her little town of Stamps, Arkansas. How they climbed the back stairs and how her grandmother asked Dr. Lincoln for help.

"Annie, you know I don't treat nigra," the dentist told her grandmother.

"Doctor, this is my grandbaby. That's all she is," her grandmother said.

"I'd rather put my hand in a dog's mouth than a nigger's mouth," the dentist responded.

There was a black dentist in Texarkana, Arkansas, and that is where the little girl and her grandmother ended up going. They rode the Greyhound bus twenty-five miles and got the child's two aching teeth extracted.

Part III

A SENTINEL EVENT

10

Deamonte's World

The Driver boys were poor Medicaid children.

Untreated cavities were common among the half-million poor Medicaid children of Maryland. The pain made 8 percent of them cry, according to a study by the University of Maryland dental school. If other children suffered, they did so more quietly. Deamonte Driver did not complain about his teeth, his mother said. Maybe he felt that it was futile to complain. Maybe he just took the pain for granted.

It was Thursday, March 8, 2007, on a cold morning in an old funeral home in Washington, D.C.'s Anacostia neighborhood. The body of the twelve-year-old lay in a casket. His mother and brothers, the rest of the family, his school friends and teachers sat numbly by.

Deamonte was remembered as a child who liked helping his grandfather, a brick mason. He adopted a squat little stray dog they called Butter, who became the family pet. He drove everybody crazy with his questions and made everybody happy with his smile. He was remembered as stubborn and wise.

Now it was time to bury him.

Deamonte grew up in poverty, yet at the same time in the shadow of great wealth and power. His grandparents' red and white house trailer in Prince George's County was about a dozen miles from the United States Capitol. The state of Maryland was rich, one of the richest states in the nation. Four months before Deamonte died, in November 2006, Prince George's County had been featured in a lavish color spread in *Ebony* magazine under the headline "America's Wealthiest Black County." The story harked back to the county's tobacco plantation past. But it was dominated by images of successful African Americans enjoying their yachts, golf courses, and gated communities.

"This county embodies what we all have envisioned as the American dream," mused one county official. "We are what America was set out to be." And like the rest of America, Prince George's County was a place of inequalities, nowhere more evident than in the mouths of the poor.

The Capital Beltway cuts an arc through Prince George's County. Inside the Beltway, clustered along the border of the District of Columbia, are many of the county's most troubled communities, plagued by crime and insecurity, unemployment, failing schools. Outside the Beltway are the golf courses and gatehouses of the county's wealthy, the glamorous places illustrated in *Ebony* magazine. There is a third part of Prince George's County, too, a rural part that lies to the south, further beyond the Beltway. It is a quieter place of forests, fallow tobacco fields, quarries, and winding two-lane roads, where hand-painted signs advertise Chesapeake Bay crabs, sold by the bushel. The rural enclave of Brandywine, home to members of the Driver family back to the tobacco days, is there.

Deamonte's mother, Alyce Driver, the daughter of Franklin T. and Jane Driver, spent her early years in a home on one of those

country roads, named for the church the family attended, Gibbons
Methodist, founded in 1884 by freed slaves. Slaves by the name of
Driver are listed in old county records, stored in the state archives.
The records also show that Alyce Driver's great-grandparents
George and Sarah Driver bought ten acres of land near the Meth-
odist church for $5 in 1921 from their neighbors the Scotts. Alyce
Driver's grandfather Charles Driver inherited the land and farmed
it. He sharecropped too on other people's fields, raising tobacco,
working long, long hours.

"He'd go down the road. He had horses. Mrs. Driver and the
kids would be sitting in front of the wagon," remembered a neigh-
bor, John Brooks, aged seventy-four.

The family picked tobacco until there was no light left in the sky.
"It would be late for harvesting tobacco," Brooks recalled. "When
Charles Driver and his family rode by in their wagon Mr. Driver
would call out, 'Man! It's getting late!'"

As Brooks recalled this memory, he stood in the old Gibbons
churchyard. He gazed down the two-lane road as if he were hearing the horses' hooves, and Charles Driver's husky shout: "Man!
It's getting late!"

"He was always in a hurry," Brooks said. "It had to be done."

He paused, as if listening to the last echoes of that vanished
world. The tobacco fields were gone and the Drivers were gone
from their land. The ten acres Charles Driver farmed so devoutly,
and his son, Franklin Driver, farmed after him, were sold in 1969,
sold for $10 and taken over by a quarry. By the time Alyce Driver
was born in 1973, her family was just renting the little house on
Gibbons Church Road. The quarrying left the land in ruins, a
field of mud pits, fenced off and posted with "No Trespassing"
signs. The old wooden Methodist church, built by freed slaves,
was replaced by a sleek brick megachurch with fourteen thousand
members and restrooms of polished stone. And the little white-
frame fellowship hall where, so long ago, the Drivers and all their
neighbors ate ham and fried chicken, was crumpling down, back to
the earth. The screen door was held shut with a single wire. Inside,

a last purple choir robe hung fluttering in the shadows. The tin roof was torn open to the sky.

John Brooks still came to mow the graveyard with his tractor. He remembered the people buried there, their marriages and families and stories. He tended the oldest graves and wondered at the strange grandeur of those lives, lived as he said "just a step from slavery." He remembered Alyce Driver when she was young, before she ran away. Alyce Driver attended the local schools in Brandywine, right up to high school. The high school lay out on the main road, leaving town. She was good at spelling and dreamed of being an accountant, maybe joining the air force reserve. But her mother beat her, she said, so she left Brandywine.

And Alyce Driver's life began to trace a new course within the Beltway. Her first two sons, Deonte and Danny, were born when she was still a teenager. As her children grew, she would eke out a living at a variety of jobs: in a grocery store bakery and as a caretaker for the elderly. Sometimes she helped her father with his brick masonry. She was strong. She liked construction work. Clarence Hendrick also worked for her father. Hendrick was "an old man with a heart of gold," Alyce Driver recalled. And when she was in her early twenties, when Deonte and Danny were still preschoolers, she had a son with Clarence Hendrick.

Deamonte was born on May 14, 1994. He was premature and tiny, weighing just two pounds fourteen ounces. But Deamonte was also a fighter. "A little champ," his mother called him. There was something old about him, too, and preternaturally wise.

"That boy had been here before," she said.

Alyce Driver would go on to have two more sons, DaShawn, two years later, and Donnell, five years after DaShawn. Around them, in those years before the mortgage crisis and the Great Recession, fortunes in Prince George's County were soaring. At its best, the county seemed like a fulfillment of many people's dreams.

"Here we are 40 years after the Civil Rights Movement—and we are the first generation to assume this kind of power—it's our time," Gary S. Murray, a Prince George's County venture capitalist and developer told *Ebony* magazine in 2006. The Prince George's County celebrated in the article was a golden place of unlimited potential where "virtually every entrance into the county has been turned into a welcoming garden. . . . One roadway median near the famed D.C. Beltway has more than 300 trees, 800 shrubs and 50,000 ornamental plants."[1]

The story featured the accomplishments of county executive Jack Johnson, who popularized the phrase "Gorgeous Prince George's" and secured the finances needed to launch the $2 billion National Harbor Project—a resort and conference center lying across the Potomac River from Washington, D.C. At the time, the development was hailed as the largest hospitality industry project outside of Las Vegas. "Through smart financial investments and an increasing tax base, the county has a $50 million surplus it is using to build new schools, raise teachers' salaries and increase county services," the article reported.

While affluent county residents who commuted to government and private sector jobs enjoyed insurance coverage and a choice of medical and dental providers, poor and working poor families grew increasingly isolated and faced dwindling access to care. The county boasted a new equestrian center with stables and riding rings for horse shows. But it lacked "a primary care safety net" where poor and uninsured people could get medical or dental care, a research report by the Rand Corporation would conclude. In 2005 and 2006, the county's single federally qualified health center reached only a fraction of the county's eighty thousand uninsured adult residents. And less-educated and lower-income residents were, Rand found, "much more likely than more advantaged residents to be uninsured, to have no regular source of care, to have missed care because of cost and to have had a dental exam more than five years ago."[2]

Alyce Driver did not get dental benefits at any of her jobs. She was going without dental care. And so were her children.

When her youngest son, Donnell, was small, Alyce Driver and the rest of her boys moved in with Donnell's father for a while. They rented a house in Fairmount Heights, a tiny, historically black Prince George's County community deep inside the Beltway.

"I had a little part-time job taking care of this elderly man. He had Parkinson's. He passed away," Alyce Driver said. "Mr. Charlie died on me."

At home, there was tension, worries about money, intermittent violence. "Things didn't go well," she said. But it was difficult to leave. Rents in the county had been rising and affordable housing was dwindling. The postwar garden apartments that first served as magnets for white flight from Washington, D.C., to Prince George's County had later become homes for black families. Now they were neglected, crime-ridden places that were being razed.

In November 2005, Alyce Driver and her sons ended up in a county emergency shelter. It was not an easy time, but Alyce Driver and her sons were together in a simple, apartment-style unit. The shelter offered social services, including job and substance abuse counseling. She saw the place as a haven from the tensions and the worries about rent. And on Thanksgiving, Clarence Hendrick, still dear to her, came to visit.

Within months, though, Deamonte's father was gone, dead of cancer.

Alyce Driver acknowledged she was struggling with addiction. When the family's time ran out at the shelter, in early 2006, she went to a rehabilitation program. Her sons were split up among the extended Driver family. Her brother and sister took the two older boys. The youngest, Donnell, went back with his father. Deamonte and DaShawn went to live with their grandparents in their two-bedroom mobile home in a grove of trees near Joint Base Andrews, the military installation that quarters the presidential aircraft Air Force One.

Deamonte was curious and loved math. He could be considered behaviorally challenging. For two years, he attended the Foundation School, a therapeutic nonprofit school just outside the Beltway, in the town of Largo. He was well liked at the school, which prided itself on intensive services and success working with children, many from poor or troubled families, and helping them succeed academically.

"We have kids who are homeless and might need medication. We do a whole lot," said school director Gina James. "We often buy uniforms for the kids. It's so much for the parents even to buy clothes."

In the summer of 2006, Laurie Norris, a lawyer for the nonprofit Baltimore-based Public Justice Center, entered the lives of the Driver family. Norris was deeply familiar with the challenges facing homeless families. She had successfully defended the right of children displaced by homelessness to remain in their local schools. The Public Justice Center was conducting a series of interviews with homeless families designed to explore their experiences with the public school system. In July, Norris contacted the Drivers as part of the survey. In August, Alyce Driver called Norris back, seeking assistance with school registration.

In September, the mother called Norris again. This time she needed help with what turned out to be a much thornier problem: finding a dentist for ten-year-old DaShawn, who was suffering from pain and swelling in his mouth. Several of his teeth had become decayed and were infected. The mother said she had previously managed to find a dentist for DaShawn, but the dentist had discontinued treatments because DaShawn squirmed too much in the dental chair. The dentist had not referred her to another provider, and Alyce Driver was not sure how to find one. She had called a toll-free number in an attempt to locate another dentist who was part of the network of providers offered by DaShawn's Medicaid managed care plan, but was not successful. She became discouraged.

"She had reached the limit of her understanding and ability to navigate Maryland's complex Medicaid system," Norris said. The lawyer joined the mother in the search. Norris soon found herself lost in the daunting maze of Medicaid managed care contractors and dental subcontractors that were the designated gatekeepers and providers of dental care to Maryland's most vulnerable children. The project of finding a dentist turned out to be a major challenge for the advocate, even equipped as she was with confidence and legal training and the support of an office and staff.

Norris began her effort by confirming that DaShawn was enrolled in Maryland Medicaid's managed care plan, and that his care was provided through United Healthcare, one of the managed care organizations serving Maryland Medicaid beneficiaries. Then she called United Healthcare's customer service number for help finding a dentist. She was transferred to Dental Benefit Providers, a separate company that administrated the plan's dental benefits.

At Dental Benefit Providers, Norris reached a customer service representative who explained that DaShawn would need to see a general dentist who would then provide a referral to an oral surgeon who would be able to give him the treatment he needed. The customer service representative also explained that the Medicaid portion of United Healthcare was actually called Americhoice. Dentists providing care would be contracted to Americhoice, not United Healthcare. The representative searched her database and gave Norris a list of several dozen general dentists located near DaShawn's grandparents' mobile home. Norris said the representative cautioned her that while the dentists were listed as belonging to the Dental Benefit Providers network, and thus under contract with Americhoice, many providers had recently dropped their contracts. And the representative warned Norris to be sure the dentist was a provider under contract with "Americhoice through the state" because only those dentists would be part of the network providing care under DaShawn's Medicaid plan.

Norris tasked her assistant with calling the dentists on the list and asking if they accepted "Americhoice through the state." The first twenty-six said no.

Norris decided to try another approach. She called the Maryland State Department of Health and Mental Hygiene help line for

Medicaid beneficiaries. The first person Norris spoke with said she could not find DaShawn in the computer and, therefore, he must be enrolled in another Medicaid managed care plan called Amerigroup, not Americhoice. Norris asked to talk with a supervisor. The supervisor found DaShawn in the database and transferred the lawyer to a supervising nurse in the department's case management unit.

Over the next five days, Norris related, the state case management nurse, a case manager from the Prince George's County Health Department's ombudsman unit and a worker at United Healthcare/Americhoice, joined efforts to find a dentist in DaShawn's network who would see him.

On October 5, 2006, DaShawn finally got in to see dentist Arthur Fridley, who cleaned his teeth, took an x-ray, and referred him to an oral surgeon. The oral surgeon said he could not see DaShawn until November and that would be only for a consultation. Six weeks later, at that appointment, Alyce Driver said she learned DaShawn would need to have six teeth extracted. She made another appointment for December. The dental office called her and asked to reschedule the appointment for January 16, 2007. But she had to cancel the January 16 appointment after finding out on January 8 that the children's Medicaid coverage had lapsed a month earlier. She suspected there had been a bureaucratic mix-up and that the paperwork to confirm their eligibility was mailed to the homeless shelter where the family was no longer staying.

That was when Deamonte got sick.

The news of Deamonte Driver's death appeared on the Metro page of the *Washington Post* on February 28, 2007, under the headline "For Want of a Dentist: Prince George's Boy Dies After Bacteria from Tooth Spread to Brain."

"Twelve-year-old Deamonte Driver died of a toothache Sunday.

"A routine, $80 tooth extraction might have saved him.

"If his mother had been insured.

"If his family had not lost its Medicaid.

"If Medicaid dentists weren't so hard to find.

"If his mother hadn't been focused on getting a dentist for his brother, who had six rotted teeth.

"By the time Deamonte's own aching tooth got any attention, the bacteria from the abscess had spread to his brain, doctors said. After two operations and more than six weeks of hospital care, the Prince George's County boy died.

"Deamonte's death and the ultimate cost of his care, which could total more than $250,000, underscore an often-overlooked concern in debate over universal health coverage: dental care."

The story went on to report the situation in Maryland and the greater Washington region: that some poor children in the state completely lacked dental coverage. Other families were traveling three hours to places such as the University of Maryland dental school to get care from dentists willing to accept Medicaid patients. Still others, like Deamonte's brother, were sometimes able to find routine services but faced difficulties obtaining help for deeper problems.

The situation was grim. Fewer than one in three children in Maryland's Medicaid program had received any dental service at all in 2005, the latest year for which figures were available at the time of Deamonte Driver's death. Fewer than 16 percent of the state's Medicaid children had obtained restorative procedures such as fillings that year.

"I certainly hope the state agencies responsible for making sure these children have dental care take note so that Deamonte didn't die in vain," Laurie Norris told the newspaper. "They know there is a problem and they have not devoted adequate resources to solving it."

State officials said that the delivery of basic dental care had actually been improving since 1997, when the state had put in place the managed care program for Medicaid, and 1998, when legislation provided funding and set higher standards for dental care under the program. But serious problems remained. At the time that Deamonte died, fewer than 20 percent of the state's dentists were reported to be accepting Medicaid patients, according to Arthur Fridley, the dentist who had seen DaShawn and who was the immediate past president of the state dental association. He said the system was in complete disarray.

"Whatever we've got is broke," Fridley said. "It has nothing to do with access to care for these children."[3]

The new governor of Maryland, Democrat Martin O'Malley, had just taken office when Deamonte Driver died. O'Malley had won a difficult race against an incumbent Republican, Robert L. Ehrlich Jr.

Before he became governor, O'Malley served as Baltimore's mayor, where he had earned a reputation as a tenacious and personable reformer. His struggles against the gun violence and addiction plaguing Baltimore had helped inspire the character of Mayor Tommy Carcetti in the television show *The Wire*. O'Malley was telegenic. He played guitar and sang in a Celtic rock band. He also had a deep affinity for the details of public administration and policy; he believed government could work if the systems worked. In 2005, when he was forty-two, *Time* magazine named O'Malley one of America's "Top 5 Big City Mayors." "Wonk 'n Roller," the headline in the magazine read.[4]

When the governor's copy of the *Washington Post* arrived bearing the news of the dental death, O'Malley reportedly held up the newspaper for the members of his cabinet to see. "What are we going to do about this?" he asked, according to a source with knowledge of the meeting.

O'Malley had not come to office focused upon Maryland's epidemic of dental disease. But he arrived in the state's capital, Annapolis, with public health on his mind. One of his goals as governor was extending health benefits to the tens of thousands of Marylanders who lacked them. He had already convinced a formidable health insurance leader, John Colmers, to serve as his health secretary. Colmers, a serious man, a first-generation American from a family of Austrian physicians, was at home in the world of cost efficiencies and quality measures. He also had a passion for public health.

Before he joined the O'Malley administration, Colmers had served as chairman of the board of the state's largest insurer, CareFirst Blue Cross Blue Shield. While at Blue Cross, Colmers had worked to restore the organization's not-for-profit status in the wake of a previous board's aborted attempt to turn it into a for-profit company and sell it. When O'Malley called Colmers in to persuade him to take the job of health secretary, Colmers was busy working on a mechanism to expand Medicaid to cover more poor uninsured adults without bankrupting the state. As health secretary, Colmers would have a chance to sell his Medicaid expansion plan to the state legislature.

Then came the news of the program's dental crisis.

"We get the news that a twelve-year-old boy died of dental sepsis," said Colmers, in an interview. "I don't remember necessarily how the news came to me. But what was clear was that it happened on my watch." In public health, prevention is always a primary focus. Still, in spite of the best efforts "horrible things are going to happen," Colmers said. "The real test is what are you going to do once that event occurs?"

With the governor's support, Colmers created a special task force. He called it the Dental Action Committee. "It was an intentional name," he said. "I wanted 'action' to be its middle name." He said he did not want a report that would end up on a shelf. He charged the group with formulating a list of remedies for the state's broken Medicaid dental program. The recommendations needed to be cost-effective and they needed to be attainable. Some would cost money, he was certain. But he was also sure that getting to the heart of Maryland's Medicaid problem would take more than money.

It would require the dentists' participation. "It was also about getting the dental profession to step up and be more responsible for providing access to the Medicaid program." Colmers asked state dental leaders, physicians, insurance and health officials, children's advocates, and academics to serve on the Dental Action Committee. Norman Tinanoff from the University of Maryland dental school was appointed. Laurie Norris was also called upon to serve. A former state dental director, dentist Harry Goodman, was named.

Jane Casper, a dental hygienist from affluent Howard County, was made chairperson of the committee. Though a quiet woman, she was known for her uncanny ability to talk dentists into accepting poor Head Start children who needed care. She was also married to a dentist with a successful suburban practice, who managed to see quite a few Medicaid children. She brought to the group her insights into many facets of dental care. She understood the pressures faced by public health providers and private practitioners. She knew poor children and families and grasped the challenges they faced in their daily lives. She had worked for years as a dental hygienist and she also knew how Maryland's dentists felt. She believed they had been badly hurt by the news of the death of a poor Medicaid child in the state.

"Dentists really do care. And they were hung out to dry with this thing," said Casper. "I think they wanted I don't want to say redemption. But it really brought it home."

During that summer, the group began convening regularly in a conference room in an aging state health department building in Baltimore.

"There was a lot of skepticism in the room," Casper recalled. "People were a little concerned, not sure about what was going to be asked of them." A couple of years before, Casper had pitched the idea of expanding the ability of hygienists to work in schools. The idea drew an angry reaction from dentists, she said. "I think they were fearful that hygienists were going to go out on their own," said Casper.

Colmers, too, knew the dentists were worried. They were worried about hygienists asking for more freedom. Like dentists elsewhere in the country, they were worried about dental therapists too. Colmers listened to the dentists' complaints about Medicaid's low reimbursement rates and cumbersome paperwork and said he would work on resolving the problems. But he told the dentists that expanding the state's dental workforce was another option he would consider.

"I was pretty clear with the dentists and said to them if at the same time we don't see a significant increase in the number of your bretheren and sisteren who are participating in the Medicaid program don't kid yourself. I will go back and work on scope of practice more broadly in that environment. If you don't want to participate and play this way that's fine. But know there will be consequences."

At regular meetings held all summer in the spartan conference room in the state office building in Baltimore, the members of the Dental Action Committee wrestled with the chimera of repairing the broken system and getting oral health care to the poor children of Maryland. The challenges were complex in a state stretching from the fishing villages of the Chesapeake Bay to the coal towns of Appalachia, a state sometimes called "America in Miniature."

And in some ways, Maryland's Medicaid dental system was America's Medicaid dental system in miniature too. It had its own history, yet its problems with funding, its problems with participation and utilization, its problems with fraud and abuse were not all that unique. The thing that made Maryland stand out was a highly publicized death that came at a critical moment in local, state, and national thinking about oral health.

Back in the 1960s, at the very beginning of Medicaid, Maryland state leaders embraced the program and the idea of providing needed dental care to the poor. Then, in a matter of months, dentists began complaining that the program was underfunded.

Maryland's Medicaid program went into place in 1966 and the state's dental program, offering generous benefits, began in earnest on July 1, 1967. A total of $650,000 was set aside to pay the dentists for the coming fiscal year. In five months, all the money was spent.

When the state legislature again appropriated $650,000 for fiscal year 1969, the vast majority of the state's dentists, members of the Maryland State Dental Association, announced they were pulling out of Medicaid.

"It is difficult for the dentists of the State to see how $650,000 will provide comprehensive dental care for 276,831 indigent citizens when the State is attempting to treat a disease with a 90 per cent prevalence," wrote the organization's president, Irving I. Abramson, in a letter to the state health commissioner quoted by the *Baltimore Sun*.[5]

An editorial writer for the *Sun* grimly assessed the dentists' revolt, seeing the breakdown as an ominous sign of larger problems with fulfilling the promise of Medicaid's social contract with the poor. "The State's Medicaid program will be two years old on July 1. Like parallel programs in most of the other states, it has been in financial trouble from the start. The reason: the rapidly rising costs of medical care and the too-low estimates of the number of indigent and medically-indigent persons who are eligible for hospital care, doctors' services and other aid under the program."[6]

In 1970, Maryland dentists were given a rate increase and drawn back into the program. But by the spring of 1972, rising Medicaid costs were causing alarm among state officials and drawing press coverage. Burgeoning dental fees got special attention. On a statewide list of per-patient claims by hospitals, doctors, and dentists, a couple of Prince George's County dentists stood out. One of them was Earlie Lee Trice, who received $34,700 for treating 152 patients, an average of $228 per patient.

In an interview with the *Washington Post*, Trice boasted that Medicaid had been a large boon to his practice in the historically black community of Glenarden. "I'm right in the middle of the ghetto. . . . I've got the most Medicaid work of any dentist in Prince George's County—I've got four secretaries. I sometimes work until midnight and I work on Sundays," said the dentist. "Trice added," the article went on to say, "that when the Medicaid dental program began in 1966 'white doctors didn't want Medicaid work because the fees were too low' and began referring patients to him. Since then dental fees have risen and his Medicaid business has continued 'to snowball.'"[7]

After that, state investigators would take another look at Trice. Over a three-year period, he billed the state for nearly $200,000 of work, more than twice the average amount claimed by other doctors and dentists during the same period. Some of the most expensive claims were for work done on adults. Ultimately, authorities charged him with fraud. In court, prosecutors pointed out that Trice claimed to have extracted thirty-eight teeth from the jaw of a single patient. An expert witness testified adult humans rarely have more than thirty-two teeth. Records were introduced showing Trice alleged to have filled thirteen teeth for a patient from whom he had earlier claimed to have extracted thirty-five teeth.[8] The 1976 trial got wide media coverage, even attracting the attention of the muckraking journalist Jack Anderson, whose syndicated column featuring the Trice scandal ran in newspapers across the country under headlines such as "Medicaid Also a Dentists' Goldmine."[9]

Trice was found guilty on twelve counts of obtaining money from Medicaid under false pretenses. He was sentenced to four years in prison. The damage to Maryland's Medicaid dental program, and the suffering of countless beneficiaries, lasted far longer.

Amid the fraud investigations, Maryland's governor, Marvin Mandel, proposed eliminating routine dental care for adults from the Medicaid program. For a while, Maryland dentists again found themselves fighting the state—this time on the side of Medicaid.

State dental association president Joseph P. Cappuccio told the Baltimore Sun that he saw the efforts to cut adult benefits as evidence that officials saw dental care as a "luxury." By then, Maryland had 427,000 Medicaid beneficiaries. A quarter of them were receiving dental services, at a cost to the state of $10.5 million. More than half the funding (66 percent) went to cover care to adult patients, Cappuccio acknowledged. Even so, dentists were taking a loss caring for Medicaid patients, he contended.[10]

Maryland lawmakers were not persuaded by his arguments. During their 1976 legislative session, under a Medicaid cost containment plan, they eliminated all dental benefits to poor adults except for emergency care.[11] The cuts left adults with few options and, in 1993, even those options were eliminated. As the legislature attempted to deal with the impact of a recession, lawmakers voted to stop reimbursing dentists even for adult emergency care.

Maryland also tried to economize on its children's program. States are not allowed to cut the number of children who are federally entitled to Medicaid. They are not allowed to cut the range of federally mandated, medically necessary benefits guaranteed by law. But they can cut the reimbursement rates paid to dentists to provide the care. So Maryland, like many other states, did that. Private dentists left the program, saying they were losing money treating poor children. Meanwhile, the state's public health safety net was inadequate. Only half of the counties in the state were offering public health dental services.[12]

It was hoped that the managed care system would be a solution. Instituted by the state in 1997, the reform was promoted as a way of giving Medicaid beneficiaries the ability to shop for care and obtain services from participating dentists, just like patients with private insurance.

Once the new system was in place, health departments in some of the counties that had been providing dental care to Medicaid children stopped. The expectation was that under the managed care system, more private practice dentists would take Medicaid children, so the county clinics did not need to. The Prince George's County Health Department stopped providing dental care to Medicaid children. Problems with access to care persisted. Some state leaders asked for additional steps to be taken. A state Office of Oral Health was established.

In 2000, the year Deamonte Driver turned six, Maryland claimed the dubious distinction of providing less dental care to Medicaid children than any state in the country. Only 11 percent of Medicaid children aged newborn to twenty enrolled for any period during that year received any dental service. Many other states were also performing abysmally. The national average was 27 percent.

Emotions ran high at the monthly meeting of the local chapter of the National Dental Association (NDA). The news of Deamonte Driver's death hit the minority dentists particularly hard. Hazel Harper remembered the dentist sitting next to her breaking down and sobbing, "We never would have turned that child away. We never would have let that boy die! It shouldn't have happened." Yet when Laurie Norris and her assistant had been searching for care for DaShawn, some of the group's members had been called.

William Milton III, with his dreadlocks and outspoken style, did not practice in Prince George's County. But he stood up and said what was on a lot of people's minds.

"They are blaming it on us. They are blaming it on the dentists." Like Milton, Harper did not work in Prince George's, but she lived in one of the county's well-groomed subdivisions. Harper was the daughter of a doctor and a former professor at the dental school at Howard University.

One of Harper's former students, Belinda Carver-Taylor, was at the meeting too. Carver-Taylor had a small office in Prince George's County, not far from the district border. It was located in a struggling shopping center, tucked behind a grocery store and pain clinic, in a storefront with a metal gate that rolled down at night. The problems of the poor were not an abstraction for Carver-Taylor. She was the daughter of a single mother who had struggled to support her family by working in a Tennessee shoe factory. After the factories started shutting down the family moved to Maryland. It was with her red and white Maryland Medicaid card that Carver-Taylor found needed dental care, relief from pain, and her career. She was in high school when a dentist extracted four badly decayed molars and made a partial denture for her.

"I was so glad to be able to eat," she remembered. The partial denture was not covered by Medicaid, but the dentist was kind. He said, "Do good in school! Keep the partial." In gratitude, she began helping around the dental office. Then she trained as a dental assistant. Then she went to dental school at Howard University, where she met Harper.

Amid the passionate discussion at the NDA meeting, the two women began to develop a plan. Children could not take themselves to the dentist. But maybe, with a mobile clinic, they could bring care to the kids.

"Hazel and Belinda took the ball and got it rolling," said Milton.

Alyce Driver's children had received routine medical care and the immunizations they needed for school. But finding the way from the health care system to the dental care system had proven too much for the Drivers.

Deamonte was dead and buried. And DaShawn still had abscessed teeth. Alyce Driver was desperate. Then she and Laurie Norris found out about the pediatric clinic at the University of Maryland School of Dentistry in Baltimore. It was Tinanoff's clinic. He said that he and the students could take care of DaShawn. They made an appointment. But Baltimore was thirty miles away. Alyce Driver had no car.

The taxi ride was a long one, full of wrong turns that were harrowing for the mother and exciting for the son. They did not realize it but they were traveling back across the historic divide, back to the place where dentistry diverged from medicine. The trip cost $80.

The world's first dental college was now a tall structure of brick and glass. It stood on West Baltimore Street, across from the University of Maryland medical school. Inside, past the check-in desk, near the elevators, stood a showcase filled with mementos of the school's past. There were old photographs and antique pearl-handled dental instruments. There was a small book bound in red leather. It contained Chapin Harris's first lecture to the school's first dental students in 1840. "Gentlemen," Harris had begun. "I shall commence with a description of the mouth."

The mother and son found their way upstairs. The pediatric clinic, with its bright hand-painted murals of smiling sea creatures and rows of cheerful banana-yellow chairs, was located on the third floor. Norman Tinanoff and the students were waiting for them.

The clinic sees thousands of poor children every year. Some have Medicaid. Some have no insurance at all. Many have serious infections. DaShawn's problems were in no way unique, Tinanoff said. "We got him taken care of."

For Alyce Driver, there were hardly words to describe the relief. "All praise to Dr. Tinanoff," she said in a tone usually reserved for prayer.

11

Riding into the Epidemic

It was on the morning of February 28, 2007, that Burton Edelstein read the name Deamonte Driver in the newspaper. Edelstein was a pediatric dentist and a professor of dentistry and public health policy at Columbia University in New York. He was in the airport. He had flown to Washington, D.C., for a meeting on Capitol Hill. He and a handful of other advocates were scheduled to press their cause with members of the Senate Finance Committee. Their business concerned the decade-old State Children's Health Insurance Program or SCHIP.

Democratic president Bill Clinton had established SCHIP back in 1997, in the wake of his failed effort to universalize the nation's health care system. The program was less ambitious than Medicare or Medicaid. It targeted only a subset of the uninsured; the children whose working poor parents earned too much to qualify for Medicaid, but who had no health care coverage. SCHIP, which by 2007 covered seven million children, was widely applauded by health advocates. But dental coverage was not a required feature of SCHIP. Most states provided dental benefits, but they were not mandated and were vulnerable to cuts.

Edelstein believed dental benefits needed to be made a mandatory part of SCHIP. Leaving them optional, he was convinced, meant that SCHIP was perpetuating a tragic and enduring disconnection between dental care and health care in America. Across the United States, in public and private programs, dental care was provided separately from other kinds of health care. It was paid for separately. People had harder times finding it. Dentists and physicians were educated separately. They seldom communicated. Patient records were kept separately. Medicaid children were very likely to get routine immunizations, but they were far less likely to get routine dental care. In intimate personal ways and in vast public ways, dental care continued to be left out.

"The mouth is part of the body," Edelstein liked to say, often in a tone of mock amazement. Yet that basic truth got regularly lost in the gap between the separate systems that had evolved to provide care for the mouth and for the rest of the body, he believed.

"To reintegrate the two systems is a tremendous challenge," Edelstein would say. Then, in a half-joking way, he would sometimes blame it all on Baltimore. "If things hadn't gone sour in the year of 1840 in Baltimore we wouldn't have to."

Heading through the airport on that February morning, the dentist hoped this would be the moment to try to begin to correct the past. The SCHIP program was due for reauthorization. Edelstein's aim was to win the mandatory inclusion of a dental benefit for children of the working poor in the reauthorized version of SCHIP. He had been working toward this goal for ten years. In 1997, he had formed a nonprofit group—the Children's Dental Health Project—to aid in the push. Others had joined the cause. Thanks to the surgeon general's *Oral Health in America* report in 2000, to which Edelstein had contributed, there was growing awareness of the nation's epidemic of oral disease.

Still, Edelstein and his fellow oral health advocates were facing an uphill battle getting their message across in Washington. These were times of deep ideological division in the halls of Congress. The 2008 elections, though more than a year away, were already looming in many minds. In the White House, President George W. Bush was wrestling with the war on terror, sending American troops to the Middle East. At home, the cost of health care was ballooning. Millions of Americans were uninsured. Democrats spoke of the importance of reauthorizing SCHIP. Some even hoped to expand the program. But asking for a dental benefit mandate was a very long shot. The president had threatened to veto any expansion of SCHIP.

Edelstein was preparing for a hard day. With his mind on the meeting on Capitol Hill, he stopped to get his shoes shined. The airport shoeshine man kept the day's newspapers on hand for his customers to read. Edelstein reached for one. That morning, the Metro section of the *Washington Post* caught his attention.

There was a photograph of Deamonte Driver. There was the story of his death. Sitting there in the shoeshine booth, Edelstein had the feeling the tide of his battle might be turning.

Others died of dental infections before Deamonte Driver, and others have died since. But it was Deamonte Driver, who died just a few miles from the U.S. Capitol, who was spoken about on Capitol Hill. His story became part of the battle over the reauthorization of SCHIP and the guarantee of dental benefits for seven million children from working poor families. And it was the boy's image, captured in a school portrait, his head cocked questioningly, his white shirt buttoned to the collar, his searching eyes, that gazed down on the lawmakers from screens in the hearing rooms of Congress.

His face became the face of millions of children. Deamonte had been a Medicaid child. The program entitled 29 million poor children—well over a third of American children—to dental care. It was care that most of them were not receiving.

"With all the resources available to us," Maryland representative Elijah Cummings thundered in one of those hearings, "how did we so thoroughly fail this little boy?"

"Look at his face," Ohio congressman Dennis J. Kucinich said. "I mean, he is just—he is really asking us what are we going to do about this. Are we going to take a stand to make sure the children of America get the dental services they are entitled to?"

Maryland senator Barbara Mikulski, trained as a social worker and old enough to recall the beginnings of Medicaid in the Johnson era, would remember the boy as a "soldier in the War on Poverty."

For lawmakers like those, the boy's death was a reminder of monumental initiatives, the grand speeches of Johnson and Roosevelt, of their assurances that America, through collective effort, could supplant the fear and pain of poverty with dignity and health. But for others, the boy's death was just more proof of the futility of such giant federal programs. For them, the welfare state itself bred and perpetuated stigma and despair. For liberals, Deamonte's rotten tooth was an emblem of the importance of fighting to strengthen SCHIP and Medicaid, programs aimed at ensuring that children received the care they needed to grow into healthy and productive adults. But for many conservatives, the stigma of the welfare state endured. For them Deamonte's rotten tooth evoked the inability of any government program to save the poor from themselves. The personal havoc wrought by one small decayed molar became part of the huge and ongoing debate over the size and scope of the nation's government.

The federal deficit was growing. Democrats blamed the Republicans' tax cuts and the costs of war. Conservatives blamed liberals for runaway domestic spending. The Deficit Reduction Act of 2006, passed with a tie-breaking vote by Vice President Richard Cheney and signed by President Bush, stood poised to cut nearly $40 billion from the nation's spending in the next five years. One of the programs targeted for billions in cuts was Medicaid.

On March 27, 2007, less than a month after Deamonte Driver was buried, the first of a number of congressional hearings was called to explore the circumstances of his death, and the vast and chronic problems with the Medicaid dental system. In stately room 2123 of the Rayburn House Office Building, the health subcommittee of the House Committee on Energy and Commerce gathered. The members of the subcommittee began with their own statements.

"The truly frightening thing about Deamonte Driver's death is the number of American children who are at risk of a similar fate," said committee chairman Frank Pallone Jr., a New Jersey Democrat. "Statistics show that the chronic infectious disease that causes cavities remains second only to the common cold in terms of prevalence in children. Unlike a cold however, tooth decay does not go away."

Pallone spoke of a "fragmented health system" failing children. And he ended his remarks with a quote from Nobel laureate and poet Gabriela Mistral: "Many things we need can wait. The child cannot. Now is the time. His bones are being formed. His blood is being made, his mind is being developed. To him, we cannot say tomorrow. His name is today."

Democratic congresswoman Lois Capps, a school nurse from California, said she had seen the epidemic of dental disease first-hand. "There are many Deamontes in classrooms today with abscesses in their teeth," said Capps. She said she hoped to move dental benefits into the limelight, not just for the children of the very poor, the Medicaid children, but for the children of the working poor, who were eligible for SCHIP. "With SCHIP reauthorization covering the uninsured at the forefront of this committee, I am hoping we can make progress," she said.

But the Democrats got no agreement from the committee's ranking member, Republican Nathan Deal, from Georgia. Deal reminded his colleagues about the wariness with which many dentists viewed Medicaid. And he firmly noted that he was opposed to adding a dental mandate to SCHIP. He introduced the members of the American Dental Association who were in the audience. Dentists would rather give care away for free than participate in burdensome public programs, said Deal. And Deal defended the need for austerity measures and stressed the importance of allowing states to decide what health care benefits to provide.

"I am afraid that many in our committee have an interest in creating mandates with SCHIP like the dental benefit in Medicaid, which would make it more difficult for states to provide health coverage appropriate to the needs and conditions of the individual states," warned the Georgia congressman, a future governor of his state.

In addition to cutting Medicaid, the Deficit Reduction Act (DRA) of 2006 gave states new powers to redefine the rules for benefits that had long been regarded as fundamental entitlements under Medicaid.[1] "The Governors' frequent frustration with the rigid structure of the Medicaid program helped inform the steps we took in the Deficit Reduction Act to provide benefit flexibility in Medicaid," said Deal.

Some state governments had already begun to use the new flexibility granted by the DRA to reduce Medicaid benefits. West Virginia had quickly gotten federal approval to begin scaling back benefits, including children's benefits for prescriptions and for hearing, vision, and dental care. For the next three years in West Virginia, in order to receive an "enhanced benefit" package similar to the old Medicaid benefit, parents were required to sign and comply with a personal responsibility contract. If after a year the state determined that the parents had failed to comply with directives for screenings, health improvement programs, or medication, or if they missed appointments, they or their children stood the risk of losing their benefits entirely. (A 2010 federal rule would end the experiment.)

Poor patients needed to do more to help themselves, said Deal. "It seems that the impediments to adequate coverage in the public programs exist not necessarily because the benefit does not exist," said Deal. "In my conversations with dentists, many cite the overwhelming administrative burdens of providing services through public programs. Moreover, many people do not recognize the importance of oral health and fail to take advantage of the benefits that are available to them. At some point, people must take responsibility for their oral health on a regular basis."

Then Pallone called upon the first witness, Burton Edelstein.

Later, the pediatric dentist would remember the extra-corporeal quality of that moment. The people in the crowded hearing room waited for him to speak. It was as if he were outside himself waiting too.

A long chain of moments in his life had led him to this chair, to this place of silence. There was that dental chair he sat in as a boy of seven or eight, growing up in Rochester, New York. The family dentist had given him a bit of elemental mercury, and he held it on a piece of cotton in his palm. It glinted there, and moved, with a restless magic. He would become a dentist, a restless and curious one. He would puzzle over his profession in ways others some-times found unsettling. He would place his hands into thousands of mouths and puzzle over the mysteries of health and decay.

There was the moment when, as an army dentist, he was exam-ining the teeth of Vietnam War orphans who had been airlifted to the United States. He was supposed to figure out how old they were, what grade they should be placed in at school, but seeing their mouths changed his feelings about tooth decay and dentistry. Some of the children had tooth decay like he had never seen before. The diseased places in their teeth were not soft and brown. They were glossy and hard with defined borders. As his dental instru-ment glided over the hard surfaces, Edelstein marveled. It was a thing that had been seen among other children in other wars.

It was arrested decay. These children had not tasted sweetness for a long time. Their teeth had remineralized. Mother Nature had won, he thought.

Dentists should be doing more than drilling teeth, he came to believe. They needed to work with nature, to stop seeing like sur-geons and to start seeing like healers. To cross boundaries, to speak new languages. They needed to work together, and work with hygienists, with pediatricians, with nurses, with dieticians, with parents, with the children themselves. But first they needed to get to the children at greatest risk, the children who did not even come into dental offices, the poorest, the most vulnerable.

After he left the army, he studied pediatric dentistry and he studied public health. He worked in Connecticut and did research with Norman Tinanoff, who was at that time at the University of Connecticut. Together they collected children's spit and pondered the riddles of tooth decay.

Then Edelstein ran a successful private practice in Connecticut for a while. He went out of his way to bring poor children to his practice. He contracted with county Head Start centers. He went to library programs and health fairs and found more poor kids. There were so many poor children in New London County who needed a dentist he had to keep growing his practice to keep the proportions right. He hired more dentists and took on more children with private insurance to balance it all out. There was a year when they counted twenty-one thousand visits. He stressed prevention. He put a medically inspired caries management protocol in place in his office.

When the state Medicaid system switched to managed care in the 1990s, Edelstein banded together with other dentists to successfully fight for better fee schedules. But there were not enough dentists treating Medicaid children, in Connecticut or anywhere else. Edelstein wanted to reform the system. He won a public policy fellowship and went to Washington. He wanted to work for national change. Instead he was there when dental benefits were left out of SCHIP.

And here he was again. People were waiting for him to testify. The story of a boy's death had captured the public imagination and had opened this window of opportunity. Edelstein drew a breath.

"My testimony is grounded in three straightforward facts," he began.

"First, tooth decay is virtually preventable" yet "it remains the single most common chronic disease of childhood in the United States and it is present in one quarter of all 2 to 5 year olds.

"Second, dental care is essential to overall health, yet for reasons that make neither biological sense nor policy sense, dental care has been legislated as an optional service, as though the mouth were not integral to the body.

"Third, preventive care is cost effective yet far [too] few children obtain the kinds of routine care that would prevent pain, infection, sleepless nights, missed meals, and poor school performance."

He made a plea to repair the broken Medicaid dental system. States could make Medicaid work, for dentists and for poor children, Edelstein testified. With federal leadership and oversight and grants to support innovations, Congress could help ensure that Medicaid was reformed, he said. Then he asked for mandated dental benefits under SCHIP.

"Put the mouth back into well-child care," he told the subcommittee. Preventive care would be far more cost-effective than treating the disastrous impact of chronic disease across the population. He noted that the cost of the two brain surgeries and the weeks of hospitalization that failed to save Deamonte Driver was a quarter of a million dollars. "Deamonte could have received preventive care for 12 years. He could have had a sealant. He could have had a filling. He could have had a root canal. He could have had a number of dental treatments, not one of which would have cost more than one-thousandth of what his hospital stay cost."

He urged members of Congress "to ensure that dental care is never again considered an optional service, as though it didn't matter, and to integrate oral health into each and every federal program that addresses children's health and well-being.

"Deamonte is sadly only one example of what happens when we fail as a nation to sustain attention to children's oral health," he said.

Other witnesses followed. Among them was American Dental Association president Kathleen Roth, a practicing dentist from West Bend, Wisconsin, and an experienced Medicaid provider.

"Like all of us, I was very shocked at the death of 12-year-old Deamonte Driver, who lived just a short distance from here," Roth said. "I believe we have an obligation to honor this child and his family by saying 'no more.' No more children unable to sleep and eat properly, no more needless deaths, no more unable to pay attention in school and no more unable to smile because of severe dental disease that could so easily be prevented and treated. If we do not resolve to reform the system now, we are ignoring the warning that this tragedy is sending us and the nation's children will continue to suffer," said Roth.

She said that every dentist she knew offered some free or discounted care. But she added, "The sad fact is that all our volunteerism and charitable efforts are not enough because charity is not a health care system."

The nation's safety net clinics were understaffed. Federal and state governments undervalued dental care, she said. Less than one percent of the nation's more than 177,686 dentists worked in health centers funded under the federal Public Health Service Act, she said. Drawing private practice dentists into Medicaid should be a priority. But the low fees and red tape needed to be addressed in states like her own, Wisconsin.

"The Badger Care reimbursement schedule is so meager that in most cases, it does not even cover dentists' overhead," she said. "The paperwork is onerous and confusing. The entire process is actually so frustrating that it discourages dentists from participating in the program at all. Ninety percent of the nation's dentists are in private practice. We need to make it possible for more of them, many more of them, to participate in Medicaid. Dentists can do more but only if the state and federal governments will give us the support that we need to do that."

After the witnesses had testified, Pallone, the Democratic committee chairman, turned to Edelstein and asked how he believed the system had failed Deamonte Driver. Edelstein spoke of the need for oversight, to ensure that care was actually available to poor children. He spoke of the need for more providers. Clinics, rural health centers, and emergency rooms were overwhelmed. Then there was the fact that disease prevention messages had not reached families.

"All of these systems had to come together for this monumental failure," he said.

—⁂—

Then it was Deal's turn to ask questions about the death of Deamonte Driver. "I never heard the mother or the parents mentioned as the ones who failed him," the Georgia Republican noted. "If we had Deamonte dying from internal bleeding that occurred because he fell while in his mother's presence and he died from that, we probably would have had a child abuse case brought against the mother but here we blame the systems. We never put personal responsibility in the equation, and I think it is an important ingredient that has been overlooked."

Deal asked Edelstein to comment.

"I want to take a moment to agree with you wholeheartedly about parental responsibility," said Edelstein. "There is no question. The question becomes when parents do seek care, which is perhaps not the case we are addressing today, but when parents do seek the care, are they able to obtain it? Too often, the answer is no."

In a May hearing, Congressman Dennis Kucinich, an Ohio Democrat and chairman of the Domestic Policy Subcommittee of the Oversight and Government Reform Committee, announced that he had asked his staff to call the dentists included on a list of Medicaid providers available to Alyce Driver. Of the twenty-four dentists listed as participating in United Healthcare, the managed care organization serving area Medicaid beneficiaries, none could have helped the family, Kucinich said. Telephone numbers for twenty-three were disconnected, incorrect, or belonged to a dentist who did not take Medicaid patients. The twenty-fourth was an oral surgeon, the congressman reported.

Government regulators, who depend on the data provided by managed care organizations to assess the effectiveness of Medicaid, "would have believed that the number of dentists who could have served Deamonte was twenty-four," said Kucinich. "But the real number is zero."

A representative from the insurance company was quick to rebut the congressman's claim. "We've got 92 dentists in Prince George's

County, and in 2006 we paid claims to 78 of them," said company spokesman Peter Ashkenaz in an interview with the *Washington Post*.[2]

Kucinich stood by the findings. Maryland was not the only state where the inquiry would find inadequate Medicaid dental provider networks. The shortage of care was aggravated by the low rates that insurers and states offered to dental providers, many witnesses asserted. Many state programs were offering dentists only a fraction of their usual and customary rates for treating Medicaid patients.

Tinanoff, from the University of Maryland, was called to testify. He spoke of the shortage of Medicaid dentists in Maryland. A telephone survey of more than seven hundred dentists listed as Medicaid providers in Maryland found that only one hundred seventy would take a new Medicaid patient, Tinanoff said. Maryland's Medicaid reimbursement rates, which ranked the lowest in the nation in 2004 for restorative procedures, kept dentists out of the program, added Tinanoff. The result was a system where few children could actually find care.

Laurie Norris, the quiet, brisk lawyer who had helped the Driver family, testified too. It had required months of diligent effort to locate a local dentist to even begin providing care to Deamonte's brother, she told the lawmakers. "It took the combined efforts of one mother, one lawyer, one help-line supervisor, and three health care case management professionals to get help for one Medicaid child."

On Capitol Hill, Democratic lawmakers insisted the Republican Bush administration was not doing enough to hold states accountable for the performance of their Medicaid dental programs.

"Federal law requires these services be made to children. You are not doing a good enough job if two out of three kids do not get pediatric dental care and they are eligible for it," California representative Henry Waxman, chairman of the powerful House Committee on Oversight and Government Reform, told a top Medicaid official. "Don't you have any responsibility for this? Do you have a suggestion for changing the law? Is there any reason you are not enforcing the law?"

Dennis Smith, who served as the director of the federal Center for Medicaid and State Operations, said it was the states' responsibility to meet the program's requirements.

But, lawmakers countered, it was also the federal agency's responsibility to offer the oversight and support states needed to accomplish the complex task. By that measure, dental services had been a neglected part of the mammoth program.

At the same time, funding for dental care represented only a small percentage of combined state and federal Medicaid spending on all health care services—slightly over 1 percent, or $2.7 billion, of total Medicaid spending in 2002, hearings revealed.[3]

The shortage of dentists serving the poor was much more acute than the shortage of physicians. In medicine, three-quarters of physicians were accepting patients in public programs, but only a quarter of dentists were, testified Frank Catalanotto of the American Dental Education Association.[4]

Yet in spite of all the problems, the lawmakers heard that a few states had made their Medicaid dental programs work. In Alabama, an initiative called "Smile Alabama!" had succeeded in getting care to tens of thousands of additional children over recent years through a concerted effort that included raising reimbursement rates to attract new dentists and giving parents, school nurses, and Head Start centers new tools to get care to children. In North Carolina as throughout the nation, medical providers were far more likely than dentists to see poor babies and children. In that state, physicians and nurses had been trained to offer dental screenings, counseling, and fluoride varnishes.

In the years between 2000 and 2006, medical offices and clinics in North Carolina had managed to provide eighty thousand dental visits to at-risk children.

While Congress was slowly ruminating on the problems on a federal level, members of Maryland's Dental Action Committee bent to the task of reforming the state system. Under instructions from the state health secretary, John Colmers, the committee met every other Tuesday afternoon throughout June, July, and August during the summer of 2007.

In September, the group delivered a plan for a broad restructuring of the state's Medicaid program. To streamline red tape for dentists and increase accountability to the people of Maryland, the committee recommended that a single administrative service organization be placed in charge of providing Medicaid dental care for the state's five hundred thousand Medicaid children. The organization would work directly under a state contract, replacing the patchwork of subcontractors that had been responsible for delivering dental care under the state's managed care system.

The group requested that public health dental hygienists be given the ability to work outside dental offices to provide care to poor children. And members recommended expanding the state's system of safety net clinics and spending millions—about half state and half federal funds—annually to increase reimbursement rates to dentists participating in Medicaid.

The recommendations "are what the state needed years ago," said committee member and state dental association president Garner Morgan. The plan was embraced by the governor and by the state legislature. While funding never reached the level the Dental Action Committee requested, Medicaid reimbursement rates were increased and hundreds of additional dentists signed up for the streamlined Medicaid program. In addition, public health hygienists were allowed to offer care to schoolchildren without a prior dentist's exam. Counties that had lacked dental clinics established them. Once the measures were in place, Maryland became an example to other state efforts to expand care to more Medicaid children.

And the stakes were raised for other states to do better. Increased attention from Congress resulted in new demands for accountability and better performance from Medicaid dental programs nationwide.

"Deamonte took us by the hand and escorted us through the health-care system and pointed out all the places where we could improve," said U.S. Representative John Sarbanes, a Maryland Democrat. A growing number of nonprofits, grassroots advocacy groups, and philanthropies rallied around the cause of dental care. They demanded wider access, testifying in statehouses and on Capitol Hill.

But the war over SCHIP wore on. In Congress, Maryland's delegation led the fight for the mandatory inclusion of dental benefits for the children of the working poor. Congressman Elijah Cummings would not let the matter rest. He became an outspoken national leader on dental issues.

Cummings grew up poor in Baltimore. "I used to think toothaches were just a part of living," he said. The son of two ministers, he brought an apostolic zeal to his mission. An imposing broad-shouldered figure with a shining bald head, Cummings exhorted his colleagues to remember the importance of dental care. "We want to keep the memory of that boy alive," he said. "We want to make sure that life comes out of his death."

Yet there was no quick resolution to the reauthorization of SCHIP. In addition to adding the dental benefits, Democrats launched an effort to expand the program to additional families from slightly higher income brackets. In October 2007, behind closed doors, President Bush did as he had promised. He vetoed the expanded SCHIP bill. The president argued the legislation represented a step toward socialized medicine, the Associated Press reported.[5] In December, Bush again vetoed the bill. Then the president and Congress agreed on a temporary fix—an eighteen-month extension just to keep the program running.

It was not until the new Democratic president, Barack Obama, took office that the children's health insurance program was reauthorized. The bill expanding the program was finally signed in February 2009. The new Children's Health Insurance Program mandated comprehensive dental benefits for the children it covered. It also permitted states to use program funds to offer dental-only supplemental coverage for children whose medical coverage did not include dental benefits.

The bill's longtime congressional champion, Cummings, hailed the event. "With this landmark legislation, we take the first steps toward ensuring that all the Deamontes out there are freed from their senseless pain and suffering."

Edelstein called it a milestone on the road to a place where "oral health is recognized as an important part of overall health."

In the fall of 2009, the U.S. GAO issued a progress report on efforts to improve Medicaid dental programs since the death of Deamonte Driver. The title of the report offered a neat summary of the agency's findings: "Medicaid: State and Federal Actions Have Been Taken to Improve Children's Access to Dental Services, but Gaps Remain."

"Children's access to Medicaid dental services is a long-standing concern," the authors wrote. "The tragic case of a 12-year-old boy who died from an untreated infected tooth that led to a fatal brain infection renewed attention to this issue."

The new report referenced past warnings about the troubled Medicaid dental system. In 2000, GAO investigators had concluded that in the vast majority of the thirty-one states they examined, fewer than a quarter of dentists were seeing at least one hundred Medicaid patients.[6] And in 2008, the GAO had informed Congress that the extent of dental disease among America's millions of Medicaid children had not decreased for decades, that millions of Medicaid enrolled children were estimated to have untreated tooth decay, and that children on Medicaid were often not receiving dental services.[7]

The authors of the 2009 report pointed to ongoing problems with provider shortages. They also observed that Medicaid children still suffered from far more untreated decay and got far less care than privately insured children. But, they observed, there were a few signs of hope. Nearly every state in the nation had taken recent steps to recruit new providers and improve access. They also found that the federal Centers for Medicare and Medicaid Services (CMS) had stepped up oversight of dental services. There were hints that the troubled program might be slowly improving.[8]

Dennis Kucinich was among the members of Congress who hailed the findings, particularly the new attention to the program by CMS.

"I believe CMS has turned a corner in their oversight of pediatric dental services since the death of Deamonte Driver," said the congressman at a hearing called to assess the progress. "But the magnitude of the underlying problem is great, and even today, there are millions of children just like Deamonte—entitled to dental care but not receiving it. The urgent job of everyone here today is to move quickly to prevent another one of them from dying from preventable dental disease."

Then, Kucinich told his own story of dental pain. "People asked me when Deamonte's death was first announced, 'Why are you so interested? It's just one person out of 300 million. You know, these things happen,'" he noted. "I remember growing up in the inner city. I was the oldest of seven. My parents never owned a home and lived in seventeen different places by the time I was seventeen, including a couple of cars. And one of the things we didn't have was dental care. I mean I remember chewing on gum balls and having them just breaking off—my teeth breaking off into the gum balls. And I can remember having dental problems that didn't get treated for a long, long time.

"And I don't want to get too graphic about it, but for those who have experienced being a child without access to dental care, you know what a nightmare it can be. Deamonte Driver. That's me. That's me as a young boy. His life was sacrificed to an uncaring system. We can't have any more Deamonte Drivers out there," he said.[9]

In Prince George's County, Maryland, officials announced that health department dental clinics would again be accepting Medicaid children. "We are expanding to include Medicaid children as patients," announced county health officer Donald Shell. "No child with a dental need will be turned away."[10]

It took time for the leaders of the local chapter of the National Dental Association to raise the money for the mobile dental clinic project. Hazel Harper and Belinda Carver-Taylor kept working.

In her own studies of dentistry and public health, and in her own experiences teaching at Howard University, Harper had thought a lot about Medicaid. Once, as a student, she had dressed up in shabby clothes and tried, as an apparent indigent, to find care. It had been a new experience for her, raised as she had been as a doctor's daughter, feeling like an outsider to the system.

Harper reached a memorandum of understanding with the county school system that would allow the mobile clinic to provide dental services to the schools. She shamed and begged colleagues to volunteer. She lined up forty-seven "dentists in action" who agreed to do shifts on the mobile clinic, offering screenings, cleanings, sealants, and fluoride treatments, and to provide care in their offices for children who needed fillings and other more complicated procedures. She scaled back her private practice in Washington, D.C., to direct the effort for a $40,000 annual salary.

Teams of school nurses and counselors were assembled to work together and with parents in twenty of the poorest schools in Prince George's County to obtain permission slips and help to make sure the children who needed follow-up care actually got it. Meanwhile, Carver-Taylor, Harper's former student, used the hours she could spare from her own dental practice in a tough part of Prince George's County to pitch in on fund-raising, even getting a team of local Mary Kay cosmetics representatives to sell lipsticks for the cause.

Finally, on a cold morning in November 2010, the new Deamonte Driver Dental Project mobile clinic made its maiden voyage. The sparkling vehicle, larger than a school bus, decorated in tropical colors and equipped with three dental chairs, pulled up in front of its very first school. It was the Foundation School where Deamonte had been a student.

"This is my dream," declared Carver-Taylor, as she waited in the stillness for the first children to climb on board. She carried the memory and the record of her own childhood pain. She herself had lost four molars to disease as a teenager. A Medicaid dentist had helped her and she had become a dentist herself.

"We are making history," she declared to another local dentist Fred Clark, a former fellow dental school classmate and student of Hazel Harper's. Clark grinned in agreement.

"It don't get better than this."

The steps of the mobile clinic folded down and the project manager, Betty Thomas, leaned out of the door and smiled at the waiting children. "Are you ready?"

Four little boys, dressed in khaki trousers and polo shirts, came in together and huddled shyly. Soon the clinic was humming with children. Thomas did oral health education in the front of the bus with the kids who were waiting on a little bench behind the driver's seat. "How many times a day are we brushing our teeth?"

The first boy to climb into Carver-Taylor's chair was quiet and polite and had four cavities. The next studied himself in her little mirror. "Hey, I got nose hairs!"

Another at first refused to open his mouth. "You're not gonna get my teeth!" he declared.

Carver-Taylor was not fazed. "Let's just count 'em," she cajoled. And he allowed her to examine him. "You got some good-looking teeth in there."

A little girl in the front of the bus started playing clapping games. "They took away my favorite toys, now I play with stupid boys!" When she got to the chair she wanted to wriggle out.

"I'm scared," she confessed. But again, Carver-Taylor turned on the charm. "Scoot back. We're gonna count your teeth. You'll get a sticker."

The work went slowly. There were fifty children signed up, and between Carver-Taylor and Clark, they only managed to see about seven in the first hour. A third dentist who had volunteered had not shown up. They kept working.

"They are gonna pull your teeth out and they are gonna give you a big shot in your gums," one boy warned another, sitting on the bench up front. Another little boy brushed the teeth of the lion puppet with the giant toothbrush. Another little boy tried to escape from the bus wearing his pink bib. He was quickly corralled and returned.

"Every time I turn around, I see another child," said Clark. "They keep popping up!"

A catering wagon drove past and Clark, hungry, hot, and tired, hurried to the front of the mobile clinic to try and get some food. Carver-Taylor stayed at her chair.

"No cavities," she told a girl. "You go over and get a sticker!"

Late in the morning, a tall hurting sixteen-year-old came in. Marcus Johnson said the pain felt like "a needle stabbing me in my teeth." The boy's case was declared a dental emergency. His mother was called and he was swept away for immediate care to a designated "dentist in action" with an office nearby. The fiftieth child to arrive was a girl who had been in Deamonte's grade. She was pretty with sad eyes and seven cavities. Then Marcus Johnson returned, smiling, with the first stage of an emergency root canal completed and another appointment scheduled.

"This makes it all worthwhile," said Betty Thomas. "To know some child who was hurting is out of pain." Suddenly the mobile clinic was so quiet there was a kind of ringing in the air. The work of the day was done. Everyone started packing things up and stowing things away as the school's afternoon bell rang. The parking lot filled up with yellow school buses. The colorful mobile clinic resembled a peacock amid a flock of ducks.

Wanda Newman, one of the school bus drivers, came to the door of the mobile clinic. "Do you have any free stuff?" she asked. "For toothaches?"[11]

Fall and winter passed. A violent spring came to Prince George's County. By the time the mobile clinic reached the troubled community of District Heights in April, the county had already experienced twenty-three homicides in the new year. District Heights Elementary School was struggling too. State tests showed students were failing to make adequate yearly progress in reading and math.

The first child to climb aboard the mobile clinic that April morning was a tiny pre-kindergartener named Tashara Tavia Morton Dodson. She had long intricate braids and serious, earnest eyes. On the left breast of her blue school uniform she wore a large button like a campaign badge. It bore the laminated photograph of a young black man and the inscription "RIP Daddy." Carver-Taylor did not comment on the button. She placed a paper bib on the child and examined her, noting the steel crowns on some of her baby teeth. She showed Tashara the little brush she was putting on the end of her handpiece to clean her teeth. Each brush had soft bristles and was shaped like a tiny animal.

"Look! We got the giraffe! Open big, big, big!" When she was done, Tashara chose a sticker that said "excellent" and stuck it on her uniform, next to "RIP Daddy."

The bench at the front of the van was full of children waiting to see the dentist. Tashara found a seat on the floor to wait to go back to school with her class. She explained the button with her father's face.

"The police killed him five times." Her father had been named Trayvon Dodson. The police said that he had been armed, possibly high, when they shot him in a park on March 7.

It was time for the preschoolers to return to their studies. Tashara and the others gathered to leave. They trailed past a row of daffodils and through the dented metal door back into their school. Older children arrived, more than expected. Carver-Taylor worked steadily, through the fourth graders, then the fifth graders, talking and joking with them.

"Open big," she told a girl wearing beads and brown eyeglasses.

"Oh lord, I remember fifth grade," Carver-Taylor said. "I had my first boyfriend. Do you have a boyfriend? Good. Wait 'til the next grade. He gave me a little Valentine and everything."

They started the day with over seventy kids on the list but one hundred showed up. Some parents did not sign the consent forms but then called in, wanting for their children to be seen, project manager Thomas explained, a little frantically.

"C'mon! Time's a-wasting!" Then she turned to the next group on the bench. "Okay. Let's talk about proper brushing."

The mobile clinic covered many miles and stopped at many schools. Carver-Taylor and her colleagues saw thousands of teeth: healthy teeth and decayed teeth and abscessed teeth. Teeth with Oreos between them. Children laughing, children weeping in terror. Fluoride varnishes and protective sealants were applied, referrals to dental offices were made, charts were filled out, parents called. Betty Thomas, wielding her giant toothbrush, showed countless children how to clean the teeth of the grinning lion puppet.

In the months after Deamonte died, Alyce Driver continued trying to overcome homelessness and rebuild her life. Then, with the help of donations raised by Laurie Norris and her Public Justice Center, she was able to rent a small house where she and her sons and her parents could all live together. Things were still not easy. She sought work, she sought to keep the bills paid. She worried about her electricity being cut off. She was afraid of the dark.

But the family managed. Alyce Driver's father still did his construction work. Her mother worked in a nursing home. Her oldest son worked at a day care center. Alyce Driver began working as a dental assistant, sometimes in Carver-Taylor's office and sometimes on the mobile clinic.

On the frigid evening of February 25, 2012, the fifth anniversary of Deamonte's death, Alyce Driver organized a memorial vigil on the steps of the Foundation School. The wind was bitter. A small knot of family and friends gathered. State dental director Harry Goodman, who had been overseeing the reforms of the state Medicaid dental system, was also there, a cap clamped down over his ears. Lawyer Laurie Norris, who was now working on a national level to hold state Medicaid dental programs accountable as a senior policy adviser at the Centers for Medicare and Medicaid Services, distributed white candles from a box in the trunk of her car. There were songs, sung against the sharp wind. It was hard to keep the candles lit. But as the sky darkened, a slender crescent moon appeared, along with Venus and Jupiter. The heavenly bodies hung there gleaming, a triangle in the deep blue.

On a weekday morning, the Prince George's County Health Department commemorated the fifth anniversary, too, with speeches and a breakfast buffet. Congressman Elijah Cummings was there. He quoted the prophet Jeremiah.

"My son is dead," he began, standing beside a large photograph of Deamonte. In the audience was Alyce Driver, dressed in her scrubs, with tears in her eyes.

The Deamonte Driver Dental Project mobile clinic was parked outside and it was offering tours to dignitaries and care to school-children. Alyce Driver took some fruit from the buffet and climbed aboard. She quietly went to work beside volunteer dentist Mfon Umoren. One by one, Alyce Driver guided children back to the dental chair, removing their woolen hats and wiping their runny noses, tucking the paper bibs under their chins, comforting the ones who were frightened. She took up the clipboard with a paper chart for each child. She listened as Umoren examined each tooth and offered her assessment. She used a red pen to mark the diseased places on the chart.

Around Alyce Driver, the mobile clinic bearing her son's name was a small, plain well-lit world, like a drop on a microscope slide. At any given time, it contained a dozen people: children giggling and whimpering, Umoren and Carver-Taylor and Betty Thomas, visiting officials from the county and the state. The instruments whirred and pulsed, and beneath their sounds there was the hum of the generator that powered the vehicle, the hum of the battle against disease, the battle for health, plain and ordinary, being fought one tooth at a time at the heart of the silent epidemic.

12

Sons and Daughters of Chapin Harris

On a brilliant October afternoon in Baltimore, the members of the newest class of the world's oldest dental college filed into historic Davidge Hall, on the University of Maryland's medical campus. Within the gloom of the aged, semicircular lecture amphitheater, they found their places. Beneath the gaze of the white busts of ancient healers, they listened to speeches. Then when they were bidden, they rose together from the steep rows of wooden seats.

The words they spoke in unison were not those of the Hippocratic Oath. But they were the words of an oath just the same: a promise to uphold the profession's principles of ethics and integrity, to place the health and well-being of patients first. "I will promote the welfare of my community by providing unbiased service to those in need and speaking out against injustice," they said. "I realize that the high regard of dentistry is borne of society's trust of practitioners and I will merit that trust."

Then, they donned their white coats. They were now professionals. They left Davidge and took the short walk to their own school, the University of Maryland School of Dentistry. Many paused at the door to pose in their white coats, alone and in groups, for photographs beside the historical marker reading "First Dental College in the World."

"It's a dream school," said Jasmine Waters. The Prince George's County native said the importance of having a beautiful smile had brought her to the career of dentistry. "I went through an awkward phase," she said. "My smile always gave me confidence."

Her new classmate Behnam Majd, who had come to America from Iran, said he hoped to dedicate his future dental career to getting care to needy Americans. "I think I owe back to the community here," he said. Then they disappeared inside, where a reception and four years of dental education awaited them.

A little more than 175 years had passed since Chapin Harris and Horace Hayden made their own short journey from Davidge Hall to start a profession from scratch, to deliver the first lectures not in the medical college with its domed anatomical theater, with its noble stench of cadavers, with its drafts and darkness and discoveries, but in the Baptist church on Calvert Street. At a time when most people, including many physicians, saw dentists as lowly manual tradesmen, at best tooth pullers, at worst charlatans, Harris was convinced that dentistry was a high calling. Though not everyone appreciated its complexity, its profound beauty, its integral role in human health, Harris insisted that dentistry deserved respect.

"Many regard it as a mere mechanical occupation, and believe that anyone possessed of a slight degree of tact and manual dexterity can practice it. But this is a mistaken view of the subject," he wrote. "Dentistry, as it exists at the present day, is a science, partaking of medicine, surgery, and the manual arts; and he who practices it, should have some knowledge of all these branches, and moreover, be possessed of a mind that naturally inclines to their study."

In terms of the need for the formal education of dentists, Harris had been determined to find a way to establish a course of studies.

But he did not seem overly concerned about whether the school was separate from the medical school or part of it.

"That a college for the education of persons for the profession might be gotten up, and that it would be well sustained I think is more than probable," Harris noted. "The same object might be accomplished by the establishing of professorships of dentistry in Medical Schools—all the branches necessary to a dental education, might be taught."[1]

The independent dental college Harris and Hayden founded would be separate from the medical school. So would nearly every American dental school that has opened since. The professions of dentistry and medicine would develop along separate paths. While medicine would expand beyond surgery in its approaches to healing, dentistry would remain largely focused upon surgical procedures to treat the symptoms of disease.

America's dental care system continues to reward those surgical procedures far more than it does prevention. That fact, and its enduring impact upon the way dentists see and address oral disease, was a topic of conversation for a handful of "Evidence-Based Dentistry Champions" who gathered for a preconference session at the American Dental Association's 2015 annual meeting. The subject under discussion was dental sealants. The coatings, which are applied with a small syringe or brush, have been found to be highly effective in preventing decay when placed upon the biting surfaces of children's newly erupted permanent molars. Research has also found that sealants can be useful in delaying or stopping the progress of decay, if applied early in the disease process to "noncavitated lesions" or soft spots in tooth enamel.

Even after the American Dental Association's Council on Scientific Affairs issued a 2008 clinical recommendation supporting the usefulness of the treatment for children, adolescents, and adults, dentists have been slow to accept the practice.[2] A 2011 study found that fewer than 40 percent of dentists surveyed were following the recommendation.[3] The reluctance among many dentists to place a sealant on a demineralized area on a tooth persists. They remain far more likely to drill.

"There is a mental block," said Montana dentist and researcher Jane Gillette. "Dentists want to pick up a handpiece and start drilling in teeth. Sometimes more conservative treatment is more patient-friendly," she noted. But conservative treatment comes as a challenge to the dentists' worldview. "We are surgeons. We are trained to drill teeth. The nonsurgical approach is a mind-bender for us."

Elliot Abt, a dentist and adjunct associate professor of oral medicine at the University of Illinois, put the conflict more bluntly in a PowerPoint presentation. "You take this out of the practitioner's hand," he noted, showing a slide of a dental drill. "You take this out of his pockets," he added, showing a stack of money.

Some over the years have disputed whether the physicians of Davidge really rejected Harris and Hayden's plan to teach dentistry at the college of medicine. Some have questioned whether the medical men sent the dentists away with the haughty admonition that the "subject of dentistry was of no consequence." Yet the story of the "historic rebuff" has lived on. It has been used to explain the isolation of dentistry, to criticize it, and also to justify it.

J. Ben Robinson, the son of a confederate Civil War veteran and a 1914 graduate of the dental school who served as dean there for nearly three decades, told the story as a fierce paean to dental independence. The physicians never sent Hayden and Harris away, insisted Robinson. Dentistry was separate, from the beginning, by choice, he said. The profession remained separate by nature.

"I know that the founding of the independent Baltimore College of Dental Surgery was not, *as has been alleged*, an alternative resorted to by the founders, after their request to have dental education included in the medical school organization was rejected," Robinson wrote.

"Instead, the founding of an independent college was a deliberate move made to establish a separate system of dental education

that would serve the special needs of an autonomous dental profession," Robinson contended in an essay published in the *Journal
of the American Dental Association*. "I know that the facts of dental
history confirm the view that while dentistry and conventional
medicine 'have their roots in the same biological soil,' the dental art
in its true sense has never been an integral part of the conventional
medical art.

"I know that the main cause of the natural separation of the
two arts is that dental diseases, defects and disorders *are not self
reparative*, as are those of other parts of the human system and,
therefore, cannot be cured or corrected by the use of therapeutic
agents commonly applied or prescribed by the conventional medical practitioner."[4]

Robinson was widely known and respected in the profession.
He had served as the president of the American Dental Association.
He was eighty years old when his essay was published in 1964. It
appeared at a tense moment for organized dentistry, as federal officials moved forward with plans for a national health care program
for the elderly. The Medicare program was signed into law the
following year. Like Robinson, the architects of the huge federal
health care program would draw a sharp line between medical care
and dental care. Medicare would deliver a full range of medical
services to generations of American elders, but it would not address
their dental needs. In Medicaid, a dental care entitlement for children would be added, as a kind of afterthought.

It is hard not to wonder if America's health care system—and the
state of its oral health—would be different today if Harris and
Hayden had stayed at Davidge and founded a dental department
within the medical school; if dentists were, from the start, routinely
educated along with other health care providers; and if they went
into the world with more intimate ties to the world of medicine
and to the larger health care system. If that road had been taken,
more dental care might be provided in the way it is offered in a
clinic run by Chase Brexton Health Services, a federally qualified

health center headquartered in a restored Gilded Age insurance building in downtown Baltimore.

Chase Brexton, which got its start three decades ago as a volunteer-run gay health clinic responding to the AIDS crisis, now offers care to the wider community. It serves more than thirty thousand patients annually. Its "medical home model" represents a growing trend in health care design. At Chase Brexton, dental services are available under the same roof as medical and mental health care. Doctors, nurses, and dentists talk to one another. They can literally bring patients to one another. Such face-to-face referrals, sometimes called "warm handoffs," hold promise for addressing some of the fear and anxiety millions of Americans experience when seeking dental treatment, researchers say. Dental records are integrated with medical and mental health records as well, helping providers to see the patient as a whole person.

"We are always trying to improve the way we integrate dental care into primary medicine. It's never really done well anywhere," said dental director Brooks Woodward, himself a graduate of the world's oldest college of dentistry. "We are a rare institution where you can get on an elevator and see primary medicine, ob-gyn, behavioral health, and dentistry all on the same placard on the wall."

Patients do not always receive their dental care at the clinic. A Chase Brexton public health dental hygienist goes out into the field, making the rounds of county nutrition centers and schools, delivering preventive services and oral health education to new mothers, infants, and children. It is the kind of approach Surgeon General David Satcher endorsed in *Oral Health in America*, where he reframed oral disease as a public health concern, to be addressed by prevention, by community-based interventions, by interdisciplinary teams.

Since the surgeon general's report was issued in 2000, factors ranging from breakthroughs in the study of the human oral microbiome to new federal, state, and nonprofit health initiatives have continued to challenge the traditional isolation of dentistry. They have furthered research into the associations between oral and systemic diseases, supported wider dental services in community health clinics, and spurred innovations in the dental workforce.

Dental caries can often be prevented with oral hygiene, education, and dietary changes, with skills that can be taught by doctors, nurses, dental hygienists, social workers, dieticians, and lay health workers such as promontoras de salud, many experts have argued. Armed with new skills, hygienists like Tammi Byrd who are trained to restore decayed teeth using minimally invasive techniques may continue to press the boundaries of scope of practice, preventing and treating disease in schools, nursing homes, and poor communities. Alaskan dental health aide therapists drill and fill teeth in villages that have gone without routine dental care for generations. But the DHATs who now provide care to 40,000 Alaska Natives also do preventive work, swabbing mouths with povidone iodine, applying sealants, and delivering cups of fluoride rinse to schoolchildren. Therapists are also being tried on tribal lands in Washington and Oregon. A variation of the dental therapist model is now at work in Minnesota. The model has been approved in Maine and in Vermont and is under active discussion in other states, in spite of the continuing opposition of organized dentistry. A handful of advocates are quietly talking about launching an effort to bring dental therapists to Maryland. Progress has been made in expanding care in Maryland. But the state could do far better, they say.

As of August 2015, more than 1,385 dentists were enrolled in the state's Medicaid dental program, Maryland Healthy Smiles— up from 649 in August 2009. And according to the most recent figures contained in a fall 2015 report to the state legislature, more than 54 percent of Maryland children enrolled in Medicaid for any part of fiscal year 2014 received at least one dental service. Despite a steep increase in the number of children enrolled in the state's Medicaid program in recent years, utilization rates have continued to climb.[5]

Not all of the dental services were provided by dentists. Medicaid children in Maryland and across the country remain more likely to see a physician or a nurse than a dentist. As some other states have done, Maryland now trains and reimburses medical providers to administer preventive fluoride varnish treatments to infants and toddlers. As of June 2015, these providers had administered nearly 144,000 fluoride varnish treatments to poor children in Maryland. In addition, school-based dental sealant programs targeting schools in poor neighborhoods have been launched in fourteen counties across the state.

In spite of the prevention efforts, the costs for the care have gone on rising. Sitting in his office in the world's oldest dental college, Norman Tinanoff held up a sheet of paper. "This is my Rosetta stone," he said, displaying a graph that showed steep and steady escalation in spending on Medicaid dental services. In 2007, the year Deamonte Driver died, the state spent $43 million on Medicaid dental care. By 2011, spending on the program had risen to $153 million. By 2014, the cost was up to $159 million. The sealants, fluoride varnishes, and routine dental checkups were still not reaching thousands of Maryland children. The burgeoning cost of treating disease is unsustainable, Tinanoff said.

Nationally in 2016, dental leaders hailed as great news the finding, reflected in federal data, that between 2000 and 2012, the percentage of Medicaid children receiving at least one dental service had climbed from 29 percent to 48 percent. But more than half—roughly 18 million—received no care in 2012 and the system continues to fail in reaching millions of poor children—children who are at the highest risk for disease.

Down in Baltimore's Fells Point area, a shipbuilding center in the days of Chapin Harris, pleasure boats now ride at anchor. In the once-pestilential lowlands by the water, condominium projects now rise. The city is no longer the gilded mecca it once was. But new immigrants still come, as they did in the nineteenth century, and struggle for a foothold.

Dental school professor Clemencia Vargas has continued to bring her Spanish-speaking dental students down to Fells Point to

provide dental care to children who might not otherwise get attention. At a school called the Wolfe Academy, under Vargas's watch-
ful eye, five young women in colorful scrubs, wearing blue gloves
and holding wooden tongue depressors, were hard at work, sitting
astride a couple of the long wooden benches in the school cafeteria,
examining the children a few at a time.

"*Abre. Abre,*" the dental students said, gently, running their
gloved fingers over the children's teeth and gums, some as perfect
as pearls, others with soft rotten places. For some of the children, it
was the first dental service they had received in their lives. When
they were finished with their exams, they carefully carried away
their new red and blue toothbrushes.

The teeth are tools we have been given to survive. We use them for
eating, for speaking, even for defending ourselves. Their mineral
beauty is a kind of gift. There is the uncanny way they are part of
us. The unsettling ways they leave us.

The teething pains of infancy herald the appearance of the baby
teeth, the deciduous teeth. Their shedding and replacement with
the permanent teeth are part of our passage from childhood to
adolescence. The eruption of the third molars, the wisdom teeth,
signals the advent of young adulthood. As time goes on, our aging
is reflected in our teeth. They wear and darken. The gums recede
and we grow "long in the tooth." Time and disease take their toll.

During our lives, their enamel is demineralized and remineralized in regular cycles. They are washed and cleaned by the saliva.
When we brush, we disrupt the plaque that lives on them. Fluoride
can help strengthen them. What we eat and drink can make them
more vulnerable to decay. So can neglect. So can the lack of professional care. Infection takes hold. Beyond a certain point the teeth
cannot be repaired.

In small ways and large ways the teeth call us back to ourselves.
They call us back to suffering, to beauty, to our time on earth.

Mamé Adjei had an eventful year reigning as Miss Maryland USA. She traveled the state, talking to schoolchildren and smiling at charity events. On a trip to Los Angeles early in the year, she finished second in a competition for the title of America's Next Top Model. In July, she went to Baton Rouge, Louisiana, to vie for the title of Miss USA 2015 and, with it, a chance to compete for the crown of Miss Universe.

Then presidential candidate and Miss Universe Organization owner Donald Trump cast a long shadow over the competition. Longtime Miss USA broadcaster NBC shelved plans to air the show. Scheduled hosts, judges, and musical performers pulled out in protest of anti-immigrant remarks that Trump made in announcing his campaign. In spite of the controversy, Adjei competed. Strutting boldly down the runway, dressed in a daring, jet-black gown, she made it to the final round of the national competition. She was crowned fourth runner-up.

In the fall of 2015, she returned to the suburban ballroom where her career as Miss Maryland USA began exactly a year before. She thanked her managers and coaches, her friends and relatives. She thanked the dentists who made her smile brighter. She thanked the Almighty for guiding her journey. She expressed her gratitude to the state itself.

"Maryland, it was my honor to be your queen," she said, "God bless you." She received a standing ovation. And when the pageant was over, Adjei posed and smiled for photos with the other contestants, with the winners and the losers, and with starstruck little girls. As the chairs were being stacked up in the ballroom and the crowd was drifting away, she was still smiling.

In essential ways, Maryland's adult Medicaid system has not yet recovered from the Earlie Trice fraud scandal, back in the 1970s. In 2016, Maryland remained one of only a small handful of states across the country that provided no adult dental benefits under Medicaid. In the western part of the state, where President Lyndon

B. Johnson spoke when he was launching his War on Poverty, the people of Appalachia are still poor. And their teeth still tell the story.

At a free weekend dental clinic at the Allegany County fairgrounds, the low mountains turned russet in the sunlight. In the exhibit hall, the hurting patients waited in the rows of folding chairs. Years without routine care left many in deep dread. For many, rare meetings with dentists had gone badly.

"It's a little scary, to get your gums cut and your teeth broke off. The sound of the cracking in your jaw is frightening," said construction worker Aaron Thrasher, thirty-two.

Not far away, a young woman was doubled over, wordlessly. Things had been hard for her, behind the white curtain. She would need more extractions, explained her companion, Keith Lambert, a fifty-five-year-old carpenter. He, himself, had no teeth left to lose. "I've got false teeth already," he said.

At a nearby table, volunteer dental technicians worked to craft replacements for the teeth that were extracted at the free clinic. The Bunsen burners flared and the curing pot steamed as they worked, skillfully shaping white artificial teeth to add to patients' upper and lower plates.

Lambert watched them quietly, sadly. "I wish I had my old teeth back."

Meanwhile, local health advocates in the mountain community continued to work to instill oral health literacy and deliver more prevention. The nonprofit Allegany Health Right applies for grants so it can pay local dentists to provide office visits to poor adults. The group employs a community health worker to bring oral health education to disabled and unemployed workers at day programs and job centers. The efforts may be having an impact. Unlike in many other places across America, emergency room visits are down in Allegany County.

"It's a handful of people trying to change the culture around oral health," said Susan Stewart, executive director of the Western Maryland Health Education Center. She helped organize the free clinic where up to four hundred patients were expected to be seen. She did not pretend one clinic would meet the need. "It's a Band-Aid until there is a full Medicaid benefit."

Stewart was not the only advocate to say it was time adult Medicaid dental benefits were restored in Maryland. Early in 2016, leaders of the Maryland Dental Action Coalition (MDAC), the group that evolved from the committee appointed to reform the state's children's program, made a trip to the state capitol in Annapolis. Thanks to reforms put in place since the death of Deamonte Driver, Maryland had become an example to the nation in getting dental care to Medicaid children, they told the lawmakers. Then they asked for the funding of Medicaid benefits for adults.

They left the chamber hopeful. But they knew more work lay ahead. "This is the opening volley," predicted MDAC board chair Salliann Alborn.

The story of Deamonte Driver continues to be told, not just in Maryland but around the country. It has become part of an ongoing movement. It is part of a larger narrative.

The same week Deamonte Driver died in Maryland, a six-year-old collapsed on a school bus in rural Gulfport, Mississippi. It happened just a few minutes after the bell rang at Lizana Elementary, as the school bus trundled down a country road. The driver stopped the bus. An older student tried, without success, to revive little Alexander Callender. Police and paramedics were called. Then the staff back at the school was alerted.

"They called me into the office and asked me if I had a little boy in my room named Alex and if there was any way I could get in touch with his mother," recalled his teaching assistant, Amanda Knight. "I remember pulling his file."

The boy had seemed fine that day. He had been one of her favorites. She had helped him use his scissors. He was left-handed. They had talked and giggled. "There was nothing during the day that led me to think there was anything wrong," she recalled. After the call came, Knight hurried down the road toward the place where the bus had stopped. The ambulance had taken the child.

"He was already gone," remembered Knight.

He had recently had two teeth extracted but the dental infection had persisted. It had spread to his brain, the Harrison County coroner found. "Septic. Yes. Septicemia," Knight said.

Seated outside the elementary school, Knight looked out over the lawn to a place where a small bench had been placed as a memorial to him. She found no broad public health lesson contained in the tragedy. For her, it was about God's hand and how it inexplicably moved that day, her heart and how it broke that day. Nothing in her training prepared her for such a thing, for one of her children dying.

"They teach you how to love them. They teach you how to take care of them. They teach you how to make them smile. How to get them to learn things. But I promise you not one time in any of the classes in any of the books did it ever mention what are you supposed to do when one of your babies passes away."

After the bench was dedicated, the boy's mother moved away. She could not be reached to talk any more about her son. But Mississippi dental hygienist Marsha Parker has not stopped speaking about Alexander Callender. She has crisscrossed the levees and driven the lonely wooded roads and the state highways with a battered and mended teaching puppet and storybooks in her backseat. She keeps packs of crackers and a GPS on her dashboard. When her GPS runs out of directions, she takes it as a good sign. It means she is bringing an oral health message to someone who might otherwise not hear it.

"I'm gonna reach somebody who wouldn't be reached," she said. At a rural Head Start program, in a small schoolhouse set back from the road, she gets out of her car. She hauls her bag of supplies into the school. The children gather around and listen to her read a storybook about taking care of their teeth. When she pulls out her puppet named Charlie, they line up eagerly to take their turn, to hold the big toothbrush and help him brush.

"You are so lucky, Charlie, to have these boys and girls brush your teeth," she tells the puppet.

Over the miles, Marsha Parker carries a school picture of little Alexander Callender, with his blond cowlick and his smile. She keeps it in a protective plastic notebook sleeve, along with a picture of Deamonte Driver. She tells the stories of the two boys to young women expecting babies and to municipal officials discussing water fluoridation. She tells the stories to anyone who will listen. Then she hands around the plastic notebook page, with the faces of those two lost children.

Alyce Driver keeps the picture of her dead son in the living room. It is set on a special shelf. Deamonte's head is cocked to the side. His eyes are searching, questioning. He is twelve years old. His brothers have kept growing. His oldest brother, Danny, has a child of his own—a curly-headed baby boy who is passed around, cuddled, and hugged. A boy named Deamonte.

Acknowledgments

This book would not have been written without the kindness and patience of many people. Both those who offered background information and those who have been named generously shared their knowledge, opinions, experiences, wisdom, and stories. A Knight Science Journalism Fellowship that allowed me to spend an academic year attending classes at the Harvard schools of dental medicine and public health provided immeasurable help in the reporting of this book. The Knight fellowship as well as a fellowship from the Dennis A. Hunt Fund for Health Journalism offered guidance and assistance with the costs of reporting and travel. The staff of institutions including the National Library of Medicine, the National Archives, and the Library of Congress aided with research. Larry Akey provided invaluable technical support and wisdom. At different stages in its development, literary agent Albert LaFarge as well as Chester Douglass, Peggy Gallos, Roberta Haber, and Kathy Kincade took on the task of reading the manuscript and offered deep insights that made it better. At The New

Press, the brilliant Marc Favreau helped bring this project to life and nurtured it to completion. Profound thanks are due to the entire New Press team, including Diane Wachtell, Maredith Sheridan, Julie McCarroll, Sharon Swados, Emily Albarillo, and Sarah Scheffel. Thanks and love also to Jeffrey Frey and to my son, Harry Frey, who has grown from childhood to manhood inspiring me and encouraging me in this work.

Notes

Preface

1. American Dental Association Health Policy Institute, "The Oral Health System: A State-by-State Analysis," 2015, www.ada.org/~/media /ADA/Science%20and%20Research/HPI/OralHealthCare-StateFacts/Oral -Health-Care-System-Full-Report.pdf.

2. Nikki Rousseau and others, "Your Whole Life Is Lived Through Your Teeth: Biographical Disruption and Experiences of Tooth Loss and Replacement," *Sociology of Health and Illness* 36 no. 3 (2014): 462–76.

3. Neeta Mehta, "Mind-Body Dualism: A Critique from a Health Perspective," *Mens Sana Monographs* 9 (January–December 2011): 202–9.

4. U.S. Department of Health and Human Services, *Oral Health in America: A Report of the Surgeon General* (Rockville, MD: U.S. Department of Health and Human Services, National Institute of Dental and Craniofacial Research, National Institutes of Health, 2000), 2.

1. Beauty

1. *Holy Bible New Revised Standard Version* (New York: Oxford University Press, 1989), 693.

2. Bill Dorfman, *Billion Dollar Smile* (Nashville: Rutledge Hill Press), 2–3.

3. Wells Fargo Bank, "Industry Perspective: US Dental Practices," 2011, www.burkhartdental.com/sites/default/files/files/news/dental_offices_9 _2011.pdf. Also see "Cosmetic Dentistry Roundtable," *Dental Economics* 92 (January 2002) and "Cosmetic Dentistry Roundtable," *Dental Economics* 92 (April 2002).

4. National Institute of Teeth Whitening, "Teeth Whitening Industry's Annual Revenue in 2015 Totals $11 Billion," niotw.com/teeth-whit ening-industrys-annual-revenue-in-2015-totals-11-billion.

5. Chapin A. Harris, *The Dental Art: A Practical Treatise on Dental Surgery* (Baltimore: Armstrong & Berry, 1839), 26.

6. Richard A. Glenner, Audrey B. Davis, and Stanley B. Burns, *The American Dentist: A Pictorial History with a Presentation of Early Dental Photography in America* (Missoula, MT: Pictorial Histories Publishing Co, 1990), viii.

7. Susan Sontag, *On Photography* (New York: Farrar, Straus and Giroux, 1973), 85.

8. Charles Pincus, "Building Mouth Personality," *Alpha Omegan* 42 (October 1948): 163–67.

9. Ibid.

10. Claudia Levy, "Shirley Temple Black, Actress and Diplomat, Dies at 85," *Washington Post*, February 11, 2014.

11. Shirley Temple Black, *Child Star: An Autobiography* (New York: McGraw Hill, 1988), 233.

12. John F. Kasson, *The Little Girl Who Fought the Great Depression: Shirley Temple and 1930s America* (New York: W.W. Norton and Company, 2014), 6.

13. Charles Pincus, "Cosmetics—The Psychologic Fourth Dimension in Full Mouth Rehabilitation," *Dental Clinics of North America* 11 (March 1967): 71–88.

14. Elizabeth Haiken, *Venus Envy: A History of Cosmetic Surgery* (Baltimore and London: Johns Hopkins University Press, 1997), 146.

15. Richard D. Lyons, "End of Most Tooth Decay Predicted for Near Future," *New York Times*, December 20, 1983.

16. Warren Berger, "What's New in Cosmetic Dentistry," *New York Times*, October 11, 1987.

17. Laurie Essig, *American Plastic: Boob Jobs, Credit Cards and Our Quest for Perfection* (Boston: Beacon Press, 2010), 36.

18. Chris Herren, Tim Armentrout, and Mark Higgins, "Body Dysmorphic Disorder: Diagnosis and Treatment," *General Dentistry* 51 (March–April 2003): 164–66.

19. Gordon Christensen, "I Have Had Enough!" dentaltown.com, Septem-

ber 2003, www.dentaltown.com/Dentaltown/Article.aspx?aid=455&i=25
&st=I%20have%20had%20enough.

2. Suffering

1. Robert Wood Johnson Foundation and University of Wisconsin Population Health Institute, "2015 County Health Rankings Virginia," www.countyhealthrankings.org.

2. Health Resources and Services Administration Data Warehouse, data warehouse.hrsa.gov/GeoAdvisrr/ShortageDesignationAdvisor.aspx.

3. Elham Emami and others, "The Impact of Edentulism on Oral and General Health," *International Journal of Dentistry,* published online May 8, 2013, doi: 10.1155/2013/498305.

4. Southwest Virginia Graduate Medical Education Consortium, "Report to the Virginia State Assembly," January 2008.

5. Andrew D. Wade and others, "Early Dental Intervention in the Redpath Ptolemaic Theban Male," *International Journal of Paleopathology* 2 (December 2012): 217–22; Jeffrey H. Schwartz, Jaymie Brauer, and Penny Gordon-Iarsen, "Tigaran (Point Hope, Alaska) Tooth Drilling," *American Journal of Physical Anthropology* 97 (May 1995): 77–82; Charlotte Robert and Keith Manchester, *Archeology of Disease* (Ithaca, New York: Cornell University Press, 2005), 82.

6. American Dental Association Health Policy Institute, "Fewer Americans Forgoing Dental Care Due to Cost," October 2014, www.ada.org/~/media/ADA/Science%20and%20Research/HPI/Files/HPIBrief_1014_6.ashx.

7. Liz Hamel and others, "The Burden of Medical Debt: Results from the Kaiser Family Foundation/New York Times Medical Bills Survey," January 5, 2016, kff.org/health-costs/report/the-burden-of-medical-debt-results-from-the-kaiser-family-foundationnew-york-times-medical-bills-survey.

8. Teresa A. Dolan and others, "Access to Dental Care Among Older Adults in the United States," *Journal of Dental Education* 69 (September 2005): 961–74.

9. Mary Otto, "Dentist of the Back Roads," *Washington Post,* February 23, 2008.

10. U.S. Government Accountability Office, *Oral Health: Efforts Underway to Improve Children's Access to Dental Services, but Sustained Attention Needed to Address Ongoing Concerns,* Washington, D.C., November 2010.

11. American Dental Association Health Policy Institute, "The Oral Health Care System: A State-by-State Analysis," December 9, 2015.

12. C.S. Lewis, *A Grief Observed* (New York: HarperCollins, 1994), 9.

13. Barbara Bloom and others, "Oral Health Status and Access to Oral Health Care for U.S. Adults Aged 18–64: National Health Interview Survey, 2008," *Vital Health Statistics* 10, no. 253 (July 2012), 1–22.

14. Robert E. Pawlicki, "Psychological/Behavioral Techniques in Managing Pain and Anxiety in the Dental Patients," *Anesthesia Progress* 38 (July–October 1991): 120–27.

15. Ilana Eli, *Oral Psychophysiology: Stress, Pain and Behavior in Dental Care* (Boca Raton, Florida: CRC Press, 1992).

16. American Dental Association Health Policy Institute "The Oral Health Care System: A State-by-State Analysis," December 9, 2015.

17. Robert Wood Johnson Foundation and University of Wisconsin Population Health Institute, "2015 County Health Rankings Virginia," www.countyhealthrankings.org.

18. Charlotte Lewis and James Stout, "Toothache in US Children," *Archives of Pediatrics and Adolescent Medicine* 164 (November 2010): 1059–63.

19. Stephanie L. Jackson and others, "Impact of Poor Oral Health on Children's School Attendance and Performance," *American Journal of Public Health* 101 (October 2011): 1900–906.

20. Clemencia Vargas and others, "Dental Pain in Maryland School Children," *Journal of Public Health Dentistry* 65 (Winter 2005): 3–6.

21. Leonard Cohen and others, "Toothache Pain: Behavioral Impact and Self Care Strategies," *Special Care Dentistry* 29 (July 2009): 85–94.

3. Emergencies

1. Dental Access Now, "It's an Emergency! Too Many Ohioans Go to Emergency Rooms for Oral Health Care Needs," September 2014, uhcanohio.org/sites/default/files/DAN%20Emergency%20Report%20-%20FINAL.pdf.

2. Veerasathpurush Allareddy and others, "Hospital-Based Emergency Department Visits Involving Dental Conditions," *Journal of the American Dental Association* 145 (April 2014): 331–37.

3. Kathryn R. Fingar and others, "Medicaid Dental Coverage Alone May Not Lower Rates of Dental Emergency Department Visits," *Health Affairs* 34 (August 2015): 1349–57.

4. Jane Brody, "Avoiding Emergency Rooms," *New York Times*, April 15, 2013.

5. Elizabeth E. Davis, Amos Deinard, and Eugenie W.H. Maiga, "Doctor, My Tooth Hurts: The Cost of Incomplete Dental Care in the Emergency Room," *Journal of Public Health Dentistry* 70 (Summer 2010): 205–10.

6. Stanford Medicine New Center, August 3, 2015, med.stanford.edu/news/all-news/2015/08/medicaid-dental-coverage-may-not-prevent-tooth-related-er-visits.html.

7. William J. Gies, *Dental Education in the United States and Canada: A Report to the Carnegie Foundation for the Advancement of Teaching* (New York: Carnegie Foundation for the Advancement of Teaching, 1926), 137.

8. Mary Otto, "Safety-net Clinics in Your Community May Benefit from New Federal Dental Care Grants," *Association of Health Care Journalists blog*, July 13, 2016, healthjournalism.org/blog/2016/07/safety-net-clinics -in-your-community-may-benefit-from-new-federal-dental-care-grants.

9. Richard A. Glenner, Audrey B. Davis, and Stanley B. Burns, *The American Dentist: A Pictorial History with a Presentation of Early Dental Photography in America* (Missoula, MT: Pictorial Histories Publishing Co, 1990), 71.

10. Burton Lee Thorpe, "A Biographical Review of the Careers of Hayden and Harris," *The Dental Cosmos* 47 (September 1905): 1047–57.

11. Chapin A. Harris, *The Dental Art: A Practical Treatise on Dental Surgery* (Baltimore: Armstrong & Berry, 1839), 52.

12. Andrea C. Shah and others, "Outcomes of Hospitalizations Attributed to Periapical Abscess from 2000 to 2008: A Longitudinal Trend Analysis," *Journal of Endodontics* 39 (September 2013): 1104–10.

13. Joana Cunha-Cruz and others, "Recommendations for Third Molar Removal: A Practice-Based Cohort Study," *American Journal of Public Health* 104 (April 2014): 735–43; Elise Oberliesen, "Dentists Debate Need to Extract Wisdom Teeth," *Los Angeles Times*, January 2, 2015.

14. Pew Center on the States, "A Costly Dental Destination: Hospital Care Means States Pay Dearly," February 2012, www.pewtrusts.org/en/research -and-analysis/reports/2012/02/28/a-costly-dental-destination.

4. The World Beneath Our Noses

1. Georges Cuvier, *Discourse on the Revolutionary Upheavals on the Surface of the Earth* (Arlington, Virginia: Richer Resources Publications, 2009), 59.

2. Tanya M. Smith and others, "Earliest Evidence of Modern Human Life History in North African Early Homo Sapiens," *Proceedings of the National Academy of Sciences* 104 (April 10, 2007): 6128–33.

3. Christine Austin, Tanya Smith, and others, "Barium Distributions in Teeth Reveal Early-Life Dietary Transitions in Primates," *Nature*, published online May 22, 2013, doi: 10.1038/nature12169. Published in final edited form in *Nature* 498, no. 7453 (June 13, 2013): 216–19.

4. James M. Byers, *From Hippocrates to Virchow: Reflections on Human Disease* (Chicago: ASCP [American Society of Clinical Pathologists] Press, 1988): 34.

5. Clifford Dobell, *Anthony van Leeuwenhoek and His "Little Animals"* (New York: Dover Publications, 1960), 239.

6. William John Gies and Henry S. Pritchett, *Dental Education in the*

United States and Canada (New York: Carnegie Foundation for the Advancement of Teaching, 1926), 28–29.

7. Thomas Bond, "To the Graduates of the Baltimore College of Dental Surgery, delivered at the Commencement, March 9, 1841," *American Journal of Dental Science* 1, nos. 11 and 12 (1841): 241–57.

8. Chapin A. Harris, *The Dental Art: A Practical Treatise on Dental Surgery* (Baltimore: Armstrong & Berry, 1839): 167–68.

9. Willoughby D. Miller, "The Human Mouth as a Focus of Infection," *Dental Cosmos* 33 (September 1891), 689–713.

10. Malvin E. Ring, *Dentistry: An Illustrated History* (New York: Harry N. Abrams, 1985), 271–72.

11. William Hunter, "The Role of Sepsis and Antisepsis in Medicine," *Dental Cosmos* 60 (July 1918): 585–602.

12. F. St. John Steadman, "A Case of Rheumatoid Arthritis Twice Cured by the Removal of Septic Teeth," *Journal of the Royal Society of Medicine* 7 (June 1914): 21–28.

13. R.A. Hughes, "Focal Infection Revisited," *British Journal of Rheumatology* 33 (April 1994): 370–77.

14. Nigel Nicholson and Joanne Trautmann, *The Letters of Virginia Woolf, Volume 2, 1912–1922* (New York and London: Harcourt Brace Jovanovich, 1976), 529.

15. Virginia Woolf, *On Being Ill: With Notes from Sickrooms by Julia Stephen* (Ashfield, Massachusetts: Paris Press, 2012), 3.

16. Charles H. Mayo, "Focal Infection of Dental Origin," *Dental Cosmos* 64 (November 1922): 1206–8.

17. Andrew Scull, *Madhouse: A Tragic Tale of Megalomania and Modern Medicine* (New Haven: Yale Press, 2005).

18. C. Edmund Kells, "The X Ray in Dental Practice," *Journal of the National Dental Association* (March 7, 1920): 241–72.

19. William John Gies and Henry S. Pritchett, *Dental Education in the United States and Canada* (New York: Carnegie Foundation for the Advancement of Teaching, 1926), 9.

20. William J. Gies, "The Dental Education Problem," *Journal of the American Dental Association* 11 (February 1924): 97–108.

21. "Gutless, Glandless, Toothless," *Journal of the American Osteopathic Association* 19 (May 1920): 335.

22. Russell L. Cecil and Murray Angevine, "Clinical and Experimental Observations on Focal Infection, with an Analysis of 200 Cases of Rheumatoid Arthritis," *Annals of Internal Medicine* 12 (November 1938): 577–84.

23. Editorial, "Dental Education at Columbia University," *Journal of the American Dental Association* 32 (September 1945): 1150–52.

24. Editorial, "They Cannot Speak for Themselves," *Oral Hygiene* 33 (September 1943): 1244–45.

25. Proceedings, Dental Centenary Celebration, Scientific Sessions, Baltimore, Maryland, March 18–20, 1940.

26. "Testimony of the American Dental Association on Wagner-Murray-Dingell Bill," *Journal of the American Dental Association* 33 (June 1946): 743–54.

27. Steven L. Schlossman, JoAnne Brown, and Michael Sedlak, *The Public School in American Dentistry* (Santa Monica, California: Rand Corporation, 1986), 14.

28. Jessica L. Mark Welch and others, "Biogeography of a Human Oral Microbiome at the Micron Scale," *Proceedings of the National Academy of Sciences* 113, no. 6 (February 9, 2016): E791–E800, doi: 10.1073/pnas.1522149113.

29. Floyd Dewhirst and others, "The Human Oral Microbiome," *Journal of Bacteriology* 192 (October 2010): 5002–17.

30. P.D. Marsh, "Are Dental Diseases Examples of Ecological Catastrophes?" *Microbiology* 149 (February 2003): 279–94.

31. Remco Kort and others, "Shaping the Oral Microbiota Through Intimate Kissing," *Microbiome* 2, published online November 14, 2014, doi: 10.1186/2049-2618-2-41.

32. Michael Glick, *The Oral-Systemic Health Connection; A Guide to Patient Care* (Hanover Park, Illinois: Quintessence Publishing Company, 2014), 63.

33. Mary Otto "Diagnostic Dental Codes: Are We There Yet?" DrBicuspid.com, December 4, 2012, www.drbicuspid.com/index.aspx?sec=ser&sub=def&pag=dis&ItemID=312134.

34. Mary Otto, "Shedding Light on the Link Between Periodontitis, Diabetes, CVD, and More," DrBicuspid.com, February 15, 2012, www.drbicuspid.com/index.aspx?sec=ser&sub=def&pag=dis&ItemID=309710.

35. Wu Liu and others, "The Earliest Unequivocally Modern Humans in Southern China," *Nature*, published online October 14, 2015: 696–99, doi: 10.1038/nature15696.

36. Gregorio Oxilia and others, "Earliest Evidence of Dental Caries Manipulation in the Late Upper Paleolithic," *Scientific Reports* 5 (article 12150), published online July 16, 2015, doi: 10.1038/srep12150.

5. The Birth of American Dentistry

1. Burton Lee Thorpe, "A Biographical Review of the Careers of Hayden and Harris," *The Dental Cosmos* 47 (September, 1905):1047–57.

2. Ibid.

3. Joseph Fox and Chapin Harris, *Diseases of the Human Teeth: Their Natural History and Structure with the Mode of Applying Artificial Teeth* (Philadelphia: E. Barrington and G.D. Haswell, 1846).

4. John Hunter, *A Practical Treatise on the Diseases of the Teeth; Intended as a Supplement to the Natural History of Those Parts* (London: Printed for J. Johnson, 1778).

5. James Hall, "Popular Tales: An Event in the Life of a Dentist," *New York Mirror* 10 (April 6, 1833): 313.

6. Chapin A. Harris, *The Dental Art: A Practical Treatise on Dental Surgery* (Baltimore: Armstrong & Berry, 1839).

7. Frederick Douglass, *Narrative of the Life of Frederick Douglass, an American Slave* (New York: Doubleday & Co, 1963), 32.

8. George H. Callcott, *A History of the University of Maryland* (Baltimore: Maryland Historical Society, 1966), 103.

9. Roger Forclaz, "A Source for 'Berenice' and a Note on Poe's Reading," *Poe Newsletter* 1, no. 2 (October 1968): 25–27.

10. Edgar Allan Poe, *The Essential Tales and Poems of Edgar Allan Poe* (New York: Barnes & Noble Books, 2004), 40.

11. Thomas E. Bond Jr., "Obituary Notice of Prof. Horace H. Hayden," *American Journal of Dental Science* 4 (June 1844): 221–30.

12. J. Ben Robinson, "Dr. Horace H. Hayden and His Influence on Dental Education," *Dental Cosmos* 74 (August 1932): 783–87.

13. James McManus, "First Dental College in the World," *Connecticut Magazine* 11 (July–September 1907): 429–38.

14. Horace H. Hayden, *Geological Essays: Or an Inquiry into Some of the Geological Phenomena to Be Found in Various Parts of American and Elsewhere* (Baltimore: Printed by J. Robinson for the Author, 1820).

15. J. Ben Robinson, *The Foundations of Professional Dentistry* (Baltimore: Waverly Press, 1940), 46.

16. William Simon, "History of the Baltimore College of Dental Surgery," *Transactions of the Fourth International Dental Congress 1904* (Philadelphia: S.S. White Dental Manufacturing Company, 1905), 295.

17. Lawrence Parmly Brown, "New Light on Dental History," *Dental Cosmos* 62 (August 1920): 936–58.

18. Simon, "History of the Baltimore College of Dental Surgery," 298.

19. Robinson, *The Foundations of Professional Dentistry*, 64.

20. Robert O'Shea, "Dentistry as an Organization and Institution," *Milbank Memorial Fund Quarterly* 49, no. 3 (1971): 13–28.

21. John M. Hyson Jr., *Baltimore's Own: The World's First Dental School 1840–2006* (Baltimore: University of Maryland Dental School, 2006), 26.

22. Chapin A. Harris, "Introductory Lecture," *American Journal of Dental Science* 1 (January 1841): 198–211.

23. Hyson, *Baltimore's Own*, 39.

24. Bond, "Obituary Notice of Prof. Horace H. Hayden."

25. National Institute of Dental and Craniofacial Research (NIH), "Dental Caries (Tooth Decay)," www.nidcr.nih.gov/datastatistics/finddatabytopic/dentalcaries.

6. Separate Lives

1. Clemencia Vargas and others, "Oral Health Status of Preschool Children Attending Head Start in Maryland, 2000," *Pediatric Dentistry* 24 (March 2002): 257–63.

2. American Dental Association, "Principles of Ethics and Code of Professional Conduct," 2016, www.ada.org/~/media/ADA/Publications/Files/ADA_Code_of_Ethics_2016.pdf.

3. Bruce Peltier, "Codes and Colleagues: Is There Support for Universal Patient Acceptance?" *Journal of Dental Education* 70 (November 2006): 1221–25.

4. Bruce Peltier and Lola Giusti, "Commerce and Care: The Irreconcilable Tension Between Selling and Caring," *McGeorge Law Review* 39, no. 3 (2008): 785–800.

5. Editorial "The King-Anderson Bill," *Journal of the American Dental Association* 68 (March 1964): 448.

6. "Critics Denounce Medicaid in Marathon Albany Hearing," *Post-Standard*, Syracuse, New York, May 25, 1966.

7. Sara Rosenbaum "Caring for Flint: Medicaid's Enduring Role in Public Health Crises," *Commonwealth Fund blog*, February 22, 2016, www.commonwealthfund.org/publications/blog/2016/feb/caring-for-flint.

8. American Dental Association Health Policy Institute, "The Oral Health Care System: A State-by-State Analysis," December 9, 2015.

9. U.S. Government Accountability Office, *Oral Health: Efforts Underway to Improve Children's Access to Dental Services, but Sustained Attention Needed to Address Ongoing Concerns,* Washington, D.C., November 2010.

10. American Dental Association Health Policy Institute, "The Oral Health Care System: A State-by-State Analysis," December 9, 2015; American Dental Association, "Characteristics of Private Dental Practices: Selected 2013 Results from the Survey of Dental Practice, February 2015, www.ada.org/~/media/ADA/Science%20and%20Research/HPI/Files/HPIData_SDPC_2013.ashx.

11. T.L.Finlayson and others, "Maternal Self-Efficacy and 1–5 Year Old Children's Brushing Habits," *Community Dentistry and Oral Epidemiology* 35 (August 2007): 272–81.

12. Mahyar Mofidi and others, "Problems with Access to Dental Care for

Medicaid-Insured Children: What Caregivers Think," *American Journal of Public Health* 92 (January 2002): 53–58.

13. Joanna Bisgaier and others, "Disparities in Child Access to Emergency Care for Acute Oral Injury," *Pediatrics* 127 (June 2011): 1428–35.

14. U.S. Department of Health and Human Services, Health Resources and Services Administration, "Dental Health Professional Shortage Areas (HPSA)," datawarehouse.hrsa.gov/Tools/MapToolQuick. aspx?mapName=HPSADC.

15. U.S. Department of Health and Human Services, Health Resources and Services Administration, National Center for Health Workforce Analysis, "National and State-Level Projections of Dentists and Dental Hygienists in the U.S., 2012–2025," Rockville, Maryland, February 2015.

16. Marko Vujicic, "Rethinking Dentist Shortages," *Journal of the American Dental Association* 146 (May 2015): 347–49.

17. Centers for Medicare and Medicaid Services, "Dental and Oral Health Services in Medicaid and CHIP" and "Primary Care Access and Preventive Care in Medicaid and CHIP," February 2016, www.medicaid.gov/medicaid -chip-program-information/by-topics/benefits/downloads/2015-dental -and-oral-health-domain-specific-report.pdf.

18. Cassandra Yarbrough, Kamyar Nasseh, and Marko Vujicic, "Why Adults Forgo Dental Care: Evidence from a New National Survey," American Dental Association Health Policy Institute, November 2014,www.ada.org /~/media/ADA/Science%20and%20Research/HPI/Files/HPIBrief_1114_1 .ashx.

19. B. Bloom and others, "Oral Health Status and Access to Oral Health Care for US Adults Ages 18–64," *National Health Interview Survey 2008*, National Center for Health Statistics Vital Health Statistics Series 10, no. 253 (2012).

20. National Association of Dental Plans, "Who Has Dental Benefits?," www.nadp.org/Dental_Benefits_Basics/Dental_BB_1.aspx.

21. Seth Seabury and others, "Trends in the Earnings of Health Care Professionals in the United States, 1987–2010," *Journal of the American Medical Association* 308 (November 2012): 2083–85.

22. Bradley Munson and Marko Vujicic, "General Practitioner Dentist Earnings Down Slightly in 2014," *Health Policy Institute Research Brief*, American Dental Association, March 2016, www.ada.org/~/media/ADA /Science%20and%20Research/HPI/Files/HPIBrief_1215_1.ashx.

23. U.S. Bureau of Labor Statistics, "Dentists: Occupational Outlook Handbook," www.bls.gov/ooh/healthcare/dentists.htm (accessed August 2016).

7. Adventurers and Auxiliaries

1. Chapin A. Harris, "Address Delivered Before the American Society of Dental Surgeons," *American Journal of Dental Science* 4 (September 1843): 3–22.

2. Institute of Medicine, *Advancing Oral Health in America* (Washington, D.C.: The National Academies Press, 2011), 104.

3. George Wood Clapp, *The Rise and Fall of Oral Hygiene in Bridgeport* (New York: The Dental Digest, 1929), 5.

4. E. Baeumer, "The Occupational Diseases of Dentistry," *Dental Cosmos* 56 (January 1914): 123–24.

5. Dr. Kuhn, "The Causes for Failures in Crown and Bridge Work," *Dental Cosmos* 56 (January 1914): 122.

6. Alfred C. Fones, "The Origin and History of the Dental Hygienist Movement," *Journal of the American Dental Association* 13 (December 1926): 1809–21.

7. C.M. Wright, "Plea for a Sub-Speciality in Dentistry," *International Dental Journal* 23 (April 1902): 235.

8. Wilma E. Motley, *History of the American Dental Hygienists' Association, 1923–1982* (Chicago: American Dental Hygienists' Association, 1986), 27.

9. Alfred C. Fones, "Report of Five Years of Mouth Hygiene in the Public Schools in Bridgeport, Conn.," *Dental Cosmos* 61 (July 1919): 608–18.

10. Steven L. Schlossman, JoAnne Brown, and Michael Sedlak, *The Public School in American Dentistry* (Santa Monica, CA: Rand Corporation, April 1986), 13.

11. Fones, "Report of Five Years of Mouth Hygiene."

12. "High Professional Honor Bestowed on Dr. A.C. Fones," *Bridgeport Telegram*, Bridgeport, CT, May 4, 1927.

13. "Dental Hygiene Workers Are Kept Busy on Playgrounds of City," *Evening News*, Harrisburg, PA, August 21, 1929.

14. Schlossman, Brown, and Sedlak, *The Public School in American Dentistry*, 25.

15. Proceedings of Societies, *Dental Cosmos* 61 (December 1919): 1099.

16. Thomas J. Barrett, "A New Species of Dentist: Do We Want It?," *Dental Cosmos* 61 (December 1919): 1205–12.

17. Proceedings of Societies, *Dental Cosmos* 61 (December 1919): 1225–35.

18. William J. Gies and Henry S. Pritchett, *Dental Education in the United States and Canada* (New York: Carnegie Foundation for the Advancement of Teaching, 1926), 79.

19. "The Reaction of Two Great Associations," *Journal of the American Dental Association* 21 (October 1934): 1846–50 and "The Question of Dental

Care for the Indigent," *Journal of the American Dental Association* 21 (November 1934): 2036–39.

20. Testimony of the American Dental Association on Wagner-Murray-Dingell Bill (S1606) as reprinted in *Journal of the American Dental Association* 33 (June 1, 1946): 743–54.

21. "Dental Hygienist Bill Hits Strong Opposition," *Berkshire County Eagle*, Pittsfield, MA, March 1, 1950.

22. Ralph Lobene, *The Forsyth Experiment* (Cambridge, MA: Harvard University Press, 1979), vii.

23. Ibid., 1.

24. Ibid., 7.

25. Andy Miller, "Lawmaker Blasts Dental Group," *Georgia Health News*, January 27, 2016.

26. Paul J. Nietert, W. David Bradford, and Linda M. Kaste, "The Impact of an Innovative Reform to the South Carolina Dental Medicaid System," *Health Services Research* 40 (August 2005): 1078–91.

27. Alison Borchgrevink, Andrew Snyder, and Shelly Gehshan, "The Effects of Medicaid Reimbursement on Access to Dental Care," National Academy for State Health Policy, March 2008.

28. News release, State of South Carolina Office of the Governor, May 26, 2000.

29. J. Samuel Griswold, letter to Tammi O. Byrd, August 3, 2000.

30. Burford Duff Jr., "New State Law Has Some Real Teeth to It," *Index-Journal*, Greenwood, SC, February 13, 2001.

31. United States of America Before the Federal Trade Commission, "In the Matter of South Carolina State Board of Dentistry," Docket No. 9311, November 25, 2003.

32. Associated Press, "Dental Hygienist Sues to Protect Her Business," *Gaffney Ledger*, Gaffney, SC, August 6, 2001.

33. Elham T. Keteeb and others, "Teaching Atraumatic Restorative Treatment in U.S. Dental Schools: A Survey of Predoctoral Pediatric Dentistry Program Directors," *Journal of Dental Education* 77 (October 2013): 1306–14.

8. The System

1. Angela Ericson, "White Out: How Dental Industry Insiders Thwart Competition from Teeth-Whitening Entrepreneurs," Institute for Justice, 2013.

2. Ibid.

3. Supreme Court of the United States, *North Carolina State Board of Dental Examiners, Petitioner, v. Federal Trade Commission*, no. 13–534, February 25, 2015.

4. Carl F. Ameringer, *The Health Care Revolution: From Medical Monopoly to Market Competition* (Berkeley and Los Angeles, CA: University of California Press, 2008).

5. Wayne King, "Dentist in Battle on Gum Disease Ad," *New York Times,* May 2, 1984.

6. Gustav P. Chiarello, "FTC Competition Advocacy: A Point Where Professional Regulation Intersects Competition and Consumer Protection Policies," PowerPoint presentation, April 28, 2010, www .nationaloralhealthconference.com/docs/presentations/2010/Gus%20 Chiarello-Third%20World%20Dentistry.pdf.

7. Press release, "FTC Staff Submits Comment to the Commission on Dental Accreditation Regarding its Proposed Standards for Dental Therapy Education," Federal Trade Commission, December 4, 2013.

8. Mary Otto, "Plans Progress to Accredit Dental Therapist Training," *Association of Health Care Journalists* blog, August 18, 2015, healthjournalism .org/blog/2015/08/plans-progress-to-accredit-dental-therapist-training.

9. American Dental Association, "American Dental Association Comment on the Kellogg Foundation Report 'A Review of the Global Literature on Dental Therapists,'" April 10, 2012, www.ada.org/en/press-room/news -releases/2012-archive/april/american-dental-association-comment-on-the -kellogg.

10. American Dental Association, "Health Care Reform Update," undated letter to members.

11. Mary Otto, "US Budget Issues Put Oral Care Programs in Peril," DrBicuspid.com, July 25, 2011, www.drbicuspid.com/index.aspx?sec=ser &sub=def&pag=dis&ItemID=308195.

12. American Public Health Association, "Support for the Alaska Dental Health Aide Therapist and Other Innovative Programs," APHA Public Health Policy Statement Database, apha.org, accessed May 31, 2016.

13. Alaska Dental Society, "Second Class Dental Care for Alaska Natives Deserves a Ferocious Reaction," *Anchorage Daily News*, September 18, 2005.

14. Philip Nice with Walter Johnson, *The Alaska Health Aide Program* (Anchorage: Institute for Circumpolar Health Studies, 1998), 1.

15. David A. Nash and Ron J. Nagel, "Confronting Oral Health Disparities Among American Indian/Alaska Native Children: The Pediatric Oral Health Therapist," *American Journal of Public Health* 95 (August 2005): 1325–29.

16. Libby Roderick, editor, *Do Alaska Native People Get Free Medical Care?* (Anchorage: University of Alaska/Alaska Pacific University, 2008).

17. Cara James, Karyn Schwartz, and Julia Berndt, *A Profile of American Indians and Alaska Natives and Their Health Coverage* (Henry J. Kaiser Family Foundation, 2009), kaiserfamilyfoundation.files.wordpress.com/2013/01/7977.pdf.

9. Color Lines

1. Bruce A. Dye, Gina Thornton Evans, and others, "Dental Caries and Tooth Loss in Adults in the United States 2011–2012," NCHS Data Brief, no. 197, Hyattsville, MD: National Center for Health Statistics, May 2015.

2. U.S. Commission on Civil Rights, "Title VI One Year After: A Survey of Desegregation of Health and Welfare Services in the South," 1966.

3. Max Schoen, "Dentist Liberty Versus Patient Equity," Third-Annual Dunning Symposium, Columbia University School of Dental and Oral Surgery and School of Public Health, New York, NY, April 1983.

4. Author interview with Marvin Marcus DDS, Professor Emeritus, University of California Los Angeles School of Dentistry, June 9, 2014.

5. Associated Press, "Civil Rights Congress Hits Bridges' Judge," *Evening Independent*, St. Petersburg, FL, November 25, 1949.

6. Harvey Schwartz, editor and curator of ILWU Oral History Collection, "Harry Bridges: An Oral History about Longshoring, the Origins of the ILWU and the 1934 Strike," ILWU Oral History Collection, July 27, 2004, www.ilwu.org/oral-history-of-harry-bridges.

7. Hearings Before the Committee on Un-American Activities, House of Representatives, Eighty-second Congress, First Session, September 21, 1951, Washington, D.C.: U.S. Government Printing Office, 1951.

8. Max H. Schoen, "Response to Receiving the John W. Knutson Distinguished Service Award," *Journal of Public Health Dentistry* 51 (Summer 1991): 181–83.

9. Ibid.

10. "Politics, Trends and Geography," *Journal of the Southern California State Dental Association* (September 28, 1960): 269.

11. U.S. Department of Health, Education and Welfare, "Report on the Dental Program of the ILWU-PMA: the First Three Years," Washington, D.C.: U.S. Government Printing Office, 1962.

12. Max H. Schoen, "Group Practice and Poor Communities," *American Journal of Public Health* 60 (June 1970): 1125–32.

13. Ibid.

14. Clifton O. Dummett, "Retrospective on Community Dentistry and Public Health at the University of California 1966–1976, Part 2," *Journal of the National Medical Association* 90 (May 1998): 301–16.

15. Robert L. West, "Dean Ingle's Plans for U.S.C. School of Dentistry," *Trodent* (Winter 1972): 1.

16. Nickolas Chester, "From Your President," *Trodent* (Winter 1972): 3–4.

17. "Dr. Ingle Named Officer of Academy of Sciences," *Trojan Family* (December 1972): 1.

18. Schoen, "Response to Receiving the John W. Knutson Distinguished Service Award."

19. Max Schoen, "Dentist Liberty Versus Patient Equity," Third-Annual Dunning Symposium, Columbia University School of Dental and Oral Surgery and School of Public Health, New York, NY, April 1983.

20. Ibid.

21. Albert H. Guay and others, "Evolving Trends in Size and Structure of Group Dental Practices in the United States," *Journal of Dental Education* 76 (August 2012): 1036–44.

22. Elizabeth Mertz and Edward O'Neill, "The Growing Challenge of Providing Oral Health Care Services to All Americans," *Health Affairs* 21, no. 5 (2002): 65–77.

23. National Association of Dental Plans, "Who Has Dental Benefits?," accessed August 28, 2016. www.nadp.org/Dental_Benefits_Basics /Dental_BB_1.aspx.

24. Jihong Liu, Janice Probst, and others, "Disparities in Dental Insurance Coverage and Dental Care Among US Children: The National Survey of Children's Health," *Pediatrics* 119 (February 2007): S12–21.

25. Kamyar Nasseh and Marko Vujicic, "Dental Benefits Coverage Rates Increased for Children and Young Adults in 2013," Health Policy Institute Research Brief, American Dental Association, October 2015, www.ada.org/~/media/ADA/Science%20and%20Research/HPI/Files /HPIBrief_1015_3.ashx.

26. Algernon Austin, "Obamacare Reduces Racial Disparities in Health Coverage," Center for Global Policy Solutions, December 16, 2015, globalpol icysolutions.org/wp-content/uploads/2015/12/ACA-and-Racial-Dis parities.pdf.

27. Nasseh and Vujicic, "Dental Benefits Coverage Rates Increased for Children and Young Adults in 2013."

28. U.S. Government Accountability Office, "Dental Services: Information on Coverage, Payment and Fee Variation," Washington, D.C., September 2013.

29. Clifton O. Dummett and Lois Doyle Dummett, *Afro-Americans in Dentistry: Sequence and Consequence of Events*, published by the authors, 1978.

30. Gunnar Myrdal, *An American Dilemma: The Negro Problem and Modern Democracy* (New York: Harper & Bros., 1944).

31. Paul B. Cornely, "Segregation and Discrimination in Medical Care in the United States," *American Journal of Public Health* 46 (September 1956): 1074–81.

32. Clifton O. Dummett, "Homage to the NMA: The NDA Story (1895 to 1975)—Part 2," *Journal of the National Medical Association* 89 (August 1997): 555–63.

33. "Dentist Breaks Color Line," *Baltimore Afro-American*, November 23, 1968.

34. "Thirty State Agencies—White Only," *Baltimore Afro-American*, August 22, 1970.

35. Harvey Webb Jr., "Problems and Progress of Black Dental Professionals," *Quarterly of the National Dental Association* 34, no. 4 (1975): 147–54.

36. Institute of Medicine, *Advancing Oral Health in America* (Washington, D.C.: National Academies Press, 2011): 100–101.

10. Deamonte's World

1. Kevin Chappell, "America's Wealthiest Black County" *Ebony* (November 2006).

2. Nicole Lurie and others, *Assessing Health and Health Care in Prince George's County* (Santa Monica, CA: Rand Corporation, 2009).

3. Mary Otto, "For Want of a Dentist," *Washington Post*, February 28, 2007.

4. Mark Thompson, "Wonk 'n Roller: Martin O'Malley/Baltimore," *Time*, April 18, 2005.

5. Lowell E. Sunderland, "Dentists to Leave Medicaid, To Do Needed Work on Own," *Baltimore Sun*, May 21, 1968.

6. Editorial, "Medicaid in Trouble," *Baltimore Sun*, May 28, 1968.

7. Edward Walsh, "Costs Climb for Medicaid in Maryland," *Washington Post*, April 14, 1972.

8. Ron Davis, "Dentist Is Guilty of Fraud." *Washington Post*, August 13, 1976.

9. Jack Anderson, "Medicaid Also a Dentists' Goldmine," *Washington Post*, April 1, 1978.

10. "Medicaid Cuts Upset Dentists," *Baltimore Sun*, November 16, 1975.

11. *Maryland Register*, vol. 3, no. 16 (August 4, 1976): 862–65.

12. Njeri M. Thuku and others, "Breaking the Cycle in Maryland: Oral Health Policy Change in the Face of Tragedy," *Journal of Public Health Dentistry* 72 (Winter 2012): S7–12.

11. Riding into the Epidemic

1. Sara Rosenbaum and Paul Wise, "Crossing the Medicaid-Private Insurance Divide: the Case of EPSDT," *Health Affairs* 26 (March and April 2007): 382–93.

2. Mary Otto, "Health on Boy's Death Shows Little Dental Care for the Poor," *Washington Post*, May 3, 2007.

3. Statement of the American Dental Education Association, "One Year Later: Medicaid's Response to Systemic Problems Revealed by the Death of Deamonte Driver," Before U.S. House Oversight and Government Reform Subcommittee on Domestic Policy, February 14, 2008.

4. Statement of Frank Catalanotto, American Dental Education Association, Before U.S. House Oversight and Government Reform Subcommittee on Domestic Policy, October 7, 2009.

5. Jennifer Loven, "Bush Vetoes Child Health Plan," Associated Press, October 3, 2007.

6. U.S. General Accounting Office, "Oral Health Factors Contributing to Low Use of Dental Services by Low-Income Populations," GAO-00-149, Washington, D.C., September 2000.

7. U.S. Government Accountability Office, "Medicaid: Extent of Dental Disease in Children Has Not Increased and Millions Are Estimated to Have Untreated Tooth Decay," GAO-08-1121, Washington, D.C., September 2008.

8. U.S. Government Accountability Office, "Medicaid: State and Federal Actions Have Been Taken to Improve Children's Access to Dental Services but Gaps Remain," GAO-09-723, Washington, D.C., September 2009.

9. Dennis Kucinich, "Opening Statement: Medicaid's Efforts to Reform Since the Preventable Death of Deamonte Driver," Before U.S. House Oversight and Government Reform Subcommittee on Domestic Policy, October 7, 2009.

10. Mary Otto, "For Too Many Maryland Children, Too Few Trips to the Dentist," *Washington Post*, December 27, 2007.

11. Mary Otto, "Smile! Four Years After a 12-Year-Old Boy Died from an Untreated Tooth Abscess, a Mobile Clinic Named in His Memory Brings Volunteers to Help Prince George's County Children," *Washington Post*, February 22, 2011.

12. Sons and Daughters of Chapin Harris

1. Chapin A. Harris, "Observations," *American Journal of Dental Science* 1 (no. 3, 1840): 49–57.

2. American Dental Association Council on Scientific Affairs, "Evidence-Based Clinical Recommendations for the Use of Pit-and-Fissure Sealants: A Report of the American Dental Association's Council on Scientific Affairs," *Journal of the American Dental Association* 139 (March 2008): 257–86.

3. M. Tellez and others, "Sealants and Dental Caries: Dentists Perspectives on Evidence-Based Recommendations," *Journal of the American Dental Association* 142 (September 2011): 1033–44.

4. J. Ben Robinson "This I Know: A Rejoinder," *Journal of the American*

Dental Association 68 (April 1964): 613–16.

5. Maryland State Department of Health and Mental Hygiene, "Maryland's 2015 Annual Oral Health Legislative Report," October 30, 2015.

Index

About the Author

Mary Otto is the oral health topic leader for the Association of Health Care Journalists. She began writing about oral health at the *Washington Post*, where she worked for eight years covering social issues including health care and poverty. She lives in Washington, D.C.

Celebrating 25 Years
of Independent Publishing

The Studs and Ida Terkel Award

ON THE OCCASION OF HIS NINETIETH BIRTHDAY, STUDS TERKEL AND his son, Dan, announced the creation of the Studs and Ida Terkel Author Fund. The Fund is devoted to supporting the work of promising authors in a range of fields who share Studs's fascination with the many dimensions of everyday life in America and who, like Studs, are committed to exploring aspects of America that are not adequately represented by the mainstream media. The Terkel Fund furnishes authors with the vital support they need to conduct their research and writing, providing a new generation of writers the freedom to experiment and innovate in the spirit of Studs's own work.

Studs and Ida Terkel Award Winners

Mary Otto, *Teeth: The Story of Beauty, Inequality, and the Struggle for Oral Health in America*

David Dayen, *Chain of Title: How Three Ordinary Americans Uncovered Wall Street's Great Foreclosure Fraud*

Aaron Swartz, *The Boy Who Could Change the World: The Writings of Aaron Swartz* (awarded posthumously)

Beth Zasloff and Joshua Steckel, *Hold Fast to Dreams: A College Guidance Counselor, His Students, and the Vision of a Life Beyond Poverty*

Barbara J. Miner, *Lessons from the Heartland: A Turbulent Half-Century of Public Education in an Iconic American City*

Lynn Powell, *Framing Innocence: A Mother's Photographs, a Prosecutor's Zeal, and a Small Town's Response*

Lauri Lebo, *The Devil in Dover: An Insider's Story of Dogma v. Darwin in Small-Town America*